THE NEW FACE OF BASEBALL

THE NEW

BASE

THE ONE-HUNDRED-YEAR RISE AND TRIUMPH

PRODUCED BY THE PHILIP LIEF GROUP INC.

 An Imprint of HarperCollinsPublishers

FACE OF
BALL

TIM WENDEL

FOREWORD BY BOB COSTAS

COLOR PHOTOGRAPHS BY
VICTOR BALDIZON

FIRST EDITION

Designed by Judith Stagnitto Abbate/Abbate Design

Printed on acid-free paper

Library of Congress Cataloging-in-Publication Data is available upon request.

ISBN 0-06-053631-4

03 04 05 06 07 DIX/QW 10 9 8 7 6 5 4 3 2 1

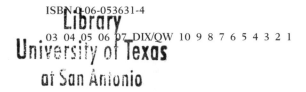

For my grandfather, who took me to my first game.

For my children, who help me still find the joy in sports.

And, again, for my wife, Jacqueline.

ACKNOWLEDGMENTS

This book would not have been possible without the help and guidance of Judy Capodanno. She's a great editor and friend. Rene Alegria and Philip Lief believed in this project when few did and only with their backing and counsel did this book become a reality.

Bill Francis, Scot Mondore and Bruce Markusen of the National Baseball Hall of Fame and Library were gracious with their time and patience, as were my traveling companions—Milton Jamail and Alan Klein. Susan O'Brian and Eric Enders were always there to help with any research issue. Sam Moore and Wade Den Hartog of the Major League Baseball Players Alumni put me in touch with many of the old-timers who were crucial in the telling of this story. Thanks to Charles Cooper, who gave me my first major-league assignment.

I am grateful for interviews to Hank Aaron, Manny Acta, Sandy Alderson, Roberto Alomar, Dusty Baker, Paul Beeston, Rod Beck, Louis Berney, Jeff Blauser, Larry Bowa, Bob Brenly, Orlando Cabrera, Jose Canseco, Rod Carew, Orlando Cepeda, Bob Costas, Don Fehr, Tony Fossas, Andres Galarraga, Nomar Garciaparra, George Genovese, Mark Grace, Ken Griffey,

Vladimir Guerrero, Mickey Hatcher, Mike Hargrove, Livan Hernandez, Tony La Russa, Omar Linares, Larry Lucchino, Edgar Martinez, Pedro Martinez, John Marzano, Luis Mayoral, Mark McGwire, Omar Minaya, Orestes Minoso, Joe Morgan, Eric Nadel, Jerry Narron, Junior Noboa, Rafael Palmeiro, Tony Peña, Rafael Perez, Lou Piniella, Jorge Posada, Kirby Puckett, Manny Ramirez, Mariano Rivera, Frank Robinson, Alex Rodriguez, Ivan Rodriguez, Mike Scioscia, Alfonso Soriano, Sammy Sosa, Fernando Tatis, Syd Thrift, Jim Thome, Luis Tiant, Carlos Tosca, Joe Torre, Jose Vidro, Omar Vizquel, Bernie Williams and Billy Williams.

Doing public relations in this day and age isn't easy, and special thanks to John Blake and Rich Rice of the Texas Rangers, Jay Stenhouse of the Toronto Blue Jays, Bart Swain and Bob DiBiasio of the Cleveland Indians, Bill Stetka and Shannon Obaker of the Baltimore Orioles, Matt Charbonneau of the Montreal Expos, Larry Shenk and Leigh Tobin of the Philadelphia Phillies and Kevin Shea and Kerri Walsh of the Boston Red Sox for their assistance.

Hope Gatto and Annie Jeon compiled the statistical pages that helped the Latino All-Century team come to life. And, in the end, we come full circle to my friend Scott Price, who put me in touch with photographer Victor Baldizon. His photographs not only grace these pages, but our discussions were the beginnings of this book.

—TIM WENDEL

CONTENTS

FOREWORD

When Major League Baseball teams posted their rosters on opening day in 2001, nearly 20 percent of the players were Latino—up from only 8 percent about fifteen years earlier. Like the country that it so often mirrors, baseball is changing. While dubbed "America's national pastime," baseball has been a part of *Latin* American society almost as long as it's been played in the United States. Since 1868, when Cuba started up its first professional baseball league, the game spread throughout the Caribbean and Latin America. But only in the last two decades have so many Latinos shared the same field with their U.S. counterparts.

Latinos now make up 12.5 percent of the U.S. population, and more and more, baseball reflects our nation's *beisbol* connections. In case you're not convinced, stats will show that the Latino influence has touched every part of the game. At the plate, among today's hitting leaders you'll find such names as Sammy Sosa, Alfonso Soriano, Bernie Williams, Alex Rodriguez, Vladimir Guerrero and Manny Ramirez. On the mound, this generation's pitchers include potential Hall of Famers Pedro Martinez and Mariano Rivera. And on the field, over the last five years approximately one-third of Gold Glove winners have been of Latino descent.

Since the United States' inception, we've prided ourselves on being a melting pot—a place where talent, not connections or family linkage, has been the bottom line. While that may be difficult to argue in some fields, it still rings true for baseball. Today's superstars come not only from the projects of the inner city or the fields of the heartland, but more and more can trace their family tree back to the shores of the Dominican Republic, Panama, Puerto Rico, or Cuba.

Unlike past generations, when homegrown athletes dominated the sport, today's baseball franchises turn to their scouts for prospects from around the globe, with major priorities in Central America and the Caribbean. To many young boys in that part of the world, baseball is seen as a road out of poverty, much like basketball is to disadvantaged African-Americans. The wealth of talent to be culled from those parts of the world is now obvious, with many of the highest-paid players in the game being of Latino descent—signaling team-owner recognition of both talent and fan appeal. Perhaps a future step will involve the big leagues tapping into the baseball fever that is so evident in Latin America. In recent springs, we've seen exhibition games involving major league ball clubs in Mexico, the Dominican Republic, and even Cuba.

When significant numbers of Latinos finally began openly joining the ranks of major-league teams in the '50s and '60s, they encountered some of the same discrimination faced by their African-American counterparts. They experienced the added alienation of coming from a different country and a different culture, and, of course, many also faced a significant language barrier. Now many of today's stars make their home in this country and experience the unreserved support of their team's fans.

Take a look at this year's All-Star ballot and you'll find at least one star of Latino descent at every position in both the National and American Leagues. Surely this will be the case next year, in the next decade, and long after, for the game of baseball has truly become an international sport, and nobody arrives more eager to play and ready to make an impact than those from the Caribbean and beyond. They are the latest wave of immigrants to make a home for themselves in this land. Here is their story. Say hello to the "new face of baseball."

—BOB COSTAS

INTRODUCTION

O nly for a short while was the game ours and ours alone. While baseball in the United States dates back to before the Civil War, to the opening of the Western frontier, by the era of Babe Ruth our national pastime had been carried far beyond our ever-burgeoning borders.

In Cuba, baseball took root more than a century ago and is still played today with an aggressiveness and hustle reminiscent of the St. Louis Cardinals' "Gas House Gang" or that golden era in the 1950s when three ball clubs—the Yankees, Dodgers, and Giants—made New York the capital of baseball. Nostalgic for good old days when everyone took the extra base and few managers dared wait, fingers crossed, for the miracle of the three-run homer? The old game, the way it was supposed to be played, can still be found in Havana and throughout the Caribbean to Venezuela and Colombia.

The game of baseball—where an out is an out, a strike is a strike—will always belong in some basic way to the United States. But what many Americans don't realize is that our national pastime also belongs to the rest of the world, and has for some time. From Cuba, the sport soon found a home in

Mexico, Puerto Rico, and the Dominican Republic, the country where scouts currently flock to view the best in young baseball talent.

"In my country, the dreams about baseball are as strong as they used to be in America," says Omar Minaya, who was born in the Dominican Republic and made history when he became the first Latino general manager in the major leagues for the Montreal Expos in 2002.

That these dreams about baseball can extend beyond borders, even reach past the barriers of language, is truly a wonder in a world that's seemingly eager to break along class and racial lines at every turn. To watch a ball game in Havana or Santo Domingo is a chance to be carried back in time. That impromptu game of pepper down the third base line before the game, the way the base runner raced from first to third without a backward glance? Yes, that's how they used to do it in the old days. And that is how we are beginning to see it played more and more here today, thanks to the flow of talent coming from Latino countries. Ironically, players from outside the United States are bringing baseball back home and with their speed, grace, and impressive athleticism, redefining major parts of the game and how it is played. The ties can bind so tightly that when Miguel Tejada enjoyed his MVP season in 2002 with the Oakland Athletics, the newspapers back in the Dominican Republic held publication night after night, sometimes until three in the morning, for the latest report of his heroics.

Baseball has always offered the comfort of continuity, a link between generations. What we Americans haven't realized is that the game can also connect us to worlds with which we thought we had little in common. So let's consider these other dreams of baseball. The ones that began long ago with Dolf Luque and soon extended like a family tree to Orestes Minoso,

Roberto Clemente, and Orlando Cepeda, all the way to the modern era with Alex Rodriguez, Sammy Sosa, and Vladimir Guerrero. Yes, let us pursue baseball in all its configurations. For only then can we catch a glimpse of the world and our place in it.

THE NEW FACE OF BASEBALL

LOST IN
THE SHADOWS

"Walking from shadow to shadow, he reached

the end of the trees and passed into the world

of columns. Columns with blue and white

stripes, with railings connecting them: a

double gallery of portals along that royal

roadway whose Foundation of Neptune was

adorned with tritons that looked like wild dogs

pasted over with campaign posters."

◆ **ALEJO CARPENTIER,** *The Chase*

They play baseball everywhere—in the alleyways and on the narrow streets beyond the columns, in the small parks that line the wide boulevards coming into Havana and near the sweeping Malecon seawall. Everywhere they play. For in Cuba there may not be much, but there is always baseball.

Love for the game moves beyond the political and the past. In the years after the Soviet Union's collapse, baseball has become more important than ever on the island. The people know about those who have left to play in the major leagues in *El Norte*. They build makeshift radio antennas that rival the Tower of Babel in hopes of picking up the signal of a game, any major-league contest, across the Straits of Florida.

"It's like a huge curtain separates us," a fan in Havana tells me. "We can hear what is happening out there, with the sport. But we can never see. We never really know."

For centuries Havana has been called the city of columns. The nickname reflects the architecture, especially in the old part of town, near the harbor and El Morro Castle. Many storefronts are adorned with columns. They can divide the world into what is going on in the street and what is happening on the sidewalks near the shops. The columns remain symbolic of what has happened in this land since 1959, when Fidel Castro, a baseball fan, one who understands his people's passion for the game, came to power. For the figurative columns and curtains divide this land into loyalists and exiles. Who has stayed and who decided to leave.

Rafael Palmeiro was born across the harbor from old town Havana, where the city soon opens up into two-story cement-block houses and the horizon of the island's vast interior is clearly visible. Not that Palmeiro remembers much from those early days. He left Cuba with his family at the age of five. He passed beyond the columns and has never returned.

Palmeiro's father, Jose, played amateur baseball back in Cuba. But again those images have been lost to the past. Palmeiro never saw his father play. His earliest memories are of his family fleeing Cuba and moving to Miami and putting down new roots. While his father didn't speak English when they moved, they had baseball and the game offered much in their new land. Soon after the family arrived in the United States, Palmeiro's father brought him a glove and the two of them began to play catch in the small backyard. Soon they were spending late afternoons in the neighborhood park a few blocks away, where the father would pitch to Rafael and his brothers and then hit them grounders and fly balls.

"My father was a hard worker in everything he did, and he carried that into baseball for me," Palmeiro says. "He worked construction after we came to this country, and I didn't understand it back then, but the last thing he probably wanted to do during the hot days in Miami in the summer was go out and play baseball when he got home from work. But he did. His main thing was to keep us off the streets. To keep our minds on good things. I know he enjoyed baseball, that he wanted me to play baseball, but I realize now that he also did it to keep me and my brothers off the streets. We grew up in a bad part of town. We were right there in Liberty City. Tough place to grow up. But we never knew that."

The sweet swing from the left side of the plate and the defensive ability that won him three Gold Gloves were a result of those after-school workouts. But at no time did the father ever tell the son that he could be a major-leaguer. The world can be a hard place, especially when you're new to this land. Daydreams are something to be wary of.

"He was very critical of me," Palmeiro tells me. "But he did it for my own good. I think he knew I could handle it. I saw [my father] as a hero, as somebody who worked really hard and didn't accept any handouts or gifts from anyone. Just by watching him, I learned to work for the things that I wanted to achieve."

Growing up, Palmeiro dreamed of one day playing in the major leagues. But it wasn't until he was named the nation's college freshman player of the year at Mississippi State that he began to believe that his dream was a realistic one. Now in the twilight of his career, Palmeiro finds himself with more career RBIs than Mark McGwire and more Gold Gloves at first base than Willie McCovey. Barring injury, he will finish his playing days with more than 500 home runs and 3,000 hits. Nobody who has reached such heights has been refused entry into the baseball Hall of Fame in Cooperstown, New York.

"In the end those are numbers nobody can overlook," says Luis Mayoral, former consultant to the Texas Rangers and radio commentator. "I can remember when people said Raffy couldn't hit for power. You could say that he's hurt himself because he keeps things to himself. He's not after the headlines. When he played in Baltimore he was overshadowed by Cal Ripken and Roberto Alomar. In Texas, there's 'A-Rod.' Raffy's overshadowed. But nothing can take away from his numbers."

In August 2002, in an inconsequential game between the Rangers and the Indians in Cleveland, Palmeiro homered to win the contest. The homer was his thirtieth of the season, the eighth straight season he had reached that plateau. He was only the tenth player in baseball history to achieve that feat.

"I know I've been overlooked in my career," Palmeiro told me that day. "But it hasn't been unfair, because you look at guys like Mark McGwire, Ken Griffey, Sammy Sosa, and Barry Bonds. I've played with Cal Ripken, Nolan Ryan, Ryne Sandberg; I'm playing with Alex Rodriguez and Ivan Rodriguez right now. Those guys are Hall of Famers, too. I feel recognized. Maybe not as much as I should. But I don't play this game for recognition. I play this game to satisfy myself; to win, to earn respect from my teammates and opponents. If I get recognition, that's great, but inside I know I've done everything I can do."

While Palmeiro may be overlooked here, elected to the All-Star game only four times in fifteen major-league seasons, back in his native land he will always have a place of honor. At the *Esquina Caliente,* which translates as the "Hot Corner," Cubans gather every day in the best-known park in Havana to discuss baseball. Here they know him.

"A fine, fine ballplayer," one of the faithful says when Palmeiro's name is mentioned. The consensus of those who have gathered here today is that Palmeiro belongs with the best first basemen of this generation. Better career numbers than Frank Thomas or Jim Thome. Somebody who should be sharing the spotlight with Jason Giambi or Mark McGwire. He will likely finish his career with more RBIs than Hall of Famer Tony Perez. One could make the argument that he's the best Cuban player of all time. But if any of those players, even Palmeiro, walked into the throng that comes to the park every day in Havana to discuss and argue baseball, they wouldn't be recognized right away. Such is life in the city of columns. Those at *Esquina Caliente* know the statistics, maybe even the game, better than the U.S. fans. But because of government crackdowns, the barriers that have existed for a half-century between these two lands, they can hear the word of baseball, but they rarely are offered a glimpse of the stars.

Here, in *El Norte,* we wrap the game in red, white, and blue bunting and make it part of our Fourth of July and Labor Day celebrations. Baseball will always be the sport of summer, tradition, and often our youth. Anyone who doubts how interwoven it is in our national fabric need only peer out the window on that next airplane trip. You'll see baseball diamonds everywhere scattered across the country. "And every time I see [one], my heart goes out to it," poet Donald Hall once said.

While many perceive baseball as American as block parties and midsummer fireworks, its popularity reached outside our borders a long, long time ago. In Latin America it took root and blossomed into something similar and yet refreshingly diverse. Imagine baseball as *beisbol*—much more than what we once thought it was or ever could be. Soon after baseball emerged in the United States, it also found a home in Cuba. Nemesio Guillo, who had studied in the United States, returned to his homeland with a bat and baseball in 1864. He and his brother, Ernesto, founded the Habana Base Ball Club a few years later, and the game flourished. The first ballpark was built in 1874 in Matanzas, east of Havana. Amateur leagues were organized around the island's sugar mills—a tradition that would later be imitated in the Dominican Republic.

Despite a shared enthusiasm for the game, a key difference remains in the baseball's roots and ultimately how it is portrayed and remembered by its fans. In the United States, presidents throw out the first pitch on opening day. It's the sport with the most history. In the Caribbean, the game obviously has history, too. But from the beginning it was embraced by those longing for independence. For young students, would-be patriots, there was no bigger statement one could make about political orientation than to shun the Spanish-style bullfights and head into the country to play this radical new game, this game called baseball.

The working class embraced baseball, and the island would soon be remembered for having four professional winter ball teams—Habana Lions, Almendares Scorpions, Cienfuegos Elephants, and the Marianao Tigers. The New York Giants were the first to travel to Cuba, doing so in the winter of 1890. The Brooklyn Dodgers joined them in Havana a decade later to play a series of exhibition games. By World War II, the Giants and Dodgers had both held spring training in Cuba, and when the war ended the Dodgers returned in 1947 so that Jackie Robinson could enjoy a more relaxed spring training before breaking the color barrier in the major leagues. In fact baseball became so entrenched in Cuba that U.S. intelligence grew nervous when surveillance images revealed soccer fields being built during the Cold War. After all, the Cubans weren't interested in soccer. Only their new friends, the Soviets, played that game.

Of course, interest and commerce of baseball were hardly one way. Cuban Esteban Bellan became the first Latin American to play ball in the United States in 1871. Rafael Almeida and Armando Marsans were the first Cubans to play in the major leagues, signing with the Cincinnati Reds in 1911. The famous pitcher Adolfo Luque followed them to Cincinnati, which established the Reds as the Cubans' favorite major league team for several generations. A feisty right-hander, Luque didn't back down from anybody and compiled a 193–179 record in twenty seasons in the majors. In the 1919 World Series, he came in from the bullpen twice without allowing a run and the next year became a starting pitcher and remained in that role until the twilight of his career. In the 1933 World Series, his 4⅓ shutout innings in relief nailed down the victory for the New York Giants in the deciding game. Though Luque was light-skinned enough to play in the majors, he put up with his share of insults and derision. Only five foot seven, Luque had to fight for everything he got in America, where he was called "a Cuban nigger," Roberto Gonzalez Echevarria writes. Never one to back down, the diminutive right-hander gained a reputation as a headhunter—a skill he later taught to Sal Maglie. Where beanballs couldn't get his message across, Luque was ready to take matters into his own hands. Once, while on the mound for Cincinnati, he charged the New York Giants' bench after hearing one too many derogatory comments. Luque punched Casey Stengel, then a part-time outfielder, in the jaw. The incident was hailed in Luque's homeland, where he was revered. In America, Luque was nicknamed "The Pride of Havana" or the "Havana Perfecto."

Until Jackie Robinson broke down the door of racism at the game's highest level, Cubans faced the same discrimination as potential players in the United States. Those of color, regardless of ability, were left on the outside, looking in.

"EL INMORTAL"

Martin Dihigo was the best player who never reached, or more accurately was never allowed to play in, the major leagues. Eventually he went on to be enshrined in four Halls of Fame—the U.S., Venezuelan, Cuban, and Mexican. He was the first Latino player so honored in Cooperstown. At six feet one, 190 pounds, Dihigo had a major-leaguer's physique. But he was too dark-skinned for any team to take a chance on him in the time before Jackie Robinson. He went on to star for a quarter-century throughout the Caribbean and in the old Negro Leagues. According to baseball historian John Holway, Dihigo began as a shortstop for the old Cuban Stars. Ironically, he was the proto-type of the modern era—an infielder who could hit with power. But unlike the stars of this age, who include such Latinos as Alex Rodriguez and Nomar Garciaparra, Dihigo could pitch, too. Only Babe Ruth can claim such prowess on the mound and in the batter's box. Dihigo's lifetime pitching record in the old Negro League was 256–136, and he batted .316 and could play any position. In the outfield, he was a Clemente ahead of his time and often warned those on base not to run on him. Few did as word soon circulated about his impressive arm.

Like the Babe, Dihigo also had a great sense of humor. Hol-way recalled one Negro League game in which Dihigo was on third base. He suddenly shouted to the pitcher, "You balked." He continued to shout this out as he walked down the third base line and touched home plate. The pitcher never threw home and a now-laughing Dihigo continued to his dugout after scor-ing the run.

Dihigo played on the Homestead Grays for five seasons. There, he won three home run crowns and tied Josh Gibson for another. John McGraw, manager of the New York Giants, called Dihigo the greatest player alive. The Cuban great could also manage and did so throughout Latin America. Johnny Mize, who played for a team Dihigo managed in the Dominican Re-public, shared McGraw's assessment. Walter "Buck" Leonard, who played against him in the Negro League, says Dihigo "could run, hit, throw, think, pitch, and manage. You take your Ruths, Cobbs, and DiMaggios. Give me Dihigo. I bet I would beat you almost every time."

After his playing days, Dihigo became an announcer and often held court, talking baseball at Havana's Cafe Las Avenidas. He would have fit right in at the *Esquina Caliente*. But as with anything that begins and ends with Cuba, the col-umns of politics often intrude. Outspoken and humorous on the field, Dihigo kept his opinions to himself outside the lines. Nobody is sure about how he felt about the discrimination that denied him an opportunity to play in the big leagues. In addition, it's unclear what he made of Cuban leader Fidel Castro, according to Holway. But there's no doubt that Castro admired him. Once Dihigo's playing days were over, he worked in sports and baseball on the island until his death. That he stayed in his homeland, viewed by many as a sign of his part in the Castro regime, rankled those who had fled their land.

"I was disappointed in later years when he became minister of sports for Fidel Castro," says Orestes "Minnie" Minoso, who had once played on the same team with Dihigo and Luis Tiant Sr. "Those people, those times—I try not to remember them. It's only so much sadness for me."

A MAN CALLED MINNIE

Jackie Robinson became one of our sports icons when he broke the color barrier in 1947. Heralded as much for his ability to turn the other cheek as swing a bat, Robinson deserves every accolade he has received. On the eve of the fiftieth anniversary of Robinson's breakthrough, I traveled to his old neighborhood—Pepper Street in Pasadena. Unfortunately, the town remains divided by race almost as much as it was when Robinson was growing up. What was heartening was talking with those who knew him in his youth. Many remembered him as an angry young man. They still marveled at his ability to curb such frustration, to rise to a greater place in history than anyone could have imagined when as a teenager he was having constant run-ins with the authorities.

But in the afterglow of Robinson's achievement in breaking

the color barrier, it's easy to forget about those who soon followed in his footsteps, and not all of them were African-Americans. Years later, Roberto Clemente tried to explain the unique position of the Latino ballplayer at the time. He called it being "a double minority," singled out for being dark skinned and unable to speak the language.

"Before Minnie came on the scene in the late forties, there had been around fifty Latin players who had played the game, all of them light-skinned because of racial policies," writes Marcos Breton, a sportswriter with the *Sacramento Bee* and the co-author of *Away Games: The Life and Times of a Latin Ballplayer.* "None of them had ever made a real big impact on the game until Minnie. He really put Latin players on the map in Major League Baseball."

Orestes "Minnie" Minoso came to the Chicago White Sox in 1951 and was the team's first "black" superstar. He homered against the New York Yankees in his Chicago debut and joined with Nellie Fox and Chico Carrasquel to lead the new darlings of the baseball world, the "Go Go" White Sox. Although Minoso would play for three other teams during his seventeen-year major-league career, he would remain so popular in Chicago that he still serves as the team's goodwill ambassador. Decades after his final at bat, he's mentioned in the same breath with Sammy Sosa and Michael Jordan.

"Believe me when I say that Minnie Minoso is to Latin ballplayers what Jackie Robinson is to black ballplayers," Orlando Cepeda maintains in his autobiography, *Baby Bull.* "As much as I loved Roberto Clemente and cherish his memory, Minnie is the one who made it possible for all of us Latins. Before Roberto Clemente, before Vic Power, before Orlando Cepeda, there was Minnie Minoso. Younger players should know this and offer their thanks. He was the first Latin player to become a superstar."

Luis Tiant tells me that Minoso was his idol because "he was the first one to stand up for black Cubans—guys like myself. You see somebody like that make it and you have some hope. You start to believe that maybe one day you can reach the big leagues, too."

But before the Havana-born Minoso came to the United States to play ball, Jose Pasquel, who induced such stars as Danny Gardella, Mickey Owen, Sal Maglie, and Luis Olmo to play in the Mexican League, warned the young Cuban star about setting his sights on the majors. He warned that in the United States Minoso would be "treated like a dog" because he was black. Minoso came north anyway and began with the New York Cubans in the Negro League in 1945. He soon saw that Pasquel was right. The segregation was rampant in New Orleans, where the team had its spring training home.

"[In the United States] it would say no blacks, no colored," Minoso remembers. "In Cuba, it was much the same, but the sign said, Private. That's the key difference. They made them private clubs that people like me couldn't go into."

In 1949, Minoso broke in with the Cleveland Indians and spent much of that season and the next in the minors. Early in the '51 season, he was traded to the Chicago White Sox, where he was determined to become one of the team's stars despite the discrimination and bias there.

"First you had Jackie Robinson. Then Larry Doby and then you had me," he says. "I was the first black-skinned ballplayer to play in the city of Chicago. I tried to take everything as it comes. I never let the world hurt me. The world didn't break me. They used to call me terrible things, but I let it go in one ear and out the other. None of it stayed with me. I never wanted them to know my feelings on the inside. On the outside I just gave them my smile. Smile all the time."

But wasn't that difficult?

"Sure it was. But what can you do?" he tells me, comparing the insults and threats to a prolonged batting slump. "With both, you have to be strong in the mind. Not let it hurt you. Sooner or later you're going to have a slump, and that's when you need to be strong. Ted Williams told me that. He also told me I could hit, and I cannot tell you how good that made me feel. How I remembered that when I was going through difficult times, on or off the field.

"This is what the world is like, my friend. You cannot let anyone run your life because they call you names or tell you you can't play. When I played I sometimes had to play the clown. I had to listen and laugh, even if I was crying inside. But never did I let them see that it bothered me. I tried to answer with my bat. Always my bat. It's like if you're a singer. If you hear noises out there, people may not like how you're singing, are you going to stop and tell them to be quiet? Of course not. You're going to keep singing."

Minoso's persistence paid off, and he led the league in hits in 1960, and between 1951 and 1961 he scored more than 100 runs four times and more than 90 runs nine times. But such accomplishments are often overlooked because the first wave of Latino ballplayers were routinely marginalized by nicknames. In his book *The Pride of Havana: A History of Cuban Baseball,* Yale professor Roberto Gonzalez Echevarria writes that such monikers as Minnie "infantilize athletes."

"Orestes Minoso, with his proud classical name, became 'Minnie' Minoso in the United States," Gonzalez Echevarria adds. "I could not have written a whole book referring to Orestes Minoso as 'Minnie.' "

Minoso remembers the day—May 1, 1951—when he looked in one of the Chicago papers and saw that Orestes was gone and he had been dubbed Minnie forever.

Minoso had a dentist appointment that day and he asked

first the dental assistant and then the dentist what they thought about the name Minnie. Wasn't it female? Both of them told him that men and women went by the name in the United States. For the next few weeks he continued to sign his given name, Orestes, when he was asked for an autograph.

"[But] everybody wanted me to sign Minnie," he says. "After a few years I decided to change it. Now it's part of my legal name."

THE FIRST SUPER SCOUT

Minoso went on to be a seven-time All-Star and such a fan favorite that White Sox owner Bill Veeck gave him a complimentary championship ring in 1959, even though Minoso had been in a Cleveland uniform that season. Meanwhile, back in Cuba, Joe Cambria had made a name for himself by combing Minoso's homeland for major-league talent. The New York Giants and Brooklyn Dodgers may have trained and played on the island, but it was the Washington Senators, thanks to Cambria, that claimed so much Cuban talent. With many U.S. players in the military during World War II, and President Franklin Roosevelt pressing baseball officials to keep the game going on the home front, the race was on for new talent.

Born in Italy, Cambria wasn't fluent in Spanish, but he became a fixture within the baseball culture of the Caribbean. After a brief career as a minor-league infielder, he purchased the Baltimore Black Sox in the National Negro League. There, according to Gonzalez Echevarria, he learned of the potential in the Cuban market. He convinced Clark Griffith, the Senators' owner, to make him the team's Latin American scout. Cambria specialized in locating players off the beaten track, often signing prospects to minimal, even blank contracts. Stateside he had signed Mickey Vernon and Eddie Yost in this way. His philosophy was that a star or two would always surface from the wide swath he cut. It's a method that big-league clubs would emulate a half-century later in the Dominican Republic and Venezuela.

Before 1946, approximately forty Cubans had reached the majors, with Luque and Miguel Angel Gonzalez, the third base coach who waved Enos Slaughter around with the winning run in the 1946 World Series, the most prominent stars. But between 1947 and 1959, when Castro took power, Cuba became the primary source of major-league talent outside the United States. The ranks included Tony Oliva, Tony Perez, and Minoso. In 1950 alone, Cambria sent six Cuban-born pitchers to the Senators, including Carlos Pascual, the older brother of Camilo Pascual. A right-hander with a devastating curveball, Camilo Pascual led the American League in strikeouts and complete games three times. But speculation still surrounds another right-hander with a curve who somehow got away from the game's first super scout. Legend has it that Cambria took an interest in Castro in the 1940s.

I heard about this unusual scouting trip firsthand on my initial trip to Cuba in 1992. Milton Jamail, Rick Lawes, and I were guests on Radio Rebelde in Havana. Radio Rebelde began as the clandestine station for Castro's rebel army. It now specializes in game broadcasts and sports talk shows. We arrived at the station's dilapidated studios and were introduced to Edel Casas. Even though Casas had never been to the United States and had never seen a major-league game in person, he knew more baseball than the three of us put together. Give him any year, and he could recite the Cy Young winner and MVP in either league. The man was a walking baseball encyclopedia.

Milton, who teaches Latin American politics at the University of Texas at Austin, a person with whom I would take two more trips to Cuba, asked Casas about the old winter ball league, in which Habana, Almendares, Cienfuegos, and Marianao played one another in Gran Stadium. The huge bowl of a ballpark still stands, now with Soviet-style lighting, on the opposite side of town. During that golden era of Cuban baseball every team had noteworthy stars—Minoso had played for Marianao at one time, Tommy Lasorda had pitched for Almendares—and the teams played three times during the week, off on Friday and Saturday, with a doubleheader on Sunday. With so few teams, the adversaries knew one another well, and the games, especially the Sunday doubleheaders, were hard-fought and the biggest show in town.

Amaury Pi-Gonzalez, a Latino broadcaster based in the Bay Area, lived in Cuba until he was seventeen years old. He was a big fan of the Habana Lions, and their major rival was the Almendares Scorpions.

"Almendares' color was blue, like the Dodgers, and Habana was red like the Cincinnati Reds," Pi-Gonzalez says. "They'd play every Sunday, and I remembered that the one o'clock game would be Cienfuegos and Marianao—the Elephants and the Tigers. But the second game of the day would be like life or death—Almendares and Habana. It would be like Dodgers and Giants or Red Sox and Yankees these days. You saw all these great players—Minoso, Pascual, Cuellar."

Back at Radio Rebelde we talked about Cuba's baseball heyday for a while until Milton asked Casas, the Cuban baseball analyst, about Castro. Was he really a ballplayer? And the radio show host replied that Cambria met with Castro in 1942 or 1943. The Senators' scout liked Castro's size. Despite a lackluster fastball, he was a prospect who could think on the fly and, according to Casas, Cambria offered the future dictator a contract. Castro turned him down.

While that situation, if it did happen, remains baseball's

biggest what-if, one cannot underestimate how Cambria's over-all success changed the game forever. Other teams took note of his almost assembly-line procedure of signing players. That he was the first one operating in Cuba forced others to first con-sider the talent on that island and then begin to wonder if there was more to be found in Puerto Rico or the Dominican Repub-lic. But, more important, Cambria showed that Latinos could play the game. That he specialized in finding talent on the pe-riphery. That a budding superstar could be anywhere became part of our folklore. Wherever he went, Cambria sought out baseball games. If there was a sandlot game going on some-where nearby, he found it. He was always on the lookout for the next "natural."

In 1938, George Genovese, then a sixteen-year-old short-stop playing near his home in Staten Island, New York, was scouted by Cambria. It was an experience he will never forget.

"I saw this old gent with a white Panama hat and a linen suit. It seemed like his eyes were always on me," Genovese re-members. "He was stocky, no more than five eleven. At the end of the game, he hurried out and got a hold of me and the pitcher for the other team, Karl Drews. Drews later pitched for the Yan-kees. He could really throw hard.

"Cambria wanted to sign us right there on the spot. But I told him that my parents wouldn't like that. That I had to finish high school."

A few years later, Genovese signed with the St. Louis Cardi-nals out of a tryout camp. He played in three games for the Washington Senators. He had one big-league at bat and was walked and later scored a run. More important to our story, Branch Rickey named him as a minor-league manager in the 1950s. He coached such Latinos as Jose Cardenal and Jesus Alou. Later he became one of the top scouts in the game.

Throughout his career, Genovese never forgot that afternoon

in Staten Island when Cambria took an interest in him. That day taught him that a good scout or manager always looks past convention or reputation. The key was to consider everyone individually and imagine how good a player could be. What you could add to repertoire that could make him better, the team better.

"The first time I ever talked with a scout, I started with one of the tops," says Genovese, whose list of signees includes Bobby Bonds, Barry's father. "I always was thankful that it was someone of his magnitude who told me that I had the ability to be a ballplayer. Every time I considered a prospect, I tried to remember how (Cambria) had looked at me. I was just a sixteen-year-old kid. But you would have thought he'd stumbled upon the next great shortstop. I only wish it were so."

AFTER THE REVOLUTION

Some fifteen years after Castro supposedly turned down Cambria, he moved on to slightly bigger things. In January of 1959, his rebel armies took over Cuba. During the next eighteen months he would secretly steer his country toward communism and link it with the Soviet Union. Few countrymen realized what Castro had in store for the island as the rebel army tanks and soldiers streamed into the capital, to be greeted by cheering throngs. But at least one ballplayer was wary of the new regime and what the future held for his homeland.

On January 1, 1959, Orestes Minoso sat in his trademark Cadillac as the military parade tied up traffic in Havana. Passing soldiers recognized him and called for Minoso to join them. The ballplayer left his car and was about to jump onto one of the passing flatbed trucks when something stopped him. Something wasn't right. Minoso claims that from that moment on he never trusted the Castro government. In fact he began to make plans to leave the island, which proved to be a costly process, because he owned several high-rise apartment buildings and a fleet of taxis. By pulling out of Cuba, he knew he would lose a lot of money.

"Call it a gut feeling," Minoso says in his autobiography, *Just Call Me Minnie,* "but I was always suspicious of [Castro]. I kept quiet at first, but kept an eye and ear open as to where his government was heading. When I became convinced beyond doubt that he would take all freedom away from the Cuban people, I made up my mind to leave."

Of course, Minoso wasn't the only one to reach that decision. The exodus began in earnest as Castro methodically destroyed the old social order and moved Cuba rapidly toward a Marxist-Leninist way of life. In 1959, Castro abolished professional baseball on the island. Cubans would only play amateur baseball, with the country's new "maximum leader" routinely questioning national team coaches about game strategy and roster moves.

"I'm talking about politicians, such as the first secretary of the Communist Party who calls the manager and wants to know why they are not winning," Gilberto Dihigo, Martin's son, once explained to Jamail. "They are like the club owners. And, of course, the big club owner is Fidel Castro."

The Cuban revolution and the subsequent events had a profound impact upon the American baseball community. Almost everywhere the ripples spread. The Minnesota Twins, for example, had released Tony Oliva when the Bay of Pigs invasion took place in 1961. All flights back to Cuba were canceled. So the ball club decided to keep him. Three years later, Oliva became the first rookie in major-league history to win a batting championship.

George Genovese was managing with the Giants' minor-league affiliate in El Paso. On his roster was Jose Cardenal, who was born in Matanzas, Cuba. Cardenal was listed as an infielder, but Genovese soon realized that he didn't have a future at any of the infield positions.

"Jose hadn't shown much in spring training and he was about to get released," Genovese says. "So I decided to take him along with me to El Paso and make an outfielder out of him. If he couldn't make it, I'd release him then, so he could stay in this country. I knew if he went back to Cuba, he would never get out."

The move to right field paid off. Cardenal homered in his first game for El Paso and went on to hit thirty-six round-trippers that season. He played eighteen seasons in the majors, including appearances in the 1978 League Championship Series and the 1980 World Series.

Eventually the city of columns became more than an Old World nickname. The families of Rafael Palmeiro and Jose Canseco soon fled the island. A wealth of baseball talent remained, of course. The Cuban national dominated amateur competition, won the sport's first Olympic gold medal at the Barcelona Summer Games in 1992 and repeated that feat in Atlanta four years later. Still, something had been broken. The curtain that fell between Cuba and the United States remained, and on both sides the whispers began.

COMING HOME

Palmeiro's older brother, Jose, was left in Cuba when the family fled to the United States in 1971. In his early twenties, Jose Palmeiro was on the list to serve in the military. He never did because he was born with a partial left arm. But that disability wasn't on his official papers, so he had to stay.

It wasn't until twenty-one years later that Rafael Palmeiro saw his older brother again. In a visit arranged in part by Major League Baseball and the Texas Rangers, the two brothers were reunited in New York, where the team was playing the Yankees. The night Jose Palmeiro arrived in Miami, before continuing on to New York, Rafael Palmeiro had hit a home run. When Jose Palmeiro had arrived the next day at LaGuardia Airport he was still in shirtsleeves. When they arrived in the Bronx, Rafael took his brother on a tour of Yankee Stadium. As the two of them surveyed the field from the upper deck, Rafael took off his leather jacket and gave it to his brother.

"That's the moment I'll always remember," says Luis Mayoral, who served as a liaison for Latin American players with the Texas Rangers. "Normally, Raffy is a big introvert. He can be very shy. But not that day. Both of them couldn't stop smiling. That I helped facilitate that meeting, their reunion, is one of my highlights of my many years in baseball."

In the Rangers' clubhouse, Jose Palmeiro met Nolan Ryan, Ruben Sierra, and Juan Gonzalez. They had heard about and had been touched by his story. Before the game, Rafael Palmeiro remembered being nervous for the first time in a long while. "I wanted to show him that I could play the game," he says. "It was important. Family, baseball—those were the links we had with each other."

The little brother nearly duplicated his feat of twenty-four hours earlier on that cold evening—coming close to hitting another home run, only to see the wind knock the ball down at the warning track. Soon afterward, Jose Palmeiro returned to Cuba and it would be another four years before the necessary paperwork was completed that would bring him out of Cuba for good. Jose Palmeiro now lives in Miami.

No wonder Rafael Palmeiro publicly opposed the Orioles' visit to Cuba in 1999. The exhibition series struck especially close to home because he had played with the Orioles the five previous seasons. In 1998, his last year in Baltimore, he led the Orioles in home runs, RBIs, walks, and total bases. But the Orioles chose not to re-sign him.

Yet, like anything involving Cuba, if you can move beyond the obvious, find a portal between the columns, what is said next can surprise you. Ask Palmeiro, a man who lost more than two decades with his brother because of the political posturing that exists between these two lands, if he would ever consider revisiting his homeland, and he immediately nods his head.

"Once Castro is gone, I'd like to go back," he tells me. "To take a look around. I left there when I was five years old. I hardly remember a thing. I remember my brother was like a second father to me. He'd kick my butt if I got out of line."

Then the conversation turns toward a World Cup for baseball, one of the few things that the owners and players can agree about. A tournament in which everyone would play for their country. An Olympics for the national pastime.

Palmeiro has the numbers to be on such a team. Despite battling through the 2002 season with a bum ankle and an aching calf, he says he plans to play another three or four years.

"Once this game is gone for you, it's gone," Palmeiro says. "It's all I've ever wanted to do. So why put a time frame on it? As long I'm healthy and can play this game at a high level, why stop? Nolan Ryan played this game until he was forty-six. And he was a pitcher, which puts a lot more strain on the body than playing first base. I don't have to worry about running into walls or running around like a shortstop. If I can stay healthy, stay strong and focused, I can do some damage over the next few years."

All along I assumed we've been talking about the U.S. team.

With McGwire retired and Thomas in a seasons-long slump, there would be room for Palmeiro on such an all-star squad. But one last time Palmeiro surprises me. Once more we're reminded how deep the connection is between baseball and Cuba.

"The American team would be great," he says. "But what I'd really like to be on is the Cuban team. For that to happen, things there would have to really change. Change for the better."

CLEMENTE'S LEGACY

"... he'd been a boy without a man's strong
voice but with his mother's permission to stay
very late on the beach to listen to the wind's
night harps, he could still remember, as if still
seeing it, how the liner would disappear when
the light of the beacon struck its side and how
it would reappear when the light had passed,
so that it was an intermittent ship sailing
along, appearing and disappearing, toward the
mouth of the bay ..."

◆ **GABRIEL GARCÍA MÁRQUEZ,**
   The Last Voyage of the Ghost Ship

Jorge Posada grew up watching the Atlanta Braves on WTBS, Ted Turner's superstation in Atlanta. In the late 1970s, this wasn't the team that became a National League dynasty—the winner of eleven divisional titles. This was before Greg Maddux, Tom Glavine, and the Joneses—Chipper and Andruw. The Braves ball club that Posada first followed had stars like Dale Murphy, Bob Horner, Claudell Washington, even Joe Torre at the helm for a time. More often than not, the Braves ball club Posada followed was lucky to finish at .500, and it was rarely in the postseason hunt.

Posada watched those games with his father, who was then a scout for the Toronto Blue Jays. "He'd always be asking, 'What do you do in this situation? How about this one?' And I'd have no idea," Posada tells me. "But then he'd explain everything to me. Maybe later on we'd go down to the backyard and play a lot of catch. Or we'd go to this field just a couple of blocks up from our house and he'd hit me grounders and flies. Just the two of us."

Father and son also watched the network games from *El Norte* on Saturday afternoons and during the postseason, and Posada's favorite player eventually became George Brett. ("I loved how he had pine tar all over his bat and batting gloves.") Still, like anyone who grew up in Puerto Rico, Posada was told about one more ballplayer—the legendary Roberto Clemente.

"Of course I never saw Clemente play in person," said Posada, who was born in 1971. "But my dad had some old footage of him. He'd show it to me and tell me the story of Clemente. Everyone where I come from knows his story, the way he could play."

The son of a sugar plantation foreman in Carolina, Puerto Rico, Clemente was discovered during an open tryout at Sixto Escobar Stadium in San Juan. Although he was still in high school, Clemente was easily the best player in attendance. The Dodgers' Al Campanis first signed the Puerto Rican prospect to a $10,000 contract in 1954, prompting Clemente's father to tell his son to buy himself "a good car and don't depend on anyone."

At that time any player signed to a contract greater than $4,000 had to be on the parent club's roster or risk being drafted by another club at the end of the season. Campanis told his minor-league people to hide Clemente for a year in their system so he could gain some experience. That ploy backfired in more ways than one. Sent to Montreal, Clemente was benched whenever he got too hot at the plate. It was a situation that he didn't fully understand and he threatened to go home. In the end, such deception didn't pay off for the Dodgers anyway. Pittsburgh Pirates president Branch Rickey had heard about Clemente and sent his super scout, Howie Haak, who would later sign such Latino stars as Manny Sanguillen and Tony Peña, to investigate. On Haak's recommendation, the last-place Pirates selected Clemente in a draft the next spring. Perhaps that's why years later Campanis was more than willing to outbid the Yankees for Fernando Valenzuela. He had learned how easily a talented player can slip from one's grasp.

Clemente admitted that he didn't know where Pittsburgh was when he first joined the Pirates in 1955. Pittsburgh certainly wasn't located anywhere near the top of the National League standings. Still, Clemente joined a promising nucleus of players—Bill Mazeroski, Dick Groat, and Vernon Law—and the Pirates soon found themselves in the 1960 World Series, where they upset the Yankees. While the baseball world will never for-get Mazeroski's stunning series-ending home run, insiders and students of the game noticed Clemente's spirited play.

"I remember the way he ran out a routine ground ball in the last game," Yankees pitcher Whitey Ford told Phil Musick in *Who Was Roberto? A Biography of Roberto Clemente.* "It was something most people forget, but it made the Pirates' victory possible."

That season Clemente batted .314 with sixteen home runs and led NL outfielders with nineteen assists. Yet he finished eighth in the MVP balloting.

"Roberto worked as hard as anybody on the team in 1960, and he was brokenhearted at finishing no better than eighth in the balloting," Mazeroski later said. "Our shortstop, Dick Groat, was the winner. Our third baseman, Don Hoak, finished second. Roberto was as valuable as either of them. It affected him as a person and made him bitter."

Others would contend that the MVP slight made the bud-ding superstar more moody, perhaps more prone to discuss his various injuries with anyone who asked, and in the long run it probably made him more driven to succeed. In any event, Amer-ica had its first Latino superstar with warts. Clemente could be a walking contradiction. He wasn't all smiles like Minoso. Not only would Clemente test the fans' and his teammates' patience, he would also test their ability to forgive. One could argue that if he hadn't died young, debates about his character, his person-ality quirks, would still be taking place. For how much are we ex-pected to forgive to have the chance to witness plays and on-field artistry that borders upon the unbelievable? That de-bate still rages within the game.

In their book *Away Games*, Marcos Breton and Jose Luis Vil-legas contend that matters began to come to a head in the years after World War II. Jackie Robinson had broken the color barrier, and those who had followed, among them Minoso, had pushed the door wide open. But managers and even fans sometimes didn't know what to think of this new wave of players led by Clemente, Orlando Cepeda, and the Alou brothers. They were dark-skinned like the other new superstars, Willie Mays and Hank Aaron. But they came from a completely different world, with far different ways of coping with the pressure of major-league play.

America's approach to baseball, then and arguably now, was routinely corporate, often rigid, even militaristic. The Latino way often sought the humor in a pressure situation. Whereas the U.S. approach stressed the team first, always the team, the Latino philosophy acknowledged that baseball invariably breaks down into one-on-one confrontations. It's the pitcher versus the hitter. The base runner first versus the pitcher, who tries to hold him close to first base, and then it quickly shifts to the would-be base stealer against the catcher. On defense, it's the hard-hit ball versus the fielder. Breton and Villegas tell a story about the old San Francisco Giants, the most star-crossed ball club of the early 1960s. Once Felipe Alou struck out four times in one game. In some circles, it's called the "golden sombrero." While such a disastrous day would have left most American players publicly downcast and disconsolate, the Latinos on the Giants joked and crowed at Alou. By the end of the game most of them were laughing along with him—doing their best to help him forget a bad day at the office.

"We Latins get more excited than Americans," Clemente once explained to Musick. "We have a lot of pepper blood."

THE STRUGGLE FOR RESPECT

Roberto Clemente first reported to the Pirates' spring training camp in 1955. On the first day, he was labeled as a "hot dog" by the one of the local papers. When he spoke, the newspapermen often quoted him phonetically, incorporating his accent. So, for example, if he said the word "This," they would spell it "Theez." "Hit" became "Heet." This made the promising right fielder sound less intelligent, and Clemente soon decided that most writers were only out to embarrass him. So began his rocky relationship with the Pittsburgh media specifically, and American society in general.

"I don't think much of the sportswriters," Clemente once said. "If I'm good enough to play, I have to be good enough to be treated like the rest of the players."

His frustration extended to Jim Crow segregation that he experienced in the minors and then on an annual basis when the Pirates headed to Florida for spring training. But unlike Minoso, Jose Cardenal, and the other Latino players who had come before him, it wasn't in Clemente's nature to shrug such things off. Longtime Pittsburgh sportswriter Myron Cope once remarked that Clemente "walked naked to the world."

And that was part of the allure. For here was a ballplayer who treated games as an actor would performances on Broadway. An aristocrat among tobacco-chewing good old boys. He moved with the quiet elegance of a dancer and the originality of a freethinker.

Clemente "broke the cultural rules of the game," writes Earl Shorris in *Latinos: A Biography of the People.* "He was a sixties man wearing spikes, ethnically proud, racially unafraid, graceful afield and in his life. Clemente loved fast cars, fine clothes, and the poor. He was Martí, Manolete, Machito, and Muhammad

Ali, and he could hit! He was not humble in the Anglo world. His name was Roberto; he refused ever to be called Bob."

While other outfielders would cut off a hard-hit smash up the line, stop, steady themselves and then throw the ball back to the infield, Clemente would grab that rocket destined for the fence, pirouette in one motion, and fire the ball back in.

"You'd watch him and find yourself saying to the guy next to you, 'Did you see that?' " says Frank Robinson.

"I never saw a player quite like Roberto Clemente," former player and now television analyst Tim McCarver told Fox Sports. "You were in the presence of greatness."

Throughout the 1960s, Clemente felt he rarely got his due, especially from the national media. He led the National League in hitting three times before he won the MVP award in 1966. It would be the only time he would win the award in his eighteen-year career. Clemente was often overlooked because he played in Pittsburgh and, arguably, because he was a Latino and proud of it. Clemente, like many artists, could be incredibly open about what was on his mind, humble one moment, arrogant the next. One time Cope asked Clemente how he was feeling, and before he knew it the Pirates star had flopped down on the floor and was explaining how much his back hurt and his neck ached and the various stretches he needed to do. Recognizing a story that would have people talking, Cope wrote a piece for *Sports Illustrated* about Clemente the hypochondriac. The piece included an illustration of the player that detailed all of his ailments. The medical descriptions ran from head to toe. Clemente considered the article another example of the sportswriters' bias against him specifically and Latinos in general.

In the late 1960s, the Pirates ball club began to change with the times. Scout Howie Haak continued to bring in talent from outside the country, and soon the Pittsburgh roster included such Latinos as outfielders Matty Alou and Manny Mota and catcher Manny Sanguillen. Harry Walker, who told Clemente that he was the man, replaced hard-driving manager Danny Murtaugh at the helm. The right fielder was already acknowledged as a star, but why settle for that? Why not try to be the best the game had to offer? Better than Mays or Aaron.

At the end of the 1961 season, Roberto Clemente and Orlando Cepeda sat side by the side in a Cadillac convertible and were paraded through San Juan, Puerto Rico. They were two of the best everyday players in baseball. Between them, they had captured the National League Triple Crown. Clemente had led the league with a .351 batting average, while Cepeda had hit 46 home runs and 142 RBIs, a San Francisco Giants record.

"Clemente was more of an introvert," says Bruce Markusen, an author of books about both men and an historian with the Baseball Hall of Fame in Cooperstown. "[Clemente] wouldn't show his sense of humor until he knew you. He was much more comfortable around friends and family. Whereas Cepeda has always been very outgoing. When you meet him, he makes you feel like he's known you for twenty years."

Both men were destined for greatness. Yet they would take very different, often difficult paths to get there. Clemente would struggle for recognition, even respect, in small-market Pittsburgh, before dying tragically before his time. Cepeda would become the star that fell to earth. The one who seemingly threw everything away, only to watch the baseball world take a long time to forgive his situation, his dizzying descent from national hero to persona non grata. For fourteen years, 1981 to 1994, Cepeda was the only eligible player with an average above .295 and with more than 300 home runs who was not in the Hall of Fame. Fifteen times he didn't receive sufficient votes from the Baseball Writers of America. His last time he was seven votes shy. That's why when he was named to Cooperstown in 1999, by a vote of the Veterans Committee, it was as much a vindication for him as it was for anybody who has struggled, who has made mistakes.

Born in Ponce, Puerto Rico, Cepeda broke in with the San Francisco Giants in 1958. He led the league in doubles and was named rookie of the year. He was known as "Cha-Cha" for his love of salsa music and "Baby Bull" for his family legacy and the serious intent he brought to the plate. That he would have been an instant hit at the major-league level shouldn't have surprised anyone who knew his family roots. He was the son of Perucho "The Bull" Cepeda—the Babe Ruth of Puerto Rico.

"Nobody was as good as my father," Cepeda tells me. "I never came close." Like many Latino stars of his era, Cepeda swung a R43—the same model bat that Ruth first popularized. Armed with such tradition, following in his father's footsteps, Cepeda combined with Willie Mays to form the most potent one-two power tandem in baseball from 1958 to 1964. Together they hit 488 home runs—9 more than Hank Aaron and Eddie Mathews recorded with the Braves.

While Bay Area fans soon embraced Cepeda as their favorite (Mays was seen as too entrenched with the franchise's original incarnation at New York's Polo Grounds), the Puerto Rican slugger rarely got along with the Giants' coaching staff. After Bill Rigney was fired during the 1960 season, Cepeda had tumultuous relationships with managers Alvin Dark and then Herman Franks.

"To be blunt, on many occasions Alvin made my life a living hell," Cepeda told Herb Fagen in his autobiography, *Baby Bull*. "Things got so bad at times that there were days I didn't want to go to the ballpark.

"What's ironic is that during those times of stress, my numbers were steadily improving. By the age of twenty-four, I was already 17 home runs ahead of Hank Aaron's pace at a similar age. During my first six years [1958–1963], I hit 191 home runs, drove in 650 runs, and hit at a .310 clip."

Baseball historian Bill James said that before the Baby Bull's "knees started giving him trouble, Cepeda's offensive statistics are closely parallel to Hank Aaron's at the same age."

For a groundbreaking article in 1960 for *Look* magazine, the muscular Cepeda was photographed in the nude from the waist up. Similar beefcake shots of Reggie Jackson and Nomar Garciaparra would be taken in future decades. Cepeda had been told that the *Look* article would detail why he was the best right-handed hitter in baseball. Instead the story allowed Dark to explain why he thought Cepeda would never be the team player Mays was. Perhaps Dark didn't appreciate moments like trying to get a teammate to loosen up after he'd struck out four times in a game. In the article, the San Francisco manager went as far as to say that Jim Davenport and Harvey Kuenn meant more to the overall success of the team than Cepeda.

"[In] my heart of hearts," Cepeda said, "I believe that Alvin Dark tried to destroy me emotionally."

Almost two decades later, Dark would explain that he had simply been sticking up for Willie Mays. He acknowledged that his "endless praising of Mays hurt Orlando Cepeda. He was a favorite son in San Francisco, and I shouldn't have diminished him. I didn't intend to, I was only out to uplift Willie Mays, but he was on the other end of the seesaw. I didn't handle Orlando very well. But I was as tough on myself as I was on anybody, and I felt if a guy wasn't doing all he should, it was my job to tell him. I think now that if I'd been able to get to Orlando sooner, I wouldn't have had the problems that came up, the 'race' issues."

A religious man, Dark once said that God didn't create men equal. He "gave every race and ethnic group special attributes."

The Giants eventually fired him in large part because of his inability to communicate with Latino players. But his departure did not come soon enough to save Cepeda's career in San Francisco. Compounding matters was the deteriorating condition of Cepeda's knee. A weight had fallen on it during a workout after the 1962 season, and neither Dark nor Giants management at first knew the severity of the injury.

"Because I knew that the team would give me flak, I didn't tell a soul other than my wife," Cepeda explained. "I was determined not to let Dark get on my case any more than he already did."

Instead, Cepeda tried to play through the injury. To help with the pain, he began to smoke marijuana—a vice that eventually would cost him dearly.

Even though his numbers didn't fall off that much—in the 1963 and 1964 season he still hit better than .300 and had thirty home runs—the telling statistic was how few times he could patrol the outfield. Before the injury he had played eighty games there. He took pride in playing the outfield. Now with the bum knee he played only a handful of games there, and with first baseman Willie McCovey coming into his own, Giants management decided Cepeda was expendable. Nineteen games into the 1966 season, two years after Dark was let go, they traded him to the St. Louis Cardinals. The next year, Cepeda and another newcomer, Roger Maris, were the offensive catalysts of St. Louis's world championship team. That season Cepeda became the first unanimous choice for the National League MVP Award.

RECOGNITION AT LAST

After finishing with a .500 record in 1967—the same season Cepeda and the St. Louis Cardinals won the World Series—Roberto Clemente and the Pirates began to turn heads in the National League. In 1970 they reached the postseason, only to be swept by the Cincinnati Reds in the National League Championship Series. But the following season, Pittsburgh defeated San Francisco and went on to face the Baltimore Orioles in the World Series. Despite being a decided underdog, Clemente told his teammates not to worry.

"If you guys get me to the World Series, I'll win it," Willie Stargell remembered Clemente saying. "It was almost like he said, 'Sit down. I've got a job to do and I'll show you how it's done.'"

Even though the Orioles were often in control of that fall classic—they won the first two games and were only one victory away from winning the world championship after a dramatic game-six victory in ten innings—they didn't have an answer for Clemente. Time after time he rallied his team, hitting .414 with two home runs and four RBIs. But just as important was his play in the field. By the end of the seven-game series, Baltimore base runners knew better than to test his arm. They, as well as the rest of the nation, which enjoyed its first World Series game in prime time, had witnessed the grace of Clemente's spins and the power of his arm.

"Finally, after all those years," Nelson Briles told Fox Sports, "he got the respect."

Markusen of the Hall of Fame adds, "I don't want to say that he single-handedly led the Pirates to victory because there were other players like Steve Blass, who played a role. But Clemente did as much as one player could not only to have his team win, but to pull off an immense upset.

"The Orioles had blown the Pirates away in the first two games. It looked like it was going to be a four-game sweep. Clemente made great throws from the outfield. He hit two key home runs. He was constantly on base, constantly taking extra bases. He thoroughly dominated the stage."

In the riotous victory celebration after game seven in the Pirates' clubhouse, Clemente subtly reminded fans that a new crop of major-leaguers had arrived on the scene. Until 1970, his baseball cards had portrayed him as "Bob Clemente" even though he preferred Roberto. In the victorious clubhouse, commentators again called him Bob or Bobby. This time Clemente shrugged it off. When it was time to be interviewed on national television, the Pirates star began his comments in Spanish, thanking his parents back in his native Puerto Rico.

That one moment "made people aware of his Latino heritage," Markusen says. "It made a point of not only is this guy a great player, but he's very proud of where he hails from. That was an extremely important series not just for Clemente, but for Latin players in general."

Heading into the 1972 season, Clemente needed only 118 hits to reach 3,000 for his career. But the process stretched to the last home stand. Stuck at 2,999, Clemente finally doubled into the left-center field gap and acknowledged the standing ovation by doffing his helmet after reaching second base. In the National League Championship Series, the Pirates were edged out by Cincinnati, the team that was about to become the dynasty called "the Big Red Machine."

A survey of the rosters of the prominent teams of the 1970s reveals that almost all had significant contributions from budding Latino stars. The Reds had Cuban Tony Perez at first, Dominican Cesar Geronimo in center, and Davey Concepcion, who would inspire a new wave of young Venezuelans, at short-stop. The Oakland A's would take three consecutive world championships with Cuban Bert Campaneris at shortstop and the flamboyant Reggie Jackson, who described himself as "a black kid with Spanish, Indian, and Irish blood," leading the way. Alvin Dark, who had been criticized for his inability to communicate with Latinos in San Francisco, managed the A's to the last of their world championships in that decade and had nothing but praise for Campaneris, calling him "the best offensive shortstop since Pee Wee Reese."

Clemente, though, wouldn't be part of the continuing transformation of the game he loved or see how his adopted land had come to see the Latino athlete, a phenomenon that soon would be as important to U.S. culture as the rise of the African-American athlete a decade or so before. After the 1972 season, Clemente went home to his native Puerto Rico, where he was a national hero. When an earthquake ravaged Nicaragua, he took it upon himself to help. It's just as important for players to be good citizens as good athletes, he often told the youth of his homeland. It's now the credo of his sports complex, which his widow, Vera, runs today.

Clemente commissioned a plane and loaded it with food and supplies for those who were suffering in Nicaragua. The plane went down on New Year's Eve 1972. His body was never found.

"He died the year I was born," says Toronto Blue Jays first baseman Carlos Delgado, who grew up in Aguadilla, a beachfront city in the northwest corner of Puerto Rico. "I never saw him play, but I've seen highlights and videos. My winter team [Santurce] is the same team he played for. He's something anybody from this island will never forget."

"MAKE A DIFFERENCE"

When Cepeda's playing career ended in 1974, he returned to Puerto Rico. After Clemente's tragic death, Cepeda had become the island's reigning baseball hero. But when he was arrested at the San Juan Airport for smuggling marijuana from Colombia, Cepeda quickly became an outcast. Television commercials featuring him were immediately pulled off the air. His name was removed from neighborhood ballfields where his sons played. Before the front-page news, Cepeda had drawn 10,000 for a baseball clinic. Now few admitted to being his friend.

"With one stupid decision, everything changed," Cepeda tells me. "My life became a struggle."

He was sentenced to five years in prison, and in early summer of 1978 he entered the minimum-security federal prison at Eglin Air Force Base in Florida.

"That was the darkest moment," he says, "walking past those gates. Being locked away. Afterward, I realized it was the best thing that could have happened to me. But that moment, when I was going into jail, it was the darkest time not only for me, but also for my family. My mother, brother, and friends."

Cepeda served ten months, cleaning toilets and doing laundry, until he was paroled.

"In jail you learn that we take so many things for granted, and the small things that we don't pay attention to in life can be so huge, so important," he says. "Going to jail made me aware."

Life outside of jail wasn't any easier at first for Cepeda. His first marriage fell apart and he lost his job as batting coach and scout with the Chicago White Sox. Depressed, uncertain about his future, Cepeda found hope in Buddhism. He began to attend daily meetings of the Nichiren Shoshu sect, which employs a chanting mantra to cleanse the mind and soul. Through such practice Cepeda began to find inner peace.

"It helped me to learn not to blame anybody anymore," he says. "I learned to go forward in life. Learn that it offers so much in a positive way. We have the potential to achieve that. When you chant, you connect yourself with the universe. It's an invocation."

In 1986 Cepeda was invited back to San Francisco. That's when the final step of his redemption took place. As soon as he walked into old Candlestick Park, where he had played for eight seasons, everyone seemed to recognize him. Autograph seekers soon surrounded him. The old magic was back.

After beginning as a scout, Cepeda became the Giants' community liaison. He especially enjoys talking with kids.

"I tell them to never give up," he says. "I tell them what happened to me in my life. I tell them about Roberto Clemente. I tell them about myself and what I had to go through. How you have only opportunities, no excuses. I tell them to be somebody. Make a difference."

TAKING ROOT

Those who have followed in Clemente's and Cepeda's footsteps, taking such words to heart, today rank among the best players in the game. Puerto Rico remains a rich source of baseball talent despite the influx of talent from the Dominican Republic, Venezuela, and elsewhere. But, like Clemente and Cepeda, ballplayers from this land have occasionally clashed with the cultural perceptions of America. While it's easy now to appreciate what Jackie Robinson and Orestes Minoso did in earning a place in the major leagues, most of the time human beings aren't as saintly. All of us are contradictions. Only a few have the courage to be honest about their foibles—to walk naked in the world like Clemente. One of the unspoken things in baseball is that Latinos are often considered too demonstrative—perhaps too moody to be trusted for the long haul. Such preconceptions have been a part of baseball since Latinos began to strive for larger roles in the game.

"Roberto Clemente was my hero," says Roberto Alomar. "When you know what he went through, it helps with whatever can happen to you."

But can every transgression be forgiven because of what Clemente once explained was pepper blood? Alomar may be the ultimate example of how willing fans and baseball people are to forget an unfortunate situation. In 1996, in an argument at home plate, Alomar spat on umpire John Hirschbeck. The confrontation happened during the final weekend of the season as Baltimore fought to clinch the American League wild card. The Orioles' magic number was down to two after they won the opener of the four-game series. In the first inning of the game on September 27, 1996, Hirschbeck called Alomar out on a called third strike. Replays showed the pitch to be several inches outside.

Afterward Alomar told Hirschbeck, "You can't call that a strike."

"It was a strike," retorted Hirschbeck, who has the reputation for being one of the more confrontational umpires.

"It was outside," Alomar said.

"Do your job," the umpire replied. "Swing the bat."

"I'll do my job," Alomar snapped. "You do yours."

In most cases the incident would have ended there. Alomar returned to the Baltimore dugout. But when Hirschbeck heard him continue to complain, he ejected the All-Star second baseman. That brought Alomar back to home plate with Orioles manager Davey Johnson right behind him. That's when things got ugly. Alomar and Hirschbeck exchanged profanities, and the All-Star second baseman become so incensed he spat in the umpire's face. Even though both parties soon apologized to each other, some in the game never forgave Alomar. Just as troubling were the whispers that Alomar only played hard when he wanted to. It was said that the Hirschbeck incident had robbed the Puerto Rico native of his joy for the game.

"When he wants to play, there is nobody better," Hall of Fame pitcher Jim Palmer says. "Some guys might hit more homers, but with the glove and all, nobody is better."

When he wants to play. Alomar bristles at such criticism.

"Maybe Jim Palmer never had a bad year," Alomar tells me. "Maybe he was always perfect. I'm not perfect."

Maybe not, but Alomar's play often borders upon the extraordinary. The switch-hitting second baseman broke in with the San Diego Padres in 1988, collecting his first major-league hit off Nolan Ryan. Traded to the Toronto Blue Jays along with Joe Carter before the 1991 season, he won the first of his six consecutive Gold Gloves that year and was a mainstay of the Blue Jays' back-to-back World Series championship team.

Manager Mike Hargrove has known Alomar since Roberto and his older brother, Sandy, were kids running around the Texas clubhouse when he and Sandy Alomar Sr. were teammates there. He's made a point of following their careers, checking the daily box scores to see how they were doing. Still, Hargrove was surprised when he managed Roberto and got the chance to see him play every day.

"This game, at this level, you only need a little edge," Hargrove says, "and if there has been a player looking for an edge all the time, it's him. I saw Joe Morgan play, and Robbie Alomar is every bit as good or better than him. I don't know why Robbie was left off [Major League Baseball's] All-Century list."

Even though Hargrove has never spoken directly with Alomar about the Hirschbeck incident, he agrees that some fans will never forgive or forget.

"John has forgiven him," Hargrove says. "There is no bad blood between him and John. Does it bother Robbie? He never talks about it, so I don't really know. But I think it does at certain levels. I don't know that it bothers him that there are fans that still boo him. But in knowing him, knowing the type of person he is, I think it bothers him that he did that."

In New York, Alomar found himself as the second-best second baseman in town with the emergence of the Yankees' Alfonso Soriano. His string of All-Star appearances ended at a dozen as the Mets fell from contention. Still, some of the biggest names in the front office believe that one day Alomar will be able to turn the page.

"[He's] a sensitive kid," Seattle Mariners executive vice president Pat Gillick told *USA Today Baseball Weekly.* Gillick had Alomar on his roster in Toronto and Baltimore, and expected him to eventually get over what the *New York Times* had called "a major case of stage fright."

Montreal Expos general manager Omar Minaya, who grew up in the New York area and attended games as a kid at Shea Stadium, added that it would be a shame if the Mets missed out on their first foreign-born Latino superstar. "As a kid you went to see the Pirates to see Clemente," he says. "Someday you'd like to say you went to see the Mets because of Alomar."

BERNIE BASEBALL

One reason baseball insiders remain optimistic about Alomar's dilemma is that it took several seasons for Bernie Williams to become comfortable playing in New York. Today, though, if you visit the Yankees' clubhouse, Williams can often be found at his locker, playing his Fender Stratocaster guitar. A native of San Juan, Puerto Rico, Williams may have played on the same team with Juan Gonzalez growing up, but away from the diamond he studied to be a classical guitarist. To this day his game can be like a distant melody. The passion, the drive, may not be apparent at first. But the more you watch, the better able you are to grasp the notes.

"There isn't a day that goes by when I don't wonder, How did I get here?" he says. "My mom was a school principal, the main provider in my family. When she retired from public school system, she taught college. She wanted me to be an engineer or lawyer. In my mind I thought I'd be that or in a music conservatory. We didn't grow up rich. We were a hardworking middle-class family, and I never thought that playing sports would be how I make my living. Go figure."

Quiet and introspective, Bernie Williams appears to be ill suited to his professional surroundings. An anomaly set against the glare of bright lights, big city. Team officials and fans once wondered if the shy center fielder would ever grow into the big shoes left by such Yankee greats as Joe DiMaggio and Mickey Mantle. While in high school, Williams had been wooed by the Philadelphia Phillies and Pittsburgh Pirates before he signed with the Yankees on his seventeenth birthday. Early in his minor-league career, Williams nearly quit baseball to devote more time to his music. Yankees owner George Steinbrenner once urged his GM to trade him. But since the mid-1990s, nobody has played the game better, especially during the pressurized setting of division and league championship series.

In the '95 Division Series loss to Seattle, Williams became the first major-leaguer to homer from both sides of the plate in a playoff game. He duplicated that feat the following year as

New York won its first World Series in eighteen years. Though often criticized for being lethargic or disinterested early in his career (teammates would joke about how he would nap until a few minutes before game time), ex-Yankee Reggie Jackson applauded Williams's ability to perform on the postseason stage. He said those breakthrough years were "about Bernie battling to be accepted as a great player. He wants people to hold him in that regard." While Williams will still struggle at times, the Yankees have learned to be patient with him.

"Sometimes Bernie looks like he has some at bats that don't make sense for his ability," says Yankees manager Joe Torre. "Then, all of a sudden, when something needs to happen, it's like there's a certain amount of magic that's tied to him. We all expect it, and he's never let us down."

Opposing pitcher Pat Hentgen adds, "Of all the great guys in that lineup, he's the guy who can beat you all by himself."

Years ago my wife and I attended a minor-league game in Prince William, Virginia, then the home of the Yankees' Class A ball club. That evening we began a tradition that we later continued with our two children. At the end of the game, everybody picked his or her player most likely to succeed. In other words, the player who could someday reach the majors.

The Prince William team had Tom Tresh Jr. at shortstop and Hensley "Bam-Bam" Meulens at third. But this gangly kid in center captivated us. The one who twice ran gracefully to the fence to make running catches. The one who won the game with a home run that disappeared into the night. That player was Bernie Williams.

THE BEST SINCE BENCH

That's the great thing about baseball. It comes down to moments or snapshots that you remember for the rest of your life. Roger Angell of *The New Yorker* talks about following the playoff game between the Brooklyn Dodgers and New York Giants in 1951. The one that was eventually decided when Bobby Thomson hit "the shot heard 'round the world." Just before Thomson stepped to the plate, Angell called for his wife to come in and watch the game on television. Sometimes you have the feeling that something big is about to happen. Maybe that's how casual viewers are transformed into lifelong fans. One highlight is so memorable they can always picture it in their mind.

But behind every great play there are hours of preparation. The near obsession with the game in Puerto Rico resulted in catcher Ivan Rodriguez's always looking for ways to improve. His approach continued years after he had reached the major leagues and was instrumental in his becoming the league MVP, the award Clemente once coveted. In narrowly edging out pitcher Pedro Martinez, Rodriguez became the first catcher to win the American League MVP since Thurman Munson in 1976.

Before that '99 season, Rodriguez took his cherished Viper automobile to the Chrysler dealership in San Juan for servicing. On duty that day was Edgar Diaz, an Olympic pole vaulter who was trying to make ends meet as he prepared for international competition.

"I just told him I could help him run better," Diaz recalls.

While some athletes would have shrugged off such an offer, Rodriguez always seems to be watching and listening. Maybe that's how you improve upon excellence. Become the best catcher since the Reds' Johnny Bench. You listen while the rest of the world hurries by.

"I've always been able to throw," Rodriguez tells me. "Even when I was little, I could throw a ball. I guess it was my gift. But that doesn't mean you aren't open to other things—ways to improve."

Diaz took Rodriguez to the track and slowly refined his running style. During the off-season they worked together five days a week, and their workouts would make a decathlete wince. They ran intervals, usually 200 or 400 meters at a time. They threw the shot put. Not just with one hand, but with both hands to improve strength and flexibility. Rodriguez was a six-time All-Star before those workouts, but he became the league MVP afterward. Now seemingly in the twilight of his career, overshadowed on the Texas Rangers during the 2002 season by two other probable Hall of Famers in Alex Rodriguez and Rafael Palmeiro, it's easy to forget how Rodriguez's presence behind the plate once impacted ball games. That he won ten consecutive Gold Gloves after reaching the majors in 1991. In his MVP season, he threw out nearly 55 percent of those who tried to steal a base on his watch.

Toronto Blue Jays outfielder Shannon Stewart, a quality base stealer, remembers one of his first encounters with Rodriguez and his amazing arm. Stewart had reached first base and had just stepped off the bag to take his lead. He wasn't as far off as he planned when Rodriguez threw behind him. Stewart barely dived back to the bag safely.

"I got up and he's smiling at me, saying, 'Be ready,' " Stewart says. "It's fun and frustrating to go against him. To steal a bag you'd better get a big lead and pray the next pitch is a curveball. That's the only way you have any chance."

STAYING CLOSE TO HOME

Today, most scouts consider Clemente's homeland a baseball backwater. They will tell you it's more "cost-efficient" to look elsewhere for talent. That the Dominican Republic and Venezuela are better places to build baseball academies. But when Edgar Martinez was growing up he became convinced that he would only reach the major leagues if he stayed in Puerto Rico.

He explains that the examples of Clemente and Cepeda were there for everyone to see. "You just had to follow them," he says.

In addition, only in Puerto Rico could Martinez's grandfather attend all his games. Their relationship was always close, in large part because the boy's parents had separated only years after his birth.

In Martinez's first season in Little League on the island, he emerged as one of the best young players in Puerto Rico. That was an accomplishment, considering that Jose Lind and Carmelo Martinez hailed from Martinez's neighborhood, Maguayo. When Martinez's parents unexpectedly reconciled, suddenly eager to move their children with them to New York City, the boy refused to go. He saw his older sister and younger brother leave, but he remained because he loved his grandparents and baseball too much.

"If I'd gone back to New York with them, I probably would have never played more baseball," Edgar Martinez explains. "My younger brother stopped playing then. I probably would have, too. But you can't help but play where I come from."

Staying in Puerto Rico, to play the game year-round, allowed Martinez to perfect one of the most complex batting stances in the game—an intriguing blend of counterbalances and angles. He holds the bat up over his head, elbows high, with barrelhead pointed out toward the pitcher. The only batter I've seen with such a pronounced exaggeration, that buggy whip ready to come around, is another Latino, Julio Franco. Martinez, though, further complicates the stance by standing pigeon-toed in the box, anchoring himself on his back right foot.

"When I first saw him I questioned his arm, his power, his speed, and his position," says Roger Jongewaard, Seattle Mariners vice president of scouting and player development. "But once I saw him swing a bat, I never questioned his hitting."

Manager Tony La Russa says that Martinez has long been "one of the most complete hitters in the game. There's no set way you can pitch him. If you do, he's on everything."

"Some guys are mistake hitters, but he's a great pitch hitter, too," adds former Oakland pitcher Steve Ontiveros. "He's able to take your best stuff and drive it."

Mario Salgado died in November 1992, just months after his grandson won the American League batting crown—one of the few players ever to lead the league in batting while playing for a last-place team. The day of his funeral, Martinez's grandmother, Manuela, suffered a massive stroke. In one day he lost the two people who had raised him. Those who had allowed him to stay in Puerto Rico and play baseball.

Sometimes during a game, Martinez believes he can still see his grandfather.

"In the middle of everything, there he will be," says the slugger who averaged 42 doubles and 110 RBIs a season between 1995 and 2000. "The reason why I still play."

UNITING A COMMUNITY

"Look at the map of our backyard: Here

is Cuba. Here is Mexico. Here is

Santo Domingo. Here is Honduras.

Here is Nicaragua. . . . Look at the map,

children. Learn."

◆ **CARLOS FUENTES,** *The Old Gringo*

Walk into a major-league clubhouse and you're never sure what you'll see on television. In the expansive country clubs found in many of the new ballparks, color TVs hang from the ceilings. Late at night, after their particular contest has concluded, players will watch the last of the night's games or the highlights on ESPN or Fox as they dress. But in the afternoon, in the long hours before the next game, the fare can range from Jerry Springer to CNN to anything else going on in the sports world. During soccer's World Cup, such competition dominated these screens. In large part the players watched because the format—everyone playing for his country—is something they would like to see happen in baseball.

"People here may think that the U.S. would win easy," says Pedro Martinez, echoing the interest Rafael Palmeiro and many others have in such games, "but Puerto Rico would have the Alomar brothers. Venezuela would be right there, who knows about Cuba, and I like my country's chances."

Indeed, the roster for the Dominican Republic could have Sammy Sosa in right field and Martinez on the mound. A pretty potent combination in any short series.

The Yankees' Mariano Rivera, statistics-wise the best post-season relief pitcher of all time, watched World Cup soccer, too. He had a more vested interest besides the interest in national format and seeing other quality athletes compete. In countries such as Cuba and the Dominican Republic, baseball has always been king. Yet in Mexico, Puerto Rico, Venezuela, and Rivera's home country of Panama, soccer and baseball compete daily to attract the best athletes. Befitting a baseball Hall of Famer, Orlando Cepeda sees no comparison between the two sports.

"Baseball is the game of skill," he says, "and because we Latins have the skills, we can change our lives. Through baseball we can get a better education, we can get a better standing. In Latin countries, baseball is for the poor people. The passion to play hasn't changed from my generation to the next."

Palmeiro's sons play soccer and baseball, and he admits that he doesn't see any great skill involved in soccer.

"It's kicking a ball," he said. "Baseball demands so much more."

Still, in the clubhouse, where Rivera has settled in on this weekday afternoon to watch a replay of the U.S.-Germany match, the preeminent closer of the modern era can only laugh at such logic. "Maybe they should take another took," he says. "Soccer's much more than just kicking a ball."

While he was growing up, soccer was Rivera's first love. He was an accomplished goal scorer, and only an ankle injury in high school derailed him from pursuing the game at a higher level. In this changing world, he cautioned that baseball's powers that be should never take the Latino countries for granted. From the Caribbean down through Central America to Venezuela and Colombia, such locales may not always be baseball hotbeds. Still, Rivera does acknowledge that baseball is blessed by tradition. As Dominican-born Omar Minaya says, "The game has always been equal parts sport and religion throughout the Caribbean. Baseball is so ingrained there, I don't ever see it slipping away."

When Rivera's soccer career went south, he found that many of the same moves and coordination that he had used on the soccer field benefited him on the baseball diamond. To this day, when he's in a difficult situation, men on base, another good hitter digging in at the plate, he'll recall his old soccer mind-set: attack, be aggressive. The Yankees closer said that when he changed primary sports relatively late, it helped to know that others from his country had already succeeded at the major-league level. Roberto Kelly was playing then, so Rivera started to follow him. Then he was told about Rod Carew.

Swinging from the left side of the plate, Carew became an icon not only in Panama but also in his adopted land of America. After Clemente's tragic death, he fostered a more widespread recognition of Latinos playing the national pastime. In 1977, Carew made a season-long run at hitting .400 that saw him grace the covers of *Sports Illustrated* and *Time*. The man he was chasing was the legendary Ted Williams, who hit .406 in 1941.

"I may have been a pitcher," Rivera tells me, "but Carew is as big in my country as Clemente was in his. Guys like that show you the way."

WRONG SIDE OF THE TRACKS

Rod Carew was born on a Panama Railroad train as his mother tried to hurry from Gatun, in the Canal Zone, to Gorgas and a better hospital forty miles away. He was named Rodney Cline Carew after the doctor who had come in from the white section of the train to help deliver him. From the beginning, Carew was no stranger to segregation, and he became an outspoken critic of it.

"I've never been a militant," Carew says in his autobiography. "The black Latin players generally are not militant. I guess most of us are just happy to be here in the States and playing ball. We know that the opportunities don't exist in the Latin countries the way they do here. So we have a tendency to shut our mouths more than American blacks—like we're guests in the country. We get older, though; we change."

When Carew was fifteen, his mother moved the family to New York City. Baseball kept a young Carew off the streets and he soon blossomed into an impressive line drive hitter. After a secret workout at Yankee Stadium before a New York-Minnesota game, the Twins signed him.

"Baseball was in my family," Carew explains. "My uncles played it well. So did my brother. My sisters and father played it . . . When my mother was in grade school, she was a good softball pitcher, she told me. All I know is her front teeth are false, compliments of a line drive. I guess I inherited my fielding from her."

At first Carew struggled defensively, especially trying to turn the pivot at second base. Manager Billy Martin was instrumental in helping him improve his fielding. As a hitter, some initially criticized Carew's reluctance to swing for the fences. Latino hitters had long been characterized as "good field, no hit" players. Instead of trying to pull a ball deep down the line, more often than not, Carew was good for a well-placed line drive to the opposite field. In addition, he was the slugger of a thousand stances. Carew owned up to using at least five different stances at the plate. Dick Williams, who managed a half dozen major-league teams, grumbled it was more like twenty and that facing Carew was like "pitching to five different guys every night." Carew approached hitting in his own particular way, and eventually it took Ted Williams, whose legacy he would chase, to come to his defense.

"When I first saw Carew in the late sixties, I didn't think he had the talent," Williams told *Sports Illustrated*. "He was a little too lackadaisical to suit me. He still looks lackadaisical. It's his style. He's so smooth he seems to be doing it without trying. Some guys—Pete Rose is one, and I put myself in this category—have to snort and fume to get everything going. Carew doesn't."

Carew finished the 1977 season hitting .388—roughly seven hits shy of becoming the first player since Williams in 1946 to hit better than .400. Carew says he "wasn't terribly disappointed at falling short. I knew it was going to be hard to do, especially for my style—I wasn't walking a lot, and to hit .400 you probably have to be more selective with pitches."

Carew's .388 was fifty points higher than the next-best batting average in the majors that year. According to Baseball Library.com, that's the largest margin in history.

After becoming critical of Twins owner Calvin Griffith's skinflint ways, Carew signed with the then California Angels and later became the ball club's hitting coach. Although he said he had no ambition to manage, Carew became a mentor to many contemporary players.

"So much of my success I owe to him," said center fielder Jim Edmonds. "He was a father figure to me. I'd ask him about everything. On the [team] plane we'll talk about how to handle the press, the public life. He's been there. He knows it all."

First baseman J. T. Snow says that Carew would always have "that mentality of a player. He still thinks he could go up there and hit, and he probably could. He could hit .300."

Carew was the second Latino player after Clemente to collect his 3,000th hit. On the day Carew did so—August 4, 1985, off Minnesota's Frank Viola—he was reluctant to hold a news conference, even though he was just the sixteenth player in history to reach that plateau. A private man, Carew maintains that baseball is a team game. But, of course, he did need to talk with the media, and on that day his daughter Michelle, then seven years old, sat on his lap as the cameras rolled. It would be Michelle's situation that would endear Carew to the baseball community, especially the players he coached.

Carew retired after the 1985 season. He had led the league six times in hitting, and finished with a .328 career batting average. In 1991, he followed Clemente into the Hall of Fame. A few seasons after that milestone, Michelle Carew contracted leukemia and her father was forced to go public in a way that was totally out of character for him. Doctors determined that Michelle Carew could be saved if a donor was found that matched her bone marrow. In November 1995, Carew began a public awareness campaign, appearing on national television shows and handing out cards to strangers with the phone number of the marrow program. The donor registry's rolls increased by more than 2 million—up 1.5 million from the year before.

"I didn't want to make a spectacle out of my daughter's health," Carew once told me. "We talked about it as a family. Michelle said if it would help out other kids, then we should do it. And I said okay. She knew how tough it was for me."

Despite the increased awareness and surge in registered donors, Michelle Carew died just before dawn on April 17, 1996. Finding a match had proven next to impossible because Rod Carew is of Panamanian and West Indian descent; his wife is Russian Jewish. In a cruel irony, Carew's surviving children, daughters Charryse and Stephanie, are perfect marrow matches for each other.

After the EKG flatlined in Michelle's room, Carew embraced the group of family and friends who had gathered. Then he went into the corridor of the Children's Hospital of Orange County, California, a floor that he often walked in the previous months, speaking with other sick kids, being encouraged by their determination. At the end of the corridor, he rapped his left hand three times against the wall and then placed his forehead against it. After a few moments, he gathered himself, telling himself he was ready to move on.

But, of course, it's never that easy. A month after Michelle's death, Carew was back with the Angels, once again their hitting coach. On road trips he had trouble sleeping and he found himself walking the streets of Boston, New York, and Baltimore. In each city strangers recognized him. They came up to him and offered their condolences, saying how much his daughter's struggle had impacted their lives. Some nights he would walk the city streets until they were deserted and the world had folded into itself. He would gaze up at the night sky and talk to his little girl.

"You've done a great job, kid," he would tell her. "You're still helping people."

Carew still makes his home in Southern California. When his two former teams, the Minnesota Twins and Anaheim Angels, met in the American League playoffs, he threw out the ceremonial first pitch. Even though Carew hasn't coached at the major-league level in years, he still has a hand in it, as he likes to say. Neighborhood kids come to his door, almost asking if he can come out and play. He does—playing ball and instructing them in the nuances of the game. The Hall of Famer does so because he, like many in baseball, contends that you can never be certain about where the next superstar will come from. Just look at what's happened in recent memory, they will say. For if a slender kid from the Bronx via Panama could become the hitting star of the 1970s, just look at what followed. The next decade saw the rise of a Latino pitcher who became a national celebrity. He arrived in the majors from Mexico, a land often overlooked when it comes to baseball talent.

MEXICO'S PLACE

Many assume that baseball traveled to Mexico, Panama, Puerto Rico, Venezuela, and the Dominican Republic solely because of U.S. interaction and occasional occupation. Actually, it was the Cubans' fight for independence from Spain during the last two decades of the 1800s that spurred the game's migration and widespread popularity. Some Cubans fled the island during this violent period. Some went east to the Dominican Republic, while more headed west to the Yucatan Peninsula of Mexico. There the game found a home throughout the region. In their book *Beisbol: Latin Americans and the Grand Old Game,* Michael and May Adams Oleksak detail how amateur teams were formed among the children of the upper classes. In addition, baseball found a home among the working class, especially the Mayan field workers.

Abelardo Rodriguez almost became the first Mexican to play professionally north of the border. He was the second baseman for the University of Arizona team and was offered a contract by the Los Angeles Angels. But at his family's urging he nixed the deal to concentrate on politics. A good move, as Rodriguez was elected president of Mexico in 1932. The following year Baldomero Melo "Mel" Almada broke in with the Boston Red Sox. He batted .284 during a seven-year career that included four teams—the Red Sox, Washington Senators, St. Louis Browns, and Brooklyn Dodgers.

Until the 1940s, Mexico was a baseball backwater. Barnstorming teams from the House of David to those headlined by the likes of Jimmie Foxx and other major-league stars traveled there during the off-season. While Martin Dihigo and others who were deemed too dark skinned for the major leagues played exhibitions there against Negro League squads, and Connie

Mack's Philadelphia A's trained in Mexico City, it took the millionaire Jorge Pasquel to put Mexican baseball on the map.

In the years before U.S. involvement in World War II, Pasquel signed such Negro League all-stars as Josh Gibson and Ray Dandridge to play in his new Mexican League. Next Pasquel brought Satchel Paige and Roy Campanella south of the border. And, finally, in his most audacious move, he began to sign white major-leaguers, including catcher Mickey Owen, pitcher Max Lanier, and outfielder Danny Gardella to supplement his teams as well. In 1944, Rogers Hornsby was lured south to manage, and Pasquel invited Babe Ruth down for a well-publicized visit. When Pasquel hinted that he had the money to take a run at such legends as Ted Williams, Joe DiMaggio, and Stan Musial, MLB commissioner Happy Chandler declared the Mexican League an "outlaw" operation and that any player who signed there could face a lifetime ban. The players were reinstated in 1949 after a lawsuit by Gardella threatened the legality of the reserve clause.

In the end, Pasquel was undone by his inability to compete at the grassroots level. Most of the stadiums in the Mexican League weren't large enough for him to cover the costs of luring top-flight talent from the United States. By 1951, he had given up control of his cherished Veracruz ball club, even though it had won the league championship that year. He died in a plane crash in 1955. Still, his legacy remained as the only head of a foreign league to successfully raid the U.S. major leagues.

"Like Pancho Villa, he was not afraid to stand up to the giant nation to the north," write the Oleksaks. "These victories may be symbolic at best, but they remain important victories to the Mexican people."

Alejo Peralta, who succeeded Pasquel as the Mexican League's new strongman, fanned such nationalistic flames. His goal for the Mexico City Tigres was to have an all-Mexican roster. This sense of the Mexican League for Mexicans still exists today. Major-league teams interested in talent south of the border first have to negotiate with a player's Mexican League team before signing him to a major-league contract. As a result, the Mexican game can be passed over. As Seattle Mariners general manager Pat Gillick once said, teams go "where it's the most cost efficient." In other words, they go to the Dominican Republic or Venezuela, where baseball academies allow ball clubs to survey a larger number of players and sign the best to minimal contracts. In essence, it's the old Joe Cambria model but on a much larger scale.

LOOKING CLOSER TO HOME

Orioles general manager Syd Thrift sits at a table in the courtyard of the Hotel Nacional in Havana. Around him swirls a party reminiscent of Cuba's golden age. That time fifty years ago when any such gathering, on any night of the week, had the potential to last until dawn. In the twilight, before another sunrise, a crowd would form along the waterfront to await the evening ferry from Florida, everyone anxious to see who else had arrived to join the longest-running party on earth. Across the way, Orioles outfielder Brady Anderson huddles in conversation with Hollywood director Barry Levinson, who is one of the team's many owners below majority-owner Peter Angelos. Nearby, first baseman Will Clark smokes a cigar as thick as a lead pipe and there is talk about making tonight's last show at the famed Tropicana nightclub.

On the flight down from Miami, I spoke with Joe Morgan, the ESPN commentator and Hall of Fame second baseman, about Cuba's place in the baseball universe. If the Castro regime ended tomorrow, would the island once again become the most important supplier of baseball talent outside of the United States?

"I don't think you can ever go back to what it once was," Morgan says. "Because, let's face it, the world has progressed and, if the embargo is lifted, there are going to be things that are more important to them than baseball. At this point, I think baseball is so important to them because they don't have many other things to believe in or put their hands around. But if it was to open up and more things would be added, they would have a more well rounded life. It would mean they wouldn't be just focused on baseball."

When asked if he agrees with Morgan's assessment, Thrift nods his head gravely like Sydney Greenstreet in the movie *Casablanca*.

"If you learn anything in baseball, it's that you always have to be thinking of your next move," he tells me. "You're always asking yourself, 'Where's the talent?' Over the years we've gone as far afield as all through Latin America to Japan and Australia, even Italy. But there's only so far out there you can go. In time it all comes back around. You ask me where the next place for talent could be. It may be Mexico."

Mexico? Ask fans about players from that country and probably the only one they'll come up with is the legendary Fernando Valenzuela.

"Believe me," Thrift says, "there's some good ones down there."

Three seasons later, the Baltimore Orioles, once contenders with a roster filled with such stars as Rafael Palmeiro, Roberto Alomar, and Cal Ripken, had fallen upon hard times. In an effort to keep up with the New York Yankees and Boston Red Sox in their division, the O's spent lavishly upon top-dollar free agents. The moves backfired with several big names becoming injured, most notably Albert Belle, and many more failing to produce. Angelos decided that his ball club would go with youngsters and unknowns. Refrain from any more expensive free-agent acquisitions until the team's infrastructure was rebuilt.

By the 2002 season, the Orioles were a far cry from the veteran teams Baltimore had once embraced. Few on the roster were comparable in talent or temperament to Boog Powell or Rick Dempsey or the Robinsons, Brooks and Frank. Arguably the best-known Orioles were Jim Palmer and Mike Flanagan, and they could only be found up in the broadcast booth. Baltimore fans certainly needed a program to keep up with the changes. Dominican Tony Batista had taken over for Ripken at third base. Venezuelan Melvin Mora played multiple positions, while another Venezuelan, rookie closer Jorge Julio, turned heads throughout the league. But the best of the new faces was Rodrigo Lopez, a savvy right-hander from Tlalnepantla, a town about fifteen miles north of Mexico City. In July, as the Orioles fell out of contention for the American League wild card, Lopez became the first Baltimore pitcher in twenty-three years to win six straight decisions in a single month. The last Baltimore pitcher to do so was Dennis Martinez, who did so in May 1979, and gained enough notoriety playing baseball that he became a folk hero and would-be presidential candidate in his native Nicaragua.

"Rodrigo doing what he's done certainly brightened things around here considerably," says manager Mike Hargrove, "because he's a young guy and fits what we're trying to establish and build here."

Only twenty-six years old, Lopez had already experienced the highs and lows that a baseball career can offer. He was signed by the San Diego Padres in 1995 and spent much of the next five seasons in their minor-league system. In 2000, he made his major-league debut, becoming the ninth Mexican to play for the Padres. But he made only six starts and struggled with an 8.76 ERA, before being sent back down. He didn't return to the majors the following year and pitched his best games for the Culiacan Tomato Growers in the Mexican Winter League. He won all five of his decisions in the winter ball playoffs, including a four-hit shutout in defeating Puerto Rico to win the Caribbean Series title. By the end of the 2002 major-league season, Lopez had become the Orioles' ace. He won fifteen games, posting a 3.57 ERA. Quite a leap for a guy who began the year with just six games of major-league experience.

"Sometimes you have to look closer to home," Thrift says, "to find a few more gems."

Despite the complications, playing in the majors remains a dream for many Mexican ballplayers. In Baltimore, Lopez's battery mate during the 2002 season was often fellow countryman Geronimo Gil. In Arizona, Mark Grace may have been the regular first baseman during the team's championship run, but he spent more time on the bench the following season to make room for Erubiel Durazo, a promising slugger from Hermosillo, Mexico. While Latinos from the Dominican Republic, Puerto Rico, Cuba, and now Venezuela outnumber Mexicans in the majors, few ever had the meteoric rise of this one southpaw from Navajoa, Mexico. That gem of a player baseball men like Thrift will always search for.

Minoso, Clemente, Cepeda, Carew—each of them had excited a particular community and fans of a specific team. Perhaps that's what made Fernando Valenzuela's rise so stunning. There were other heroes in 1981. Rollie Fingers won the Cy Young and MVP awards in the American League. Nolan Ryan set a major-league record with his fifth no-hitter. Gary Gaetti homered in his first big league at bat. Yet the 1981 season belonged to Valenzuela. He raised the bar established by the

Latino greats that had come before him. For one of the few times in memory, the nation became enthralled with a ballplayer who hailed from outside our borders.

FERNANDOMANIA

Boston Red Sox shortstop Nomar Garciaparra was seven years old when Valenzuela became the most talked-about player in the game.

"He was such a big deal to anybody of Mexican descent, and that included such a huge part of Southern California. It included my family," Garciaparra says. "They are all directly from there. So they were all for Fernando."

Valenzuela was called up to the Dodgers in September 1980 and immediately showed promise. He won two games and struck out sixteen in seventeen and two-thirds innings.

"You could tell right away, from his body language, his facial expression when he was on the mound, that here was a guy who wouldn't be flustered," says Dodger utility man Mickey Hatcher, who often gave Valenzuela a ride to Dodger Stadium after the rookie reached the majors. "He had good stuff and, unlike some pitchers, he knew it."

Still, few would have guessed what a phenomenon he would be the following season. With his staff decimated by injury and illness, Los Angeles manager Tommy Lasorda had no choice but to name the twenty-year-old his opening day starter for the 1981 season. Valenzuela responded with a five-hit, 2–0 shutout. The Dodgers then hit the road and Valenzuela pitched another complete-game victory, then another shutout. In his fourth game, he picked up another shutout victory and for good measure went three-for-three at the plate.

"Any doubts you had about him were gone real quick," says Mike Scioscia, who often caught Valenzuela. "He may not have been much to look at it. He had a belly, thin legs. But he soon showed you that he could pitch."

By May 8, Valenzuela was 7 and 0 and had allowed only two runs. With five shutouts in his first seven starts, the left-hander was the biggest story in sports, and a growing legion of media followed his every move. Fernandomania was born.

"It was like the Beatles," Hatcher says.

Like a savvy Hollywood star, Valenzuela stayed cool despite special press conferences being held for him in town after town. He was willing to joke about himself, especially his couch potato physique. At five foot eleven, sometimes tipping the scales at close to two hundred pounds, he wasn't your average-looking superstar.

"Sure, I drink a few beers, but not that much," he told *The Sporting News*. "What I do is eat a lot—steaks, salads, avocados, Mexican food, carne asada, beans, rice. I do like to eat."

Garciaparra remembers that what Valenzuela brought to baseball, especially for Mexican-Americans, was "the vibe, an identity for a lot of us. I remember I had one of the T-shirts that read Fernandomania, too. It was a big part of our lives. Not just for me but for my family, too.

"He was the star, and the Dodgers were my team as a kid. It's what made my entire family Dodger fans. It didn't matter where they lived, the Dodgers had become their team. When I played back home in interleague play, my family went, 'Great. We get to see you play at Dodger Stadium.' That place still means something to them because of Fernando Valenzuela. I was coming back to the place where we'd all seen Fernando pitch."

Away from the spotlight, Valenzuela struggled to keep his focus that amazing rookie year. He moved in with Mike Brito and his family. Fans will recognize the longtime scout as the guy in a dapper white hat and summer suit who was a fixture behind the home plate screen during games at Chavez Ravine. There he methodically recorded the pitches in a thick notebook with abbreviations for everything from a fastball to a split-finger to a screwball.

When Brito first saw Valenzuela pitch in Mexico he was so entranced with the prospect he forgot to puff his trademark stogie. After quitting school at the age of fifteen, Valenzuela had turned to pro and eventually caught the attention of Avelino Lucero, manager of the Los Mayos de Navajoa club of the Mexican League. Word got back to Brito in L.A., who saw Valenzuela pitch for a team in Puebla, Mexico. Right away the Dodger scout knew that the young left-hander was mature beyond his years when it came to baseball.

"He was seventeen, but he pitched like he was thirty-five," Brito recalls. "He was one of those guys that comes along once every fifty years."

Despite Brito's glowing scouting report, the Dodgers' brass was skeptical until general manager Al Campanis went to Mexico and saw Valenzuela himself. By then the New York Yankees were in the hunt, too, and the Dodgers nearly dropped out of the bidding when the Yankees offered $100,000. After some soul-searching Campanis went to $120,000, a bid that seems ridiculously low by today's standards, and Valenzuela became one of the Dodger Blue.

Arguably, Valenzuela wouldn't have as great a success without the brief time he spent in the Dodgers' farm system. There he learned the screwball, a pitch that seems to back up as it reaches the strike zone, from farmhand Bob Castillo, who hailed from East Los Angeles. The pitch, which was first popularized by Christy Mathewson and later Carl Hubbell, became Valenzuela's best weapon. Houston Astros slugger Cesar Cedeño once said the screwball was deceptive because it would sail into the strike zone, seemingly easy to hit, and then "it would disappear on you." To further confuse opposing hitters, Valenzuela learned to throw the pitch, soon nicknamed "Fernando's Fadeaway," at two different speeds. To right-handed hitters, the pitch could have been mistaken for a slider or curveball. But instead of bearing inside, as such breaking pitches do when delivered by most left-handers, it fell away from the hitter, catching the outside of the plate.

"The screwball, because not a lot of guys throw it, became his trademark when you're talking about Fernando. But he's certainly more than that," Scioscia says. "He proved that as his career advanced. He had hurt his arm, he had lost velocity off the fastball, and the screwball wasn't as effective as it was before. But he adapted and was still successful. He learned a cut fastball. He was a real student of the game and became even more of a pitcher as his career advanced. That's a testimony to his intelligence and his aptitude. He wasn't just a guy with one great pitch and great run."

Weeks into the '81 season, Valenzuela had established himself as the ace of the Dodgers staff and was considered one of the promising stars in the game. Still, even more would be asked of him. In June 1981, the players went on strike. The work stoppage lasted sixty days and left many fans disgruntled. But when the game returned to the field, Valenzuela picked up where he left off. By having he best record in the National League West in the first half of the season, the Dodgers were awarded a spot in the Divisional Series—a best-of-five against the Houston Astros. Nolan Ryan beat the Dodgers 3–1 in the opener and the Astros won the next game, too. Even though Valenzuela started game four on just three days' rest, he pitched a four-hitter. When Jerry Reuss shut out Houston in the fifth and deciding game, Los Angeles became the first team to rally from a 2–0 deficit to win a five-game postseason series.

The Dodgers then topped Montreal to reach the World Series against the New York Yankees. Once again Los Angeles fell behind two games to none in a series, and for pivotal game three, manager Tommy Lasorda turned to his young superstar. Both rookie starters—Valenzuela and the Yankees' Dave Righetti—struggled early, but Lasorda stayed with Valenzuela even though the left-hander gave up four runs in three innings. Instead of replacing pitchers, Lasorda swapped catchers, bringing in Scioscia, who knew more Spanish than starter Steve Yeager. Valenzuela held the Yankees scoreless for the rest of the game and the Dodgers came back to win 5–4. Los Angeles went on to take the next three games and the world championship.

"What we experienced and enjoyed as a team was seeing an athlete get an opportunity he deserved," Scioscia says. "What made Fernando unique was how he handled himself in that situation. A lot of athletes that are twenty years old couldn't have handled all of that grace. It would have given them some trouble.

"But Fernando was very well grounded. He is very intelligent. He knew that his passion was to pitch, to play baseball, and that's where his focus was. He would mess around a little bit and have a lot of fun, but he knew what he wanted to accomplish and what he had to do. So, therefore, a lot of those things that could have been distractions were never present in his life."

At the end of that memorable season, Valenzuela had recorded eight shutouts and became the first rookie to win the Cy Young Award.

To longtime Dodgers announcer Vin Scully, that season will always be "the year of Fernando."

Earl Shorris also points out that there was a clear distinction between Valenzuela and the great Dodgers pitchers who preceded him, such as Sandy Koufax and Don Drysdale.

"While he unwound his cubby arm, Fernando Valenzuela, with his pre-Columbian physique and unreliable eyes, looked heavenward, as if praying to the gods for speed, deception, and a piece of the strike zone," Shorris writes in *Latinos*. "In contrast to Koufax and Drysdale, every move of Valenzuela's was part of a ritual offering to the muse; he did not play baseball, he expressed himself through the art of pitching."

Just as important, Valenzuela brought excitement and a sense of humor to a game that sorely needed it, especially in the days after the strike had ended.

"He helped people forget about the strike," Brito says. "He got them focused again on baseball."

Valenzuela also helped inspire a young Mexican-American in Whittier, California. Garciaparra, like most kids in the United States, played many sports growing up. But baseball remained his real passion.

"It's always been number one for me," he says. "It goes back to going to those Dodger games with my family. Those times when [Valenzuela] pitched and you had to watch and listen to it all."

TAPPING THE SOURCE

When Valenzuela reached the major leagues, the United States already boasted one of the largest Spanish-speaking populations in the world. Only Argentina, Colombia, and Mexico were larger. When Valenzuela pitched, he drew 9,000 more fans than usual in ballparks across the National League. Management throughout baseball couldn't help but notice. Among most attentive members was Larry Lucchino, who would become president of the San Diego Padres.

Since its inception, the ball club was considered to be located in one of baseball's poorest markets. The franchise was boxed in by the Los Angeles Dodgers' fan base to the north, the desert to the east, the Pacific Ocean to the west, and by the Mexican border to the south. But Lucchino has always excelled at thinking outside the box. In the late 1980s, as president and chief executive officer for the Baltimore Orioles, he oversaw the building of Camden Yards, the first and arguably best in the wave of "retro" ballparks. Original plans called for a more conventional-style stadium in Baltimore. In fact the B&O warehouse, which now towers over right field and houses much of the team's front office, was slated to be demolished. However, Lucchino heeded the advice of his underlings and demanded that the warehouse remain standing. That the ballpark's "footprint" fit into Baltimore's inner harbor landscape. Today Camden Yards not only boasts the warehouse, but the street between it and the ballpark has been transformed into a pedestrian mall.

When Peter Angelos and his investment group purchased the Orioles in 1993, Lucchino was forced out. He came to the Padres and began to develop the team's regional appeal. A team merchandise store was opened in Tijuana, and buses began to run to the other side of the border to bring Spanish-speaking fans to the games. In 1996, the Padres played the New York Mets in La Primera Serie, a three-game series in Monterrey, Mexico. Three years later, the ball club returned to Monterrey and opened its major-league season there against the Colorado Rockies. Mexican president Vicente Fox was presented with a San Diego Padres jersey in a widely publicized photo op. A new ballpark was championed for downtown San Diego in large part because it was closer to the Latino fans. Still, Lucchino said perhaps the team's best move in linking with fans south of the border was signing Valenzuela.

San Diego has a long baseball history with Anglo and Latino

roots, which Lucchino and his bilingual marketers began to explore. One connection long overlooked had to do with Ted Williams, a native son of San Diego and the man whose .406 batting average Carew would chase a generation later. At about the same time the Padres saw their annual Latino fan attendance jump from 50,000 in 1995 to 600,000 in 2001, plans were under way up the coast in San Francisco for a museum to honor the best Latino baseball players of all time. Williams was among the inductees, alongside such greats as Roberto Clemente and Orlando Cepeda.

In recent years, researchers at the Baseball Hall of Fame in Cooperstown, along with Ray Sanchez's reporting for the *El Paso Herald-Post,* have found that the "Splendid Splinter" was half Mexican. In fact, Williams's name is now included on the museum's T-shirt listing the names of all the Latino Hall of Famers. His mother, May Venzor, was Mexican and had family from Ciudad Juarez, Mexico. On Williams's birth certificate, Venzor's birthplace is listed as El Paso, on the American side of the Rio Grande. Mrs. Williams became a commissioned lieutenant in the Salvation Army. When the family settled in San Diego, she spent a lot of time proselytizing for the Salvation Army, especially in southern San Diego and across the border in Tijuana. In fact, one of her nicknames, according to historian Luke Salisbury, was "the Angel of Tijuana." Her time away from home often resulted in Williams and his younger brother, Danny, being on their own, and they headed to the neighborhood ball fields. But his mother's work and insistence that every human being was deserving of respect may be why Williams publicly supported the efforts of Orestes Minoso and later on Rod Carew.

Too soon after Valenzuela arrived in San Diego, he proved to be past his prime. His first season there, he went 8–3, followed by a workmanlike 13–8 campaign. By 1997 his fabled fadeaway screwball had lost its break and he struggled with a 2–8 record. Still he helped the Padres draw a crowd. Fans came out to cheer the southpaw as they would a rock band whose last hit record was many years past. His scheduled starts bordered upon the nostalgic as longtime fans remembered the 1984 All-Star Game, when Fernando struck out Dave Winfield, Reggie Jackson, and George Brett in one inning—becoming only the sixth pitcher to strike out the side in the All-Star Game. Or the 1986 season, when he threw back-to-back two-hitters and equaled fellow screwballer Carl Hubbell's record when he struck out five consecutive batters in that midsummer classic. Or that improbable night in 1990, when first Dave Stewart of the Oakland A's and then Valenzuela pitched no-hitters within hours of each other— the first time that had ever happened in major-league history.

"Bringing in Fernando was one of our best moves in San Diego," says Lucchino, whose honors include a World Series ring (Orioles, 1983), a Super Bowl ring (Washington Redskins, 1983), and a Final Four watch (Princeton, 1965). "It showed our respect for a man who was a hero to so many people."

FOURTH INNING

THE RING BEARER

"He understood that modeling the incoherent and vertiginous matter of which dreams are composed was the most difficult task that a man could undertake . . . much more difficult than weaving a rope out of sand or coining the faceless wind."

◆ **JORGE LUIS BORGES,**
"The Circular Ruins"

mar Vizquel drove along the Ontario Street side to Jacobs Field, past the entrance to the Indians' official souvenir store, and saw that a line already extended halfway up the block. Three hundred people and counting were waiting for him to arrive. ◆ "I better get over there," he said. "That's a lot more than I expected." ◆ Although his autograph session, billed as a chance to have the Indians' All-Star and Gold Glove shortstop sign copies of his autobiography, *Omar! My Life On and Off the Field,* and his new video, "Catch the Magic," wasn't supposed to begin until 12:30 in the afternoon, by 12:10 Vizquel was on the scene. Stationed by store management at a table near the cashiers, Vizquel signed books, video covers, and pieces of clothing. He posed for pictures with fans and chatted with everyone, especially the kids. Above his head, on the store monitors, replays of the Indians shortstop in action played over and over again.

"Some players never get it," says Bob DiBiasio, the ball club's vice president for public relations. "They take this style of life for granted. They never really learn how to interact with the fans. But Omar gets it. I've never seen anyone better with the way he talks to people, becomes genuinely interested in their lives and what they see in his. The fans love him in this town."

Before Vizquel, the fan favorites in Cleveland often reflected the faces that came out to watch them. Sure, there were exceptions like Satchel Paige and Cuban-born Luis Tiant, but players

such as Bob Feller, Rocky Colavito, Bob Lemon, and Lou Bou-
dreau dominate any list of Indians all-time greats. That's why
Vizquel's celebrity in this blue-collar city on Lake Erie illus-
trates how much the game has changed in the last generation
or so.

Vizquel grew up in Caracas, Venezuela. Latino baseball
began in Cuba, but it soon spread to Mexico, Puerto Rico, the
Dominican Republic, and it swept south, too, with U.S. teams
playing in Venezuela and Colombia in the years before World
War II. In those lands, the game now competes with soccer as
the most popular sport. In 1939, Alejandro Carrasquel became
the first Venezuelan to play in the majors. Joe Cambria discovered him in the Cuba leagues and his skin was light enough to
head north before Jackie Robinson. Alejandro Carrasquel
pitched for the Washington Senators and lasted a decade in the
majors, posting a 50–39 record. His nephew, Alfonso "Chico"
Carrasquel, reached the big leagues in 1950 and started the
transformation of how shortstop was played, beginning an en-
during lineage of excellence at that position. A line that now ex-
tends to Vizquel.

A graceful six-footer, Carrasquel turned double plays by
moving toward second base and throwing the ball on to first base
with a sidearm motion. Before Carrasquel, shortstops would
plant themselves on the bag and throw overhand to first. That
procedure took more time and made them sitting ducks for incoming base runners.

"I was one of the first shortstops [to] throw the ball from
second to first underhanded during double plays," Carrasquel
told Marcos Breton and Jose Luis Villegas in *Away Games*. "[Be-
fore that] somebody would always spike me. Every time! And so
I said, 'I have to defend myself.' Throwing the ball underhanded,
the runner would have to slide or get hit with the ball. The first
time I did that was to [former New York Yankees great] Hank

Bauer. He got mad. But he also got scared. He said, 'Chico, god-damn it.' "

Besides reinventing how to turn the double play, Carrasquel turned heads by going deep in the hole between second and third base to throw base runners out. He roamed throughout the infield, showing how active a shortstop could be. How the person in that position could control the defense up the middle.

"We hear so many stories about great shortstops, and there have been many outstanding ones," Orestes Minoso says. "But let me assure you that for the few years he was at the top of his game, Chico Carrasquel was the best shortstop I have ever seen."

"[He] was the first Latin player selected to start an All-Star Game. When I first came to Chicago, it was Chico's second year. I had seen so many good shortstops, but he played like no one I had ever seen before. I looked in amazement. I said to myself, Gee whiz, this guy never misses the ball! What a glove. What hands. Perfect throw to first base all the time."

In fact, Carrasquel's flair received such attention that the Boston Red Sox were reportedly interested in trading Ted Williams for the acrobatic shortstop in 1951. At his father's urging, Vizquel began by wearing number 17, Carrasquel's old number, when he started to play.

Carrasquel starred for the Chicago White Sox until 1956, when the ball club traded him to Cleveland. He played for another four years in the majors. Later, Carrasquel joined the White Sox broadcast team. Unfortunately, his accent was parodied by Garrett Morris on *Saturday Night Live* ("Beisbol been bery, bery good to me") as character Chico Escuela. The White Sox had to make room for another Venezuelan shortstop, Luis Aparicio. Carrasquel's countryman made quite an impression in his rookie year when he was the league leader in stolen bases and putouts. Aparicio combined with Nellie Fox, six years his senior, to form one of the best double-play combinations in baseball. At the plate and on the base paths, the duo set the tone for Chicago's "Go-Go" White Sox, which stunned the baseball world by winning the 1959 American League pennant. He was elected to the Hall of Fame in 1984, and Brooks Robinson called him "the greatest shortstop I saw in my thirty-odd years of playing baseball."

Former White Sox manager Al Lopez agreed, telling *Sports Illustrated,* "At shortstop, you must pick up the ball clean or you don't throw the man out. It is the most important position. First, second, third, you can knock the ball down. At third you don't need good hands. At second you don't need good hands or a good arm. At first, all you need is to be able to catch the ball. Shortstop requires the most ability: catching, arm, hands, experience. Luis has great hands, great arm, great speed. He covers ground from all the angles, positions. I've seen some great shortstops, but he does everything well."

While Vizquel, like many in Venezuela, knew the stories of Carrasquel and Aparicio, his boyhood hero was the next in the Venezuelan line of shortstops—Dave Concepcion. The shortstop on Cincinnati's "Big Red Machine" in the 1970s, Concepcion wore number 13 and soon a young Vizquel was doing the same.

"The thing about wearing number thirteen began with Concepcion," Vizquel says. "Luis Aparicio wore number eleven and Chico Carrasquel wore seventeen, so it began for me with Concepcion, because he's the one that I saw playing. The one that I liked. The one that I looked up to.

"In my mind, he should be in the Hall of Fame. Playing so many years with the Reds, the same team. Pretty much everybody else from the Big Red Machine is in the Hall of Fame, so I think they need to really consider him."

Ozzie Smith, who recently went into Cooperstown, agrees with Vizquel.

"There are some great fielders that I played with who have been overlooked," Smith says. "One for sure is Davey Concepcion. He was the shortstop on those outstanding Big Red Machines. There were so many terrific players on those Reds teams of the seventies—like Pete Rose and Johnny Bench and Joe Morgan and Tony Perez and George Foster—that I guess somebody had to be locked out. But Concepcion was as important to their winning as anyone else. You need that strength in the middle, and Concepcion provided it."

A nine-time All-Star, Concepcion seemed to get better with age, especially at the plate. Even though he hit just .205 in his second season in the big leagues, .209 in his third, Concepcion batted better than .300 three times and was among the league leaders in hits and doubles by the end of his nineteen-year career. In 1975, when Cincinnati swept Pittsburgh in the National League playoffs, Concepcion and fellow Latino Tony Perez led the way. Concepcion went 5 for 11 and homered in the deciding game, while Perez hit .417 with four RBIs. Both then starred in a taut seven-game showdown with the Boston Red Sox, which many consider the best World Series ever played.

Concepcion's accomplishments were certainly noticed by a young Vizquel and many others in his native land. In Venezuela, the position of shortstop carries a great deal of responsibility. When Vizquel was nine years old, he was chosen from 150 candidates to be the starting shortstop for a Caracas All-Star team in the nationals. From then on, he was recognized as a player who had the talent to follow Carrasquel, Aparicio and Concepcion to major leagues.

"He became the new ring bearer," says Carlos Luchsinger, the producer of Vizquel's video. "Shortstop is the top position to play in Venezuela, probably the top position in baseball in any Latin country. The precedent is there, so are the expectations. People talk about the pressure of playing in the big leagues, the

All-Star Game, the World Series. Omar has been playing with that kind of pressure since he was a kid."

Vizquel, like Concepcion, has great range and the ability to make acrobatic moves, especially in turning the double play. He, too, struggled at the plate his first few years in the majors. But by his fourth season, Vizquel had raised his average to .294 and was a skilled enough batter to twice lead the league in sacrifice bunts.

Wilson Alvarez, the winningest pitcher from Venezuela, said while there has been increased lobbying for Concepcion to join Aparicio in the Hall of Fame, Vizquel is the one he believes will one day land in Cooperstown.

"Vizquel, [Andres] Galarraga, [Magglio] Ordonez are the big idols right now in Venezuela," says Alvarez, who in 1991 was the eighth-youngest pitcher to throw a no-hitter in the majors. His memorable day was the first and so far only no-hitter I've ever witnessed. "Vizquel has put together quite a string in Cleveland. He has those Gold Gloves. He's been winning the last few years. I know he wants to finish his career in Cleveland because that's become his second home. In my opinion, Vizquel will be in the Hall of Fame. His record will speak for itself by the time he's through."

DO OR DIE PLAY

Omar Vizquel broke in with the Seattle Mariners in 1989 and by his second season he led all shortstops in fielding percentage. His statistics in the field and at the plate were improving and many in baseball took notice. Yet, so often, what we remember about sport is its defining moments. Vizquel could have continued to put up All-Star quality numbers, but what immediately gained him recognition, got everyone talking about what a great fielder he is, was one play in 1993, his fifth full season in the majors.

Mariners right-hander Chris Bosio had a no-hitter going into the ninth inning. With two out, Boston's Ernest Riles hit a slow chopper to Vizquel at short. Closing on the ball, he bare-handed it and threw on to first base in one motion to nail the fleet Riles. Bosio had his no-hitter, something a journeyman pitcher like him can treasure the rest of his days, but what everyone was talking about afterward was Vizquel's bare-handed grab. Why risk such a thing with a no-hitter on the line?

"I thought that if I catch it with my glove than the play is in doubt at first base," Vizquel says about the play forever immortalized on his video. "I felt that was the only way I had to make that play. I knew that if I could get it with my bare hand, it would be an easy out. I never think about things like that when the ball's hit. I only think how to make the play."

Not even Bosio, the recipient of such a Gold Glove play, really understood.

"He told me later, 'You're crazy, man,' " Vizquel says. "In the replays, you see that he didn't really want to look. He had his head down. He knew it was going to be a difficult play and he didn't want to look.

"But doing that bare-handed was the only way. I've made much tougher plays, back in Venezuela, back on lousy fields. That's where you gain the confidence to do something like that. I had no second thoughts. People may not believe it, but when I saw that ball coming out to me, I knew going with the bare hand was my only play. It wasn't flashy. It was the right thing to do."

EVERY LITTLE THING

Philadelphia Phillies manager Larry Bowa sits in the dugout before a mid-July game against the Montreal Expos and considers how much his old position, shortstop, has changed since he played. For Bowa was part of the last great crop of shortstops. He, Concepcion, and Ozzie Smith were once the preeminent players at that position. Bowa led the National League in fielding six times and held the league record for the fewest errors in a season at the position until Cuban-born Rey Ordonez surpassed him. Also, Bowa held the major-league record for fielding percentage at the position until Omar Vizquel bettered that.

"Shortstop is the most difficult position when you're playing in Little League and kid's ball. Usually your best athletes gravitate to that position," he says. "So obviously all those Latin players who play shortstop were the best athletes on their youth teams. That's why guys like Tejada, Vizquel, A-Rod, everyone wants to play there. It's almost a status thing.

"Then you had a guy like Luis Aparicio, who became such an icon at that position. You had Davey Concepcion, who continued that movement. When you have those types of players, they set the standard. They become somebody those that follow want to look up to, to be like them."

But has the style of play, especially at short, become too flashy for Bowa's taste?

The Phillies' manager shrugs and says, "It doesn't matter what I think. On the fields they play on as kids, with those rocks and divots, you're going to get as many bad bounces as good. So, they look at the game differently. At a basic level they may learn in a different way than American kids playing on better fields.

"All I know is that kids who grow up in Latin countries still consider baseball their number-one sport, whereas in this country there are too many other things kids can do. They don't get a chance to hone in on what they want to do. In Latin America, baseball is still the game. They concentrate on that twelve months out of the year. They have the weather, the fields—now they have the equipment from Sammy Sosa and others donating stuff over there. This is just going to keep growing."

Yankees manager Joe Torre named four shortstops (Derek Jeter, Nomar Garciaparra, Miguel Tejada, Omar Vizquel) as reserves to the 2002 American League All-Star team. All except Jeter were of Latino descent, and they joined Alex Rodriguez, who was voted to be the starter by the fans. While Rodriguez enjoyed one of the best seasons a shortstop has ever had at the plate, with 57 home runs and 142 RBIs, Rodriguez insisted he took the most pride in his defense.

"The first thing I have to think about is my defense," he says. "It may not get the highlights on ESPN or Baseball Tonight, but it may be where I can help this ball club the most."

Of the All-Star shortstops, Miguel Tejada has improved his defense the most in recent seasons. Vizquel says that the Oakland A's shortstop used "to charge every ball." Now Tejada is calmer, waiting on the ball more often and he's better positioned as a result of conversations with Vizquel and Rodriguez.

Torre acknowledges that the style of play, especially at shortstop, has changed so much since he grew up playing stickball on the streets of Brooklyn.

"[The Latinos] are not afraid," the Yankees' manager says. "They have certain characteristics, especially among the shortstops. They get a little fancy. Underhand flip, one-handed pickup—stuff like that. But that's something they've been doing since most of them were kids, and they have so much confidence in their ability, that's how they do it.

"You play on the rock fields and are able to do it—it's nothing to do that kind of play on something like this," he says, nodding out on a well-manicured big-league diamond. "This is like playing on your living room rug."

"You're always looking," says Alfonso Soriano, who was a shortstop in his teens, "for things that can help your game. Just like you admire particular players growing up, you like certain moves. You start to practice them on your own. Try to make them part of your game.

"Like sometimes I'll throw the ball [over to first] with a bit of an underhand flip. It gives me more time. That came from watching Tony Fernandez. You know how he could flip the ball over there? Real quick like? As a kid I fell in love with that move. I had to learn it. Sometimes it's what you need. Other times it's my way of remembering him. He was such a great shortstop. A hero to so many of us, so you want to pay him some respect in how you play."

WHO'S ON FIRST?

Shortstop may have been the first position where Latinos transformed how the game is played, a transformation that continues to this day. First base, with its traditionally less than athletic or slower players, also became forever altered with the help of a very talented, if not highly recognized Latino. Early in his career, Victor Pellot Power played in the outfield, second and third base, and an occasional game at shortstop. It was at first base, though, that Power began to redefine the position.

In a perfect world, Power would have been a Yankee. The dark-skinned Puerto Rican came north to play ball in 1950 and he soon caught the eye of New York Yankees scout Tom Greenwade and the ball club acquired his contract. But Power's arrival occurred in the netherworld after Jackie Robinson's signing with the Brooklyn Dodgers. While the color barrier was broken in the major leagues, it didn't mean teams were in any hurry to bring in more such prospects. Power languished at the Yankees' minor league affiliate in Kansas City. Even though he excelled there, hitting .349 to lead the American Association batting title, the Yankees still wouldn't bring Power up. The most successful sports franchise in U.S. history had yet to integrate.

At first, the reason given was that the big-league club really wanted a left-handed first baseman to take advantage of short porch to right in Yankee Stadium. But as Power continued to excel in the minors and never received an opportunity to prove himself against major-league pitching, the Yankees' management suggested that Power didn't have "the right attitude." In *Dynasty: The New York Yankees, 1949–1964,* Peter Golenbock writes, "A media blitz by the Yankees accused Power of being stupid, hot-tempered and a showboat. There was also talk that he liked white women." At least one lighter-skinned woman, according to Samuel O. Regalado, the author of *Viva Baseball,* turned out to be Power's wife, who often enjoyed wearing blond wigs.

In 1954, Power was traded to the Philadelphia Athletics for first baseman Eddie Robinson and right-hander Harry Byrd, who had lost a league-leading twenty games the year before. The next season the team moved to Kansas City, where Power had first encountered Jim Crow laws years earlier in the minors. When he and his wife went out together, the police routinely pulled them over.

"Everywhere she went with me, the Kansas City people they no like it," Power says in Jackie Robinson's book, *Baseball Has Done It.*

Until Power came along, players were taught to use both hands while fielding. While that may be good advice to Little Leaguers, it didn't make much sense at first base in the majors, where one had a better chance at errant throws by leaning out with just the glove hand. In the field, Power played farther off the bag than most first basemen and snagged many sharply hit grounders that would have found their way into right field. He went about his work with a self-confidence and assured style that would have made such other Latino pioneers as Dihigo and Luque proud. After three seasons in Kansas City, Power was traded to Cleveland early in the 1958 season. There he became an institution at first—a seven-time Gold Glove winner and a three-time All-Star. More important, his style of play redefined how the position should be played.

"I remember one writer asked me why I was such a clown, why did I catch the ball with one hand?" Power once told sportswriter Stan Isaacs. "I told him if the guy who invented baseball wanted us to catch with two hands he would have invented two gloves."

TAKING CENTER STAGE

The infield isn't the only place that has been changed by Latino glovemen. Today, shortstop may be the position of choice, the toughest and most prestigious on the diamond, but in Atlanta a young man from Curaçao, an island off the coast of Venezuela, has redefined center field as Carrasquel and Power once did at shortstop and first base. Others before him have played a shallow center. Baltimore Orioles great Paul Blair comes to mind. But Andruw Jones's ability to catch flares that elude the infielders, to run down drives to the gap, has become the stuff of legend in the South.

"He's why I come to the ballpark every day," longtime Braves announcer Skip Caray said one night after Jones dived, stretched out, and took away another would-be hit. "Just to see what he'll do next."

Jones plays such a shallow center field that Braves shortstop Rafael Furcal told ESPN, "I turn around sometimes and I say, 'Andruw, what are you doing in the infield?' And he will say, 'Don't worry. If it gets over my head, it's a home run. But if it stays in the stadium, it's an out.' "

Jones's father, Henry, taught him how to play. Together they would go down to the beach every day and the father would hit pop-ups that would carry like a knuckleball in the ocean breeze. The father taught the son to read the catcher's signs, so you know what pitch is coming. To quickly ascertain where the ball is heading, take your eyes off it and sprint to the spot where it will land in the straight line. When he's feeling on top of his game, which most hitters will complain is just about every day of the season, Jones contends that he's like Michael Jordan in basketball. He feels like he won't miss a thing.

It took Jones only two months to jump from Class A ball to the major leagues. That extraordinary leap took place in 1996 and he's never looked back. He homered in his first two World Series at bats and went on to hit twenty home runs and steal twenty bases in the same season. But, like Power, it will be the moves, this new grace, which will be remembered far longer than the string of Gold Gloves or even team championships. Throughout baseball, how to play particular positions is being reinvented. It's not something that leaps out at you. No, these are the subtle moves, the measures of economy, and more often than not, it is Latino players who are bringing them to the table.

One night I was watching a game on ESPN and saw Angels backup infielder Benji Gil range behind second base to catch a hard-hit grounder. The Texas Rangers had a man on first and Gil's only hope for an out was the force at second base. With his momentum carrying him toward the outfield, Gil tried to flip the ball behind his back, only to see it sail over the second baseman's head. Everybody was safe. At first glance, it was a nice hustle play. A nice try, but with little chance of getting the out. But then ESPN analyst Joe Morgan remembered that Miguel Tejada had faced a similar situation only nights before. With the help of a replay from Tejada's game, Morgan detailed how the Oakland A's shortstop briefly slid on one knee after he snared his grounder behind second base. As soon as the ball was in his glove, he popped back to his feet and successfully flipped the ball behind his back to second. It was the slide—something rarely seen in fielding a decade ago—that made the play work.

"The slide stops their momentum," Morgan told his television audience. "So they are in better position to throw the ball after they field it. Roberto Alomar has done this for years, and now you see guys like Tejada doing it, too."

Like Carrasquel's sidearm flip on the double play or Power's one-handed stretch, such moves may look too flashy to the uneducated eye, but the pros are always watching. They're like jazz musicians, always looking for another note or riff that can help them play the song better. And while it is happening throughout the field, nowhere is such scrutiny and imitation more prevalent than the hardest everyday position to play in baseball—shortstop.

HOW TO GRIND IT OUT

Much is made about how much baseball one can learn by playing catcher. It's been called "God's view" of the game, and certainly the list of ex-catchers who have turned to managing is long and impressive. Tony Peña and Mike Scioscia are the latest examples, and Joe Torre began his career behind the plate before moving to third base. But the shortstop, especially when it's a student of the game, can be almost as involved in the game as the catcher and pitcher. About the only thing Cal Ripken really complained about when he was moved from short to third base later in his career was his inability to see the catcher's signals. To know what the next pitch is and to position himself accordingly.

"I feel a bit lost without knowing," he said.

In fact, the position of shortstop has become so integral to the game that it has even become a training ground for potential managers. Nobody knows that better than the St. Louis Cardinals' Tony La Russa.

Growing up in a Spanish-speaking household in Tampa, he signed with Charlie Finley's Kansas City Athletics the day he graduated from high school. He received a $50,000 signing bonus. The following season he played thirty-four games for the Athletics, hitting .250. La Russa, Robin Yount, and Alex Rodriguez are the only eighteen-year-olds of the modern era ever to start a major-league game at short. La Russa did not know it at the time, but that season would be his high-water mark as a player. During the 1963 offseason, playing slow-pitch softball with friends back in Tampa, he went out to his position without warming up. In the first inning, a grounder was hit his way at short. It was deep in the hole and La Russa fielded it and fired to first base. In doing so he tore a tendon just below the shoulder. He would play with a sore arm for the next 15 years. In large part because of that injury he would bounce from the A's organization to the Braves to finish his career with the Cubs. He would appear in only 132 major-league games and retired with a .199 batting average—a hit or two below the Mendoza line. The term was first used by George Brett to describe the boundary between mediocre and truly atrocious batting averages, according to BaseballLibrary.com. It was inspired by Mexican shortstop Mario Mendoza, who hit below .200 five times in his nine-year major-league career.

Although La Russa admittedly hung on to his dream of playing shortstop far too long, he spent his offseasons attending Florida State University Law School. He received his degree and was admitted to the bar in 1979. Only four other managers— Branch Rickey, Miller Huggins, Hughie Jennings, and Monte Ward—have been lawyer-managers. All are in the Hall of Fame.

"It is said that the study of law sharpens the mind by narrowing it," George Will writes in *Men at Work,* which detailed how La Russa, pitcher Orel Hershiser, hitter Tony Gwynn, and shortstop Cal Ripken went about their respective crafts. "But then the study of anything narrows the mind in the sense of concentrating attention and excluding much from the field of focus."

La Russa remains one of the most intense individuals I've ever encountered in baseball. I was at San Francisco International Airport when he arrived from Chicago with his family to take over as manager of the Oakland A's in 1986. Granted, he wasn't happy to see me. After all, Sandy Alderson, then the ball club's general manager, had tried to keep the arrival secret. A news conference wasn't scheduled until the following day at the ballpark. But if La Russa had a short fuse, his natural curiosity moved him from carrying any lasting grudge. After being momentarily miffed that a member of the media had shown up to question him about the mediocre team that he had inherited, La Russa wanted to know how I'd decided this plane from Chicago would be the one he was on. I tried to tell him I'd been lucky. A friend with United had found the name "La Russa" on the plane's manifest.

"Inside information." He nodded. "That's the best kind."

In short order, La Russa turned a 76–86 ball club into a contender. Two years after his arrival, Oakland won the American League West with a 104–58 record. Under his stewardship, Mark McGwire became a fixture at first base, problem children Jose Canseco and Rickey Henderson enjoyed some of their best seasons, and Dennis Eckersley was moved from the starting rotation to the bullpen, where he became the top closer in the game. Baseball analyst Bill James ranks La Russa's decision to move Eckersley to the bullpen as the "most important smart move by a manager in the 1980s."

"It was something I wasn't happy about at first," Eckersley tells me. "But Tony was certain this was right. There was no way of talking him out of it, so I had to play along. Thank God I did."

As a manager, Eckersley says, La Russa is "into grinding things out. Being intense day after day. He's never lethargic. He does things right. He knows how the game should be played. He never misses anything and he lets guys know what he sees. Even though he probably won't say it, I think he takes pride with what he knows and sees about the game. In many ways, he's a real fan of the game. He's always looking and thinking."

Most mornings during the season, La Russa can be found in his office, reading glasses on, analyzing stacks of statistical information that his advance scouts and coaches produce daily. Numbers don't lie to La Russa. Certainly they can be manipulated and crunched, but he believes a basic truth remains. A paper trail stretches back to a player's first at bat and will help forecast what happens with the next one.

Dave Parker, who played for La Russa in Oakland and then was a batting coach for him in St. Louis, calls his former manager "very analytical. He will look at everybody's stats against certain pitchers, and that's what he goes on. Solely. The way he would look at certain players wasn't the way I looked at them.

Sometimes in meetings he said certain players weren't that good when I thought they were the best players that we could win with."

Any good shortstop will tell you that to succeed at the position, you must prepare and watch and then react. A shortstop doesn't have the time to bobble a ball as a second baseman does. He has to cover much more ground and be more involved in the infield's core dynamics than does the third baseman. La Russa says he loved playing shortstop. So much so that he tried to stay on that side of the game when he was habitually nursing a sore arm—the injury that probably led to two shoulder separations, a knee injury and elbow chips.

"I was terrible" is how La Russa sums up his playing career and medical past. "No excuses. Those are the facts."

And the facts also include that this manager still studies the game like he was a shortstop in the starting infield. Often television cameras will focus on him in the dugout. He's usually alone, watching the action with an intensity that a casual fan could mistake for brooding. Except for an occasional word with Dave Duncan, his longtime pitching coach, he keeps his own counsel as he follows the events in search of the next piece of inside information he can put into play.

Former Oakland center fielder Dave Henderson says playing for La Russa was like being assigned the toughest teacher in school.

"You hated that class," Henderson says, "but ten years later, you figured out it was all for your own good."

THE GREAT HOME RUN CHASE OF 1998

"The image was so overwhelming, so unforgettable, that people's common sense ended up somewhere else. No one knows what happened. The shape of their world changed."

◆ **TOMAS ELOY MARTINEZ,** *Santa Evita*

Round ball. The round barrel of a bat. Ted Williams once said that having them greet each other so that the impact was square and solid remains the most difficult feat to accomplish in sports. And any slugger who has come before or after him knows the wisdom of those words. So what do we make of those moments when ball and bat do meet just so? When they meet with such regularity that an entire nation becomes enthralled with two men in headlong pursuit of the record book. When the ball flies off the bat as if it had a mind of its own and for an instant the only role it knows is to soar over the outfield fence like a flock of geese heading for the horizon. What registers in the batter's box? What does the slugger remember?

"It's the feel," says Frank Robinson, who hit 586 home runs in his career—a member of the coveted 500 home run club. "You don't feel anything down the bat handle. I'm not trying to make a joke. That's how it is."

Robinson and I had this conversation in Houston, a few feet behind the batting cage, as the Astros prepared for their first game of the 1998 playoffs. What was still on everyone's mind was the Great Home Run Chase of that season. How Mark McGwire and Sammy Sosa had both surpassed Roger Maris's mark for the most home runs in a season—61. That they had done it with two weeks left in the season had left the nation's fans breathless, even disbelieving about what they had witnessed. Only a few days earlier, Sosa's Cubs had finished the regular season here before they advanced to the playoffs for the first time in nine years.

"What those two men accomplished was unbelievable," Robinson says. "I doubt if either one of them could have done it alone. It was almost like they pushed each other, in a friendly way. That two of them went after the record helped relieve the pressure for both of them. They were in their own little world and the rest of us were lucky to go along for the ride."

In front of us, the steady rhythm of home runs flying out of the ballpark, the cadence that had propelled the game that entire season, swelled to another crescendo as Jeff Bagwell, Craig Biggio and Moises Alou took their cuts. Robinson glanced at the batting cage, as if to reassure himself what his ears had just heard. For besides the feel in the hands, there is also a sweet smack of a well-hit ball. Robinson and the other greats will caution that each ballpark is different. The sound can sometimes fool you. But every slugger worth his salt knows the sound a home run ball makes.

Initially Robinson described it as "a gunshot." But then he searched for different words. A gunshot, in this day and age, seemed too callous for something so redemptive. As the Astros continued to hit, we paused and simply listened. Even though the stands were filling up, the clamor beginning for another game, Robinson tuned out such diversions. When Bagwell stepped back into the cage, the rhythmic rat-tat-tat of the bat hitting the balls began again.

"There it is," Robinson says, and moments later Bagwell's drive soars beyond the left-field fence. "It's like you're out in the woods and you step on a branch, a dry branch. It's that snap that goes just so. But you have to be careful. The sound comes and goes, depending upon the ballpark and crowd. You can't wait for the sound to tell you every time."

There remains a Zen to hitting home runs. Try too hard and

you'll surely fail. Begin to believe it's simply a science and body mechanics, and a lightning bolt occasionally shows itself. Kirby Puckett of the Minnesota Twins, like Sosa and Barry Bonds, reached the majors as a top-of-the-order guy. He remembers being terrified when manager Ray Miller moved him down to the third spot in the Twins' power-laden lineup.

"I wasn't a home run hitter," Puckett says. "I told Ray that. I didn't think I'd ever be a home run hitter. But he told me to relax and just hit the ball hard, and you know something? It was the strangest thing. The homers came. They were there when I needed them."

That's why baseball people like Robinson, Puckett, and Hank Aaron were as mesmerized as the rest of us by what transpired during the 1998 season, the year of the Great Home Run Chase. For not only did we have a competition of great magnitude, we watched two men grow up and embrace excellence and friendship while under the glaring light of celebrity and national attention. Once more the home runs came when they were needed.

"That's what made the season so special, so memorable," Aaron tells me. "Because, being a former home run hitter, I know, more than most, about how difficult it can be. How hard it is to hit a home run. But here they were again. The game was coming off that long strike, it needed something to regain people's attention, and somehow we were fortunate enough to have these two men step forward."

Robinson adds, "I don't have the vocabulary to describe what Mark McGwire and Sammy Sosa did. I mean seventy and sixty-six home runs. That sounds so strange. Even to me. Seventy and sixty-six. My goodness, you couldn't dream something like that up. But whether it's one or seventy, nothing else offers the kind of excitement that a home run does. Not even a perfect game. Because a home run is instant, it's so surprising. Since the days of Babe Ruth, it's been the thing that has made this game what it is."

THE HEIR APPARENT

I came to write about baseball in a roundabout way. My wife and I were living in the San Francisco Bay Area. Our home in the spring of 1987 was a thirty-two-foot sailboat. I had just returned from covering the America's Cup in Australia for the *San Francisco Examiner*—an assignment I was given in large part because I was the only sportswriter on staff living aboard a boat.

Despite the picture-postcard life (there are few things as beautiful as the fog sweeping in off the ocean and covering that city and the green hills that surround it like a curtain), we had begun to make plans to move back east, closer to where we had grown up. Jacqui had accepted a job with the *Washington Post* and I was on the verge of resigning to move back with her when my sports editor called. One of the *Examiner* baseball writers had been arrested for drunk driving. The paper was going to take him off the baseball beat for the season. My editor needed someone to be the "swing man" on baseball—covering many of the home games of the San Francisco Giants and the Oakland A's. I'd even go on the occasional road trip. How could I refuse? A generation ago, a sportswriter made his mark by covering baseball, boxing, and horse racing. With the ascendancy of football and the Olympics, baseball is the only one left from that golden era. So I called the yacht broker and told him not to be in any hurry to sell our sloop. My wife would head east without me. Our relationship would be bicoastal until the baseball season ended.

The two Bay Area teams that season couldn't have been

more different. Roger Craig, a former pitcher who had lost a league-leading twenty-four games for the New York Mets in 1962, was the Giants' manager. He and general manager Al Rosen had assembled a staff of journeyman pitchers—Mike Krukow, Mike LaCoss, Kelly Downs, and Scott Garrelts—and were preaching the virtues of the split-finger fastball. The everyday lineup had Will "the Thrill" Clark at first base, Chili Davis and Jeff Leonard in the outfield, with future Arizona Diamondbacks manager Bob Brenly behind the plate. Their team motto was "Hmm Baby." A philosophy that can be best described as "Don't worry, be happy." The ball club would fall one game shy of reaching the World Series that season.

Across the bay, Tony La Russa continued the rebuilding process that he had begun in the last half of the 1986 season after I had met him at the airport. While certain positions were taken—Jose Canseco in left field, Tony Phillips at second base, Carney Lansford at third base, Reggie Jackson returning to Oakland to take over the designated hitter spot from Dave Kingman—others were up for grabs. In spring training, even into the first weeks of the season, prospect Rob Nelson appeared to have the inside track for the first baseman's job. That left another promising youngster, Mark McGwire, seemingly destined to be sent back to the minors. McGwire could play first or third base. But with Nelson penciled in at first and Lansford, a former batting champion, at third, that didn't leave him much of an opportunity.

Still, La Russa liked what he saw in McGwire. Years later he would tell me he admired how the skinny kid at the time went about his business. With a clubhouse full of egos and brash talk, McGwire kept his mouth shut and did his best to fit in. He'd hit three home runs but only posted a .189 average in eighteen games with the A's the previous year. The only thing he wanted was a chance, and La Russa was determined to give him one.

During spring training La Russa told A's general manager Sandy Alderson he'd find enough bats for the kid. Don't send him down to the minors just yet. So when Nelson struggled to begin the season, La Russa tried McGwire at first base. The kid hit a few out and never looked back. He finished the season with forty-nine home runs, briefly reawakening the echoes of Ruth's and Maris's record pace for the most home runs in a season. Despite setting a rookie record for home runs, McGwire actually ended his season early. With a game left, he went home because his wife was expecting. Instead of trying to break the fifty-HR plateau, McGwire was there when his son, Matthew, was born.

Of all the personal virtues, the one La Russa probably treasures the most is loyalty. McGwire had come through for him, so he would return the favor. Of course, nothing could be easier than to write in Big Mac's name in the lineup when he was annually among the league leaders in home runs and RBIs. But McGwire struggled with a bad back and other nagging injuries. His swing was deemed too long and looping, and opposing pitchers targeted the holes in it to routinely get him out. In 1991, McGwire hit just twenty-two home runs and if La Russa hadn't sat him down for the last two games of the season, his batting average could have fallen below .200. Perhaps it takes a guy who finished with a career batting average below the Mendoza line to fully comprehend such embarrassment.

In 1996, La Russa left Oakland to manage St. Louis. He took his coaches, even his trainer, with him as they formed "Oakland East." Back in Oakland, McGwire was healthy and hitting again. He posted a team-record fifty-two home runs the year his friend and manager left town. The following season they were reunited, as the A's couldn't afford to retain their star slugger, who was about to become a free agent. McGwire was traded to St. Louis midway through the 1997 season for pitchers T. J. Mathews, Eric Ludwick, and Blake Stein—as lopsided a deal as the one that sent Babe Ruth from Boston to New York for $125,000 and a $300,000 loan. Reunited with La Russa in St. Louis, McGwire made his first serious run at Maris's record. He finished that season with fifty-eight home runs. La Russa believed that if it wasn't for the weeks of uncertainty in Oakland about whether he would be traded or not, followed by trying to learn about new pitchers and a new league, McGwire could have broken Maris's single-season home run record a year earlier.

In any event, the stage was set. On Opening Day 1998 in St. Louis, McGwire came up with the bases loaded in the fifth inning at Busch Stadium. He drove the first pitch from the Dodgers' Ramon Martinez over the left-field fence. His grand slam won the game and he went on to homer in the first four games of the season, which tied Willie Mays for the most consecutive games homered in to start any season.

SERVING NOTICE

Any competition needs an opponent. If McGwire had been left to duel against the ghosts of Ruth and Maris, I'm not sure he would have succeeded. He needed a foil, somebody to go toe to toe with him and allow him to keep his focus, even his sense of humor. After the first month of the season the home run leaders were McGwire, the Reds' Ken Griffey, and the Rockies' Vinny Castilla. Each of them had 11. Sammy Sosa had just 6. Yet in the Cubs' clubhouse there was excitement about how Sosa was swinging the bat. After almost daily spring training sessions with Jeff Pentland, the team's new hitting instructor, the notorious free swinger had rebuilt his stroke.

Since reaching the majors in 1989, Sosa had gained a reputation for chasing pitches out of the strike zone. Larry Himes, who traded for Sosa twice, said the slugger's strike zone "was from the top of his hat to his shoe tops. But you never got down on him because of his energy or his enthusiasm or his work habits. They were always there." Over the years Sosa reined in his free-swinging ways, but he was still susceptible to pitches on the outside half of the plate. Invariably he tried to pull them, which is why two teams (the Texas Rangers and Chicago White Sox) decided to trade him away. It allowed his detractors to label him "Sammy So-So." When Bobby Cox left him off the 1996 National League All-Star team, not many complained, even though Sosa was leading the NL in home runs midway through that season. In 1997, Sosa had hit 36 home runs, but he struck out 174 times. His 119 RBIs were tempered by the fact he had batted just .246 with men in scoring position. That average fell to .159 when he had two strikes on him.

"It was a bad year. I can do better," he told me that spring. "We can all do better. Me, this team—everybody with the Cubs."

Under Pentland's guidance, Sosa was no longer trying to pull everything—hit every pitch to the moon. The instructor incorporated a timing movement with Sosa's feet to keep the hitter's weight back at the plate. Instead of lunging too eagerly at anything hittable, Sosa would begin his swing by moving his front foot, his left leg, slightly backward. He would tap the front foot back, pause and then tap forward as the pitch neared the plate. A slugger's power comes from his legs, the weight transfer from the front to the back foot as the ball approaches. The trick is to be relaxed and time those often opposing movements and forces precisely so that the power is unleashed as the round bat meets the round ball.

"The strongest guy I ever played with was Reggie Jackson," Pentland says in Sosa's autobiography. "He held his arms low to take the tension out of his arms and hands and to allow him to use his strength when it was important. Sammy's swing at this point was what we call a maximum-effort swing—he swung too hard. I mean, he's a tremendous athlete. So just by lowering his arms, the relaxation and looseness clicked in."

While Sosa wears number 21 in honor of his ultimate baseball hero, Roberto Clemente, he admired what Jackson accomplished in his career, especially the 1977 World Series. On that cold fall night in Yankee Stadium, the man they nicknamed "Mr. October" hit three consecutive home runs off three different pitchers to give New York its first world title in fifteen years. After walking on four pitches his first time up, Jackson took Burt Hooton's first offering deep in the third inning. He followed that up an inning later by driving Elias Sosa's first fastball into the right field bleachers and then finished off the evening in style with a mammoth home run over the center field wall off the first pitch from knuckleballer Charlie Hough. Three pitches. Three home runs.

"Ruth, Clemente, Mays—I can now say I had one day like those guys," Jackson said afterward in the victorious Yankees' clubhouse.

Jackson's night was one for the ages and it reverberated for years within the Latino baseball community. Although Jackson is usually associated with African-Americans, his full name is Reginald Martinez Jackson.

"I thought of him as one of us," says Andres Galarraga, who grew up in shortstop-rich Venezuela. "He and Roberto Clemente were the ones I paid attention to as a boy. I loved it that both of them could really drive the ball. I guess that's what I saw myself doing someday. I loved how they'd thump the ball, how far they could hit it. I knew I was never going to be a shortstop. Not the way I'm built. Guys who could hit. That's what I wanted to be."

It wasn't that long ago that Latino players were considered "good field, no hit." That perception began to wane with the arrival of Clemente and Orlando Cepeda in the big leagues and then Rod Carew. By the end of the 1998 season, such stereotypes were demolished forever.

Through the first six weeks of that season, Sosa had only eight home runs. But on May 22, he connected on a deep blast to straightaway center field off Greg Maddux, the most consistent pitcher of the modern era. Maddux has won fifteen games or more for fifteen consecutive seasons. Homering off a guy like that meant a lot to Sosa, and with that blast, things soon fell into line for a memorable run at the record book.

"As Jeff said, by relaxing at the plate and shifting my weight to my back leg, I was starting to connect to right field," Sosa told Breton. "That made me even more dangerous as a hitter because I was now crushing pitches that were off the plate—pitches I used to miss."

From May 25 to June 21, Sosa hit twenty-one home runs in twenty-two games. He homered in his first and last at bats in June as he broke the major-league record set by Detroit's Rudy York in 1937 for the most home runs in a month. At the end of June, the All-Star ballots were counted. McGwire was the leading vote-getter and in the National League outfield Tony Gwynn, Barry Bonds, Larry Walker, Dante Bichette, and Moises Alou finished ahead of Sosa. But within weeks it seemed as if everybody knew who Sammy Sosa was. For the first time in its history, America was ready to embrace someone who had grown up outside its borders and far beyond its concept of who a sports hero should be.

WHAT PRESSURE?

Where others may find pressure, Sosa claims to see only opportunity.

"I never feel pressure," he once told me. "How can I be unhappy about where I am when I remember where I started?"

Growing up in the Dominican Republic, Sosa and his friends were so poor they used branches as bats and fashioned milk cartons into homemade gloves. He shined shoes to make money, and an early Texas Rangers scouting report described him as "malnourished." Sosa didn't really turn to baseball until he was thirteen, when Bill Chase, an American businessman, bought him a major-league-style blue glove. The glove was a good one. Chase recalled it cost $100, and to this day Sosa wears only blue gloves. Despite the gift, Sosa wanted to be a professional boxer until his mother, Mireya, asked him to give up fighting. Instead, Sosa turned to baseball with his characteristic zest. He began to wake up at six in the morning to practice.

"Back then I always wore cut-off jeans, and I would practice on my street by hitting dried husks of maize again and again," Sosa says in his autobiography. "I would tell my friends that I was going to be a big-league ballplayer and they would say, 'You're crazy. You're never going to amount to anything.' But I never paid them any attention because I knew I had the dedication that set me apart from the others."

Despite such self-confidence, Sosa realized he would need many things to fall into line if he was ever going to reach the major leagues. Baseball has become the ticket for so many Latinos, and Sosa was far from the only kid in the Dominican Republic who had decided the game would be his ticket out of poverty. Sosa's brother knew Hector Peguero, who ran a local amateur team. Sosa got his start there, playing in a ballpark named after Rico Carty, who had once starred for the Atlanta Braves.

Even though Sosa began to turn the heads of the locals, he knew that he wasn't going anywhere unless he signed with a major-league team. After tryouts with the Phillies, Yankees, Braves, Expos, Mets and Blue Jays didn't lead to a contract, Sosa attracted the attention of Amado Dinzey and then Omar Minaya of the Texas Rangers. The two convinced Sosa to take a detour on his way home from the Blue Jays camp in Santo Domingo and attend a tryout in Puerto Plata. That meant another bus ride, and at first Sosa didn't want to go. He was tired and it was nearly the weekend. But two friends talked him into it. Although Minaya had concerns about Sosa's lack of speed at the time, the way he swung at everything in sight, he appreciated the prospect's enthusiasm and long-term potential. Sosa signed with the Rangers for $3,500.

"Right away you had to like his aggressiveness," Minaya says. "He had this attitude that he wasn't going to let anything get in his way. But he had a lot of rough edges. He was just a skinny, sixteen-year-old kid. You see a lot of those and they may never develop. So, did I think Sammy Sosa would ever hit fifty, sixty home runs in a season, hit twenty in one month? I could make myself look like a real genius and say yes. But the truth? No. No way. It's amazing how much he's grown, as a ballplayer and as a person."

Signing a contract is one thing. Being invited to spring training is another. Throughout the Dominican Republic, many would-be major leaguers never make that next step. They're stuck on the island, playing against other prospects, until they are let go. In February 1986, Sandy Johnson, then the Rangers' director of scouting, came down to review the fresh talent. The skinny kid in right field—his arm strength and his promising power at the plate—impressed him. That kid, of course, was Sosa, and the ball club bought him a plane ticket for Plant City, Florida, at the time the Rangers' spring training home.

At the airport, Sosa told his mother two things: That he loved her and that one day he would return.

In his early years in the majors, Sosa was just trying to hang on to a job. Despite hitting his first big-league home run off Roger Clemens, the Rangers traded him fifty-eight games into the 1989 season to the Chicago White Sox. After playing the following season on Chicago's South Side, the White Sox sent him back down to Triple A after he and batting coach Walt Hriniak didn't see eye to eye on his approach at the plate. When White Sox general manager Larry Himes moved across town to the Cubs, he traded onetime MVP Jorge Bell for Sosa. While the deal was unpopular at first, Sosa methodically began to win over the fans, especially those who started to pay him homage from the right field bleachers. Himes said he admired Sosa because he played with the same kind of hustle, the type of confidence, that Pete Rose once exhibited. As the 1998 season began to unfold, amazingly, the only athlete more popular in Chicago was Michael Jordan.

The late Arne Harris saw a lot of hitters come and go during his thirty-seven years at WGN-TV in Chicago. He said nobody was better than Sosa at putting the past behind him.

"I can't ever remember a hitter who just threw out what he did in his last at bat or his last game the way he does," Harris said. "If he strikes out four times, he comes back up to the plate as happy as if he hit a home run."

And if Sosa does go yard? Drives another ball onto Waveland Avenue? You have to go back to the Babe, or at least Jeff Leonard, to find a more distinctive home run trot. Sosa jumps out of the batter's box as the ball soars toward the heavens. The stutter step at first base, the two-fingered touching of the chest, and the kiss home to his mother watching back home in the Dominican Republic.

THE MAN IN THEIR SIGHTS

By August, McGwire and Sosa had become baseball's main event. Griffey, Galarraga, and Greg Vaughn had fallen off the home run pace. In Seattle, Alex Rodriguez was headed for a forty-home-run, forty-stolen-base season. But the nightly sportscasts, the headlines in tomorrow's paper, began with Mac and Sammy. On August 19, Sosa briefly moved ahead of McGwire when he connected off the Cardinals' Kent Bottenfield. Later in the same game Sosa walked. When he reached first base, the two sluggers struck up a conversation and McGwire imitated the kisses Sosa blew to his mother after every home run. In his autobiography, Sosa said he doesn't remember exactly what was said that day when he and McGwire talked at first base and the baseball world watched. But he does remember McGwire saying, "Hey, I think we're going to do it." By the end of the game McGwire had hit two home runs to pass Sosa again, and afterward McGwire told the media that he thought the record could be broken.

Since June, McGwire had been conducting interviews only in half-hour press conferences before the first game of a new series on the road. After that he was unavailable. He became upset when a radio station in Arizona broadcast live play-by-play of his batting practice. Three days later, in Houston, cameras stretched from dugout to dugout and McGwire angrily declared that he felt "like a caged lion" and threatened to stop taking BP in the stadium where all could see. National columnists began to worry about McGwire's mental health. "[He] appears to be losing his mind," one wrote. Another called him "tortured . . . he can't embrace this the way Sammy Sosa does."

Meanwhile, Sosa didn't hold regular, organized press briefings. He could still be found at his locker, sometimes surrounded by fifty or more journalists.

"I've always been like this around the media," he said, "but you guys never gave me the chance to express myself before. Now that you know, you say 'Wow!' But I'm the same guy. I'm not gonna change."

The man they were chasing—Roger Maris—had also refused to change, and it cost him dearly. In 1961, he had broken Babe Ruth's record for the most home runs in a season. In that year, like 1998, it had been a two-man race. Maris competed with teammate Mickey Mantle throughout the summer until Mantle came down with the flu. Announcer Mel Allen gave him the name of a doctor, but it turned out that "he was one of those celebrity feel-good doctors," Mantle wrote in his autobiography, *All My Octobers.* The doctor injected Mantle too high on the hip with an unsterilized needle. By the next morning, Mantle was in the hospital with an abscess wound, leaving Maris to pursue Ruth's record on his own. The New York media couldn't accept that it would be a relative newcomer, Maris, and not Yankee favorite Mantle, who would take a run at Ruth's record of sixty home runs in one season.

Maris was considered to be as flat and simple as Fargo, North Dakota, and the northern Plains, where he had grown up. But anybody who has traveled across that land knows it's much more than a patchwork of September wheat and sugar beets. Down at ground level, the land can rise and fall like the waves on the ocean. The wind echoes down from the Canadian border, rippling everything that stands in its path.

"Roger and Mickey couldn't have been more different," said

Billy Crystal, who directed the HBO movie *61** about that season. "But their friendship grew and endured from that year. Only they really knew what they were going through. We saw the same thing happen in '98 with Sosa and McGwire."

In essence, the entire nation woke up to the fact that this was a two-man race. One hitter may have been as American as apple pie and the other from a Caribbean island most grade school children couldn't find on a map of the world. No other foreign-born athlete has ever been as revered in this nation as Sosa came to be. Pelé in soccer had his moments, as did Hakeem Olajuwon in basketball. Clemente never really became a hero in this country until after his tragic death. Yet the respect and admiration for Sosa increased almost daily during the summer of '98.

"White America was looking for a white sports hero," says Richard Lapchick of Northeastern University's Center for the Study of Sport in Society, "and Mark McGwire was that person."

Then we noticed we had two heroes in our midst that summer. For decades the sea change had been under way in our national pastime. More and more Latinos had reached the major leagues. There had been plenty of stars before Sosa—Minoso, Clemente, Concepcion, Cepeda, Carew, and Valenzuela are just a few. But it took the Great Home Run Chase of '98 for us to notice how much baseball had changed. In the 1960s and into the 1970s, the rise of the African-American athlete profoundly impacted sports and eventually society. It took Sosa to underscore a similar movement—the rise of Latinos—in baseball.

RECORD-BREAKERS

The entire baseball world held its breath when McGwire stepped to the plate on September 8 in St. Louis. On the mound was Cubs right-hander Steve Trachsel and in right field was Sosa. The day before McGwire had tied Maris's all-time mark with a first-inning home run off Mike Morgan. As McGwire had rounded the bases that day, Sosa had directed several two-fingered salutes or kisses in his direction. When McGwire reached home plate, he had hoisted his son, Matthew, the reason he had ended the '87 season prematurely, aloft for all the world to see. Later in that game Sosa had walked. When he reached first base he hugged McGwire and told him, "Don't go too far, now. Just wait for me."

Less than twenty-four hours later against Trachsel, McGwire wasn't waiting for anyone as he lined the first pitch he saw in the fourth inning over the wall. In the hoopla, Sosa ran in from right field to embrace his friend once more.

"[Sosa] has unbelievable class," McGwire would later say.

But the Cubs slugger would also provide one last twist to the home run chase. As McGwire basked in his glory, understandably exhausted from the ordeal and media scrutiny, Sosa put on one last push. He tied McGwire at sixty-two home runs. When Sosa surpassed Maris, nobody from the opposing team, the Milwaukee Brewers, hugged him or gave him a high-five. The baseball commissioner wasn't in attendance. Sosa rounded the bases almost as if it were a routine homer.

"McGwire was going crazy, like it was the end of the world," Pentland says. "Sammy went about it very businesslike."

After the game, Sosa said his only regret was that McGwire couldn't have been present to share the moment.

"Mark, you know I love you," Sosa told the media that day. "I wish you could have been here today. I know you have some feeling for me in your heart. This is for you, Mark. I love you."

In the 1950s, fan favorite and seven-time All-Star Orestes "Minnie" Minoso became the first black superstar on the Chicago White Sox. (*Courtesy Baseball Hall of Fame Library, Cooperstown, N.Y.*)

MINNIE MINOSO

MARTIN DIHIGO

Arguably one of the best baseball players of all time, Cuban sensation Martin Dihigo threw no-hitters in three different countries and played all nine positions. (*Courtesy Baseball Hall of Fame Library, Cooperstown, N.Y.*)

The legendary Roberto Clemente led the National League in batting four times during his illustrious career.

ROBERTO CLEMENTE

LUIS TIANT

In his nineteen-year career, Cuban-born Luis Tiant led the American League in shutouts three times. *(Courtesy Baseball Hall of Fame Library, Cooperstown, N.Y.)*

In the early 1980s, "Fernandomania" swept through Los Angeles, as support for the unstoppable Mexican pitcher united a racially divided community.

FERNANDO VALENZUELA

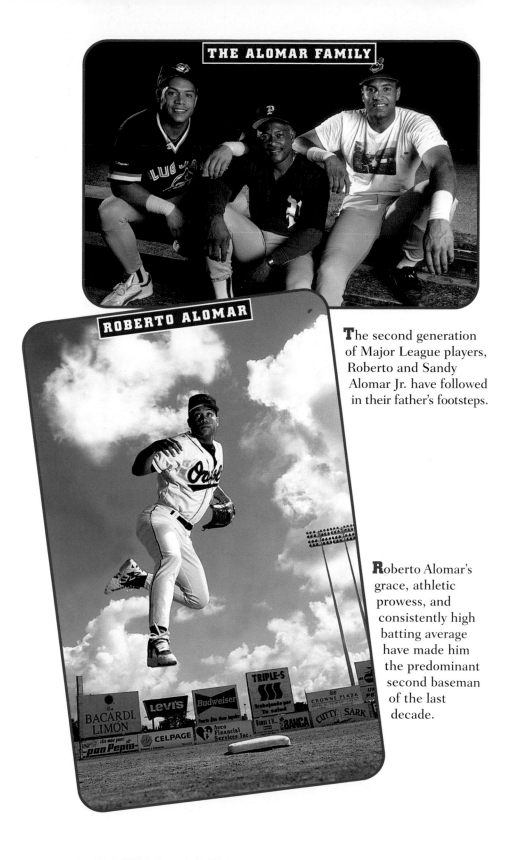

THE ALOMAR FAMILY

ROBERTO ALOMAR

The second generation of Major League players, Roberto and Sandy Alomar Jr. have followed in their father's footsteps.

Roberto Alomar's grace, athletic prowess, and consistently high batting average have made him the predominant second baseman of the last decade.

ROD CAREW

One of the greatest hitters the game has ever seen, Rod Carew hit over .300 for fifteen consecutive seasons. To this day he is a national hero in his native Panama.

JOSE CANSECO

ORLANDO CEPEDA

In 1999, after a long wait, 1960s slugger Orlando Cepeda, the "Baby Bull," was finally elected into the National Baseball Hall of Fame.

For the last five years, Carlos Delgado has been a mainstay at first base for the Toronto Blue Jays.

(*LEFT*)
Jose Canseco was in his prime during his time with the Oakland A's.

Boston Red Sox star Nomar Garciaparra is the prime example of baseball's newly defined shortstop, combining great athleticism with a strong bat.

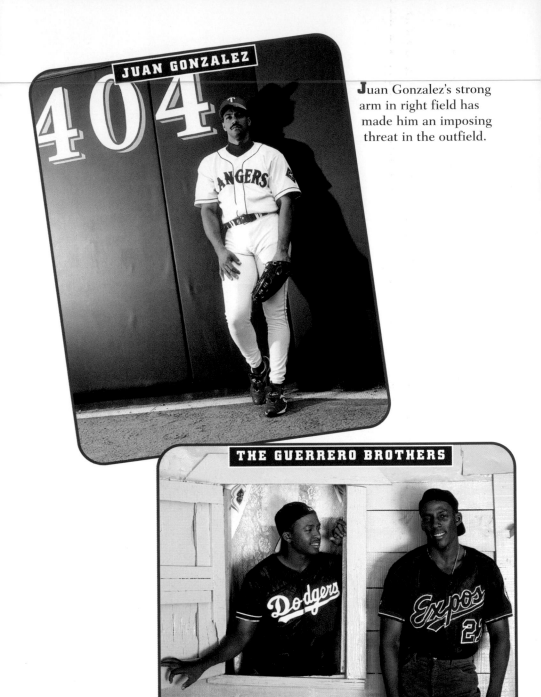

JUAN GONZALEZ

Juan Gonzalez's strong arm in right field has made him an imposing threat in the outfield.

THE GUERRERO BROTHERS

Major League brothers Vladimir and Wilton Guerrero have never forgetten their native Dominican Republic.

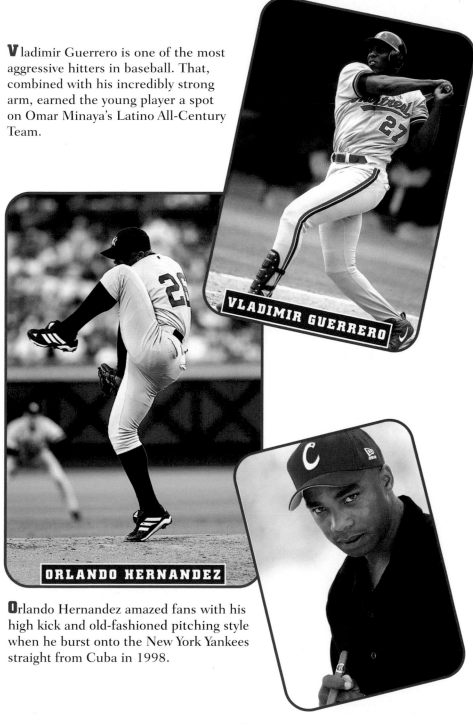

Vladimir Guerrero is one of the most aggressive hitters in baseball. That, combined with his incredibly strong arm, earned the young player a spot on Omar Minaya's Latino All-Century Team.

VLADIMIR GUERRERO

ORLANDO HERNANDEZ

Orlando Hernandez amazed fans with his high kick and old-fashioned pitching style when he burst onto the New York Yankees straight from Cuba in 1998.

Since his dramatic defection from Cuba, Orlando Hernandez has made it clear that he will never forget his homeland.

Omar Linares reportedly turned down a $40 million contract with the New York Yankees to remain in his native Cuba. The 1996 Olympic medalist has been described as "the best third baseman on the planet."

OMAR LINARES

EDGAR MARTINEZ

Unlike most players in this day and age, Edgar Martinez has spent his entire career with one team. A driving force on the successful Seattle Mariners, Martinez is known as a "virtual RBI machine," batting over .300 in seven consecutive seasons.

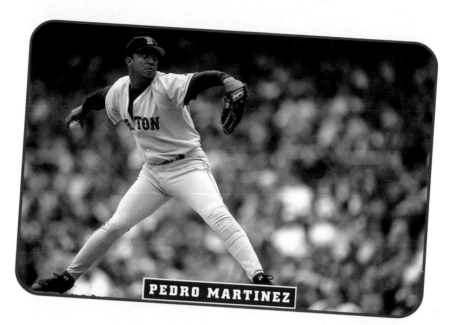

PEDRO MARTINEZ

MANNY RAMIREZ

Three-time Cy Young Award winner Pedro Martinez is one of the most imposing pitchers in baseball. With a 1.74 ERA in 2000, Martinez's arsenal of pitches made him unhittable.

Arguably one of the best hitters in the game, Manny Ramirez is known for being able to go to any field.

MARIANO RIVERA

Panama native Mariano Rivera has been one of the most dominant closers in baseball since the mid-1990s, and was the 1999 World Series MVP.

With a career total of 490 home runs, Rafael Palmeiro dispels the myth that Latino ballplayers are not sluggers.

RAFAEL PALMEIRO

In the last decade Ivan Rodriguez has become one of the most prominent catchers in the majors, with ten Gold Gloves and enormous power at the plate.

IVAN RODRIGUEZ

Sammy Sosa entertains fans at the All-Star Game's Home Run Derby.

A young Sammy Sosa already showing signs of his powerful swing.

One of the most accomplished shortstops in the Majors, Omar Vizquel has received nine Gold Gloves in his fourteen-year career.

BERNIE WILLIAMS

Thrown into the limelight with his consistent batting and great speed, Bernie Williams has quietly taken over center field for the New York Yankees.

LIVAN HERNANDEZ

Tryouts at a baseball academy in the Dominican Republic.

Only one year after his debut in Major League Baseball, Livan Hernandez was named the 1997 World Series MVP—a far cry from his life in Cuba.

TONY LA RUSSA

Tony La Russa admits to having been a mediocre player, but his true talents were revealed when he started managing.

OMAR MINAYA

The first Latino general manager in Major League Baseball, Omar Minaya accepted the challenge with gusto when it came to saving the ailing Montreal Expos.

TONY PEREZ

A leader of Cincinnati's Big Red Machine in the 1970s, Tony Perez was one of the greatest run producers in the game, retiring fourteenth on Major League Baseball's all-time RBI list.

Known for his strong arm behind the plate and his resilience as a player, catcher Tony Peña was placed on the disabled list only one time during his career.

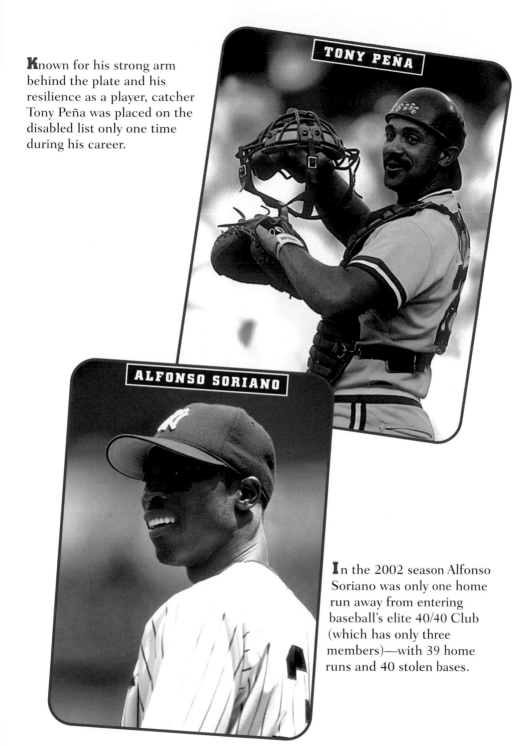

TONY PEÑA

ALFONSO SORIANO

In the 2002 season Alfonso Soriano was only one home run away from entering baseball's elite 40/40 Club (which has only three members)—with 39 home runs and 40 stolen bases.

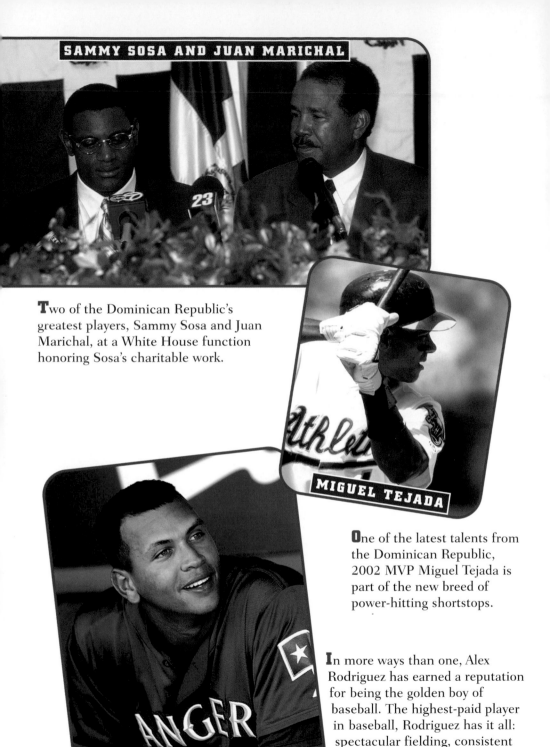

Two of the Dominican Republic's greatest players, Sammy Sosa and Juan Marichal, at a White House function honoring Sosa's charitable work.

MIGUEL TEJADA

One of the latest talents from the Dominican Republic, 2002 MVP Miguel Tejada is part of the new breed of power-hitting shortstops.

In more ways than one, Alex Rodriguez has earned a reputation for being the golden boy of baseball. The highest-paid player in baseball, Rodriguez has it all: spectacular fielding, consistent hitting, and incredible fan appeal.

ALEX RODRIGUEZ

THE FINAL DAY

Three Houston police officers protected Sosa from any more questions as he walked back to his clubhouse deep in the bowels of the Astrodome. The slugger had just completed a news conference that was orchestrated with the precision of a football halftime show. Five minutes for the dozen or so television cameras packed into the dank back room behind the Cubs' clubhouse. Another five minutes for the first wave of the print media, and then another five for the stragglers, and then that was it. The Great Home Run Chase was over. Houston's finest were on the scene to make sure that the schedule was followed and everyone behaved. The night before, proceedings had degenerated into a pushing match.

For a few moments, Sosa sat alone in front of his locker. Then his brothers, who had been traveling with him since "Sammy Sosa Day at Wrigley Field" a week before, came over to join him. One of them handed Sosa a plate of mashed potatoes and chicken, and he ate it with the fatigue of a man who had traveled far in a short amount of time.

On this same day, in St. Louis, McGwire had ended the season with an exclamation point, hitting his sixty-ninth and seventieth home runs of the season. Sosa had finished the regular season with sixty-six home runs. Sosa nodded at the TV screen hanging from the ceiling, and he and his brothers watched the other big home run of the day—Neifi Perez's dinger that forced a one-game playoff between the Cubs and San Francisco Giants to see who would go to the National League playoffs. Chicago would win the tiebreaker to reach the postseason for the first time since 1989.

"We're still alive," Sosa had told anyone who would listen only minutes before. He made it sound like the most important thing in the world, more important than beating Big Mac in the race for baseball immortality. If there is any justice in the world, McGwire and Sosa will forever be linked: a hybrid for a home-run-happy age. But this is America, after all. A place where second place usually doesn't count for much.

"When they mention Mark McGwire, they will mention me," Sosa said. "Fifty years from now I hope that they remember me, too. After all, I was there with him."

Across the Cubs' clubhouse, shortstop Jeff Blauser watched as the media began to exit.

"Sometime in the next couple of weeks, Sammy is going to be able to get away from all of this, put his feet up and relax," Blauser said. "And I tell you, he's going to find out how tired he really is. The guys in this clubhouse have been in awe of him all year. Not just for what he's done on the field, even though that is incredible. No, the guys can't believe how well he's handled all of this. It happens every day, and he's never lost it."

For the Cubs' final regular-season games in Houston, the Astrodome was packed. The area hotels were at capacity. Some had driven from as far away as New Orleans to catch a glimpse of Sosa swinging for the record books. When Sosa took off in June, hitting a major-league record twenty home runs, some of the Cubs grew worried about how this attention would impact the team and their budding national icon. However, it soon became clear, said closer Rod Beck, that Sosa had matured. He could handle the questions, the attention. It seemed he could handle anything.

"When I used to pitch against this team, I was worried about [Ryne] Sandberg and [Mark] Grace," he said. "I knew I could probably get Sammy to fish at something out of the strike zone. But this season he came in with a different attitude. Unlike a lot of guys, he's not swinging at bad balls. It kind of makes you feel good to see a guy up his game like that, become something so much more than he once was."

Many of the fans who traveled to the Astrodome on that final weekend of the 1998 season talked about the torrential rains they had encountered. The weather was a harbinger of Hurricane Georges, the fierce storm that had already raked the Dominican Republic. In looking back on the Great Home Run Race, we must remember that these two men faced far different obstacles along the way. McGwire became the heir apparent with his four home runs in the first four games of the season. All the pressure in the world was on his shoulders and he somehow found a way to rise above such great expectations.

Sosa was the guy who shows up late to the party and initially gets by with a joke and flair for the dramatic. Yet in the last week of the season much of the laughter faded for Sosa, and it had nothing to do with coming in second to McGwire or the pressure of trying to reach the playoffs. Hundreds died in his native land because of Hurricane Georges. He told me he was fortunate that most of his family had already come north for his big day in Chicago. They had either stayed on in the Windy City or joined him on the road. Before those final games of the regular season and into the night after the action was over, calls were made back home. Sosa and teammates Henry Rodriguez and Manny Alexander helped load trucks with food and supplies for the victims.

On the field, the pressure to win for the Chicago team never went away. While the Cardinals had fallen out of contention by midseason, the Cubs battled the Giants and New York Mets down the stretch. Sosa couldn't swing for the fences every time up. On the last day of the regular season in the Astrodome, with the crowd yelling for a home run every time he came to bat, Sosa had singled twice. The first hit drove in a run and the second time he put himself in scoring position by stealing second. Even McGwire conceded that Sosa had "bigger and better things on his mind."

Sosa finished his meal, showered, and put on a regal dark suit and tie. Cubs dugout coach Billy Williams watched as he filed past, again flanked by the Houston police. Williams had to shake his head, for a moment flashing back to when Sosa was such a free swinger that it seemed impossible for him to draw a base on balls.

"Sammy stayed within himself every step of the way," Williams said. "It was a helluva season and he seemed to decide early on to just enjoy the ride. He answered all the questions. He often did it with a laugh. He enjoyed himself and I think people like that about him. What we've seen this season is somebody growing up, somebody coming into his own. Everybody likes to see that, no matter how it shakes out in the end."

"SAMMY CLAUS"

In the end, McGwire was the man. Even Sosa told us so. But the kid who once shined shoes for a living had become a national treasure. Sosa was paraded through the streets of New York and applauded at a presidential State of the Union speech. Of all the stars in the national pastime, Sosa was the one seated next to the First Lady. The one who was hailed as an example of how great a land of opportunity America can be. Omar Minaya says Nelson Mandela is the only other person from a foreign land he can remember being embraced in such a way by the U.S. public. Arguably, Sosa garnered more attention than McGwire once the race was over as he simultaneously represented Latinos and the American spirit.

"I have opened the door to all of you Dominicans," Sosa said in an emotional speech after he was paraded down Broadway and given the key to New York by Major Rudy Giuliani. After choking back the tears, Sosa once again thanked his mother and told the crowd he didn't know how to repay them for their support.

"He's the greatest role model for Latino kids," said Millie Diaz, a Dominican-American from Brooklyn. "He has been a great player plus a great person."

And, somehow, despite the newfound celebrity, Sosa was still Sammy.

After the '98 season, we began a tradition at USA Today Baseball Weekly. We decided to put a prominent major-leaguer on the cover to grace our holiday issue. The only catch was we wanted the superstar to don a Santa Claus suit. Time after time we were turned down. One player said such holiday garb would make him look too fat. Many more were too busy to be bothered.

Finally, we caught up with Sosa at an inner-city high school in Washington, D.C. He was on his "Sammy Claus" tour, giving out gifts to needy kids. Sosa agreed to wear the suit for the photo session, and when he saw how the kids loved to see him decked out for the holiday, he told his handlers to call the costume shop. The rental period was extended to a week so that Sosa could wear the Santa suit on his remaining stops.

"We need to remember that every day is a gift," Sosa said. "Did you see the look on their faces? Those kids when I wore this? That's what I can give them."

TALKING
SPANGLISH

"Who is the greatest manager, really,

Luque or Mike Gonzalez?"

"I think they are equal."

◆ **ERNEST HEMINGWAY,**
  The Old Man and the Sea

'mon," Tony Peña said, flashing open his catcher's mitt and sliding down into his hurdler's stretch behind the plate. "Right here, huh?" ◆ Nothing bugs the onetime All-Star catcher, now manager of the Kansas City Royals, more than a pitcher who's tentative. Afraid to come inside with his best stuff. A pitcher who nibbles at the corners and has difficulty with his control. When Peña spots his glove, that's where he wants the pitch. Hit the glove, will ya? No ifs, ands, or buts.

On this day, midway through the 1991 major-league season, Peña was becoming especially exasperated because the guy he was catching was real raw and lacking in confidence. This guy on the mound was a real challenge. You see, I was the would-be hurler.

During the first season of USA *Today Baseball Weekly,* editor Paul White sent me on the road with the Boston Red Sox, the team Peña was playing for. I caught up with them in Chicago for a three-game series against the White Sox. I didn't know it coming in, but I was about to receive a crash course in the art of catching. Peña and I talked before and after each game. During that stretch he caught a rookie (Mike Gardiner), a journeyman (Greg Harris), and a future Hall of Famer (Roger Clemens). Peña had been in the majors since 1980, a five-time All-Star. Even though there were highlights to come as a player (most notably his walk-off home run to win game one of the 1995 American League Division Series against Boston), this catcher knew his career was coming to an end. He was already contemplating becoming a manager someday.

As part of *Baseball Weekly*'s cover story, Peña had agreed to pose in his catching gear in the Red Sox bullpen before a game in mid-July. The White Sox' Lance Johnson had been drafted to stand at the plate and hold a bat.

"Oh, I get it," Johnson said after Peña sweet-talked him out of shagging flies in right field as the White Sox took batting practice. "I'm the jerk who looks like he's striking out."

Peña nodded. "You got it."

John Zich, the photographer, had finished setting up. Everything was ready to go, except we didn't have anybody to throw the ball.

"It's on you, buddy," Peña said, lobbing the ball out to me.

I was stunned. "Me?"

"Sure thing," my new battery mate replied.

Johnson, who was already standing in the batter's box, bat in hand, looked back at Peña.

"I don't know about this," Johnson said.

That made two of us.

I shook my head. "We'll get somebody else."

"Almost out of time," Peña said. "Team stretches in ten minutes. I'll get fined if I'm not there."

"*Baseball Weekly* will pay your fine," I told him.

"You sure about that?" Peña demanded.

"I think so," I said, trying to figure if I could pad an expense account to that degree.

"Just pitch," Peña said, and I did as I was told.

Now, working off a bullpen mound in your street shoes is no picnic, especially when you haven't taken the mound since Little League. My first half-dozen offerings were feeble and drooped away to the outside of the plate. The photographer said they were so far away that he couldn't get Johnson, Peña, and the ball in the frame.

"I don't want to hit him," I said, nodding at Johnson.

I could see the headlines now: "White Sox Outfielder Injured in Freak Accident, Beaned by Sportswriter. Film at 11."

"He'll heal," Peña said.

Johnson stepped away from the plate. "Like I said, I'm not sure about this."

"It's OK," I said, now afraid he'd leave and the photo shoot wouldn't happen.

"Give the kid a chance," Peña told his fellow major-leaguer. "A few more, okay?"

With great reluctance, Johnson drew closer to the plate. But I noticed that he wasn't digging in.

"C'mon," Peña yelled out to me. "We need your best stuff. Now."

Deciding to go with a cross-seam fastball, I reared back and fired. Thankfully the ball came across the plate, almost popping Peña's glove.

"Oh, yes," Peña said, throwing the ball back to me.

For the next minutes, while the photographer snapped away, I fell under Peña's spell. He grunted and whistled, alternating between English and Spanish. Often I didn't know what he was saying, but I knew it was working. For a few precious moments in my life I was Clemens, or at least a rookie hurler like Gardiner. I was at a major-league ballpark, daydreaming that I was setting down the opposition in order. All I saw was Peña's glove, and all I heard was him barking at me.

"That's it, my friend," as another pitch somehow found the target. "Now do it again. Really bring it now."

The photo shoot was a success. Johnson lived to play another day and Peña wasn't fined. Later I told him I must have been okay. After all, he never had to come out to the mound and scold me about my location.

"Yes, yes," he said. "You pitched real good."

And I so much wanted to believe him.

From the Dominican Republic, Peña was a star in the 1980s and faded to journeyman status the following decade. Throughout his eighteen-year career, he was known for his showmanship and his perpetual smile. In a way, it was easy to underestimate him, as it was with many Latinos. The terminology that was once applied to African Americans—instinctive player, natural ability—were now hung on this new wave of players from the Dominican Republic, Cuba, Venezuela that was becoming a force in the game. Call someone a natural and the flip side of that would-be praise is that he doesn't work as hard to learn the game's nuances. Many may have missed it back then, but Peña knew the game inside and out. He was so confident in his knowledge that he wasn't afraid to embrace the unorthodox. Years later, when his Royals team was trying to end the Oakland A's record twenty-game winning streak, he intentionally loaded the bases with Miguel Tejada coming to the plate. Although Tejada promptly singled in the winning run, Peña had set up a potential inning-ending double play. First as a player and later as a manager, he's not afraid to play the fool if it has a chance of producing the result he wants.

Soon after I arrived in Chicago in 1992, I found Peña in the Red Sox dugout on one knee, breaking in a new catcher's mitt by pounding on it with one of Jack Clark's bats.

"It's the caveman technique," said pitcher Matt Young.

Clark walked by and gave Peña a curious look.

"Maybe I'll knock some hits into it," Peña said.

Clark only shrugged and nursed his pregame cup of coffee.

After a half hour of hammering, Peña held up the glove, so supple that he would use it in tonight's game.

"So, I'm a cuckoo head," he said. "But it works."

Indeed, Peña's approach would be dismissed as too unconventional, dare we say too Latin, for some. For a sore arm, Peña would rub lamb's grease on the injured limb. For impromptu meetings on the mound he used to get so worked up that his words tumbled out half in English, half in Spanish.

"We call it Spanglish," said ex-Red Sox closer Jeff Reardon, "and sometimes Tony's the only one who understands it."

Miguel Angel Gonzalez was the first Latino manager in the major leagues. He, like Peña, was a great defensive catcher with a curiosity about how the game worked. In 1938, Gonzalez was named interim manager for the St. Louis Cardinals. Yet he would be better remembered as the third base coach when Enos Slaughter came around with the winning run in the 1946 World Series. (Most sources agree that Gonzalez gave Slaughter the stop sign and wanted him to hold at third.) In addition, Gonzalez used the phrase "good hit, no field" on an early scouting report for the Cards. Those four words would stereotype many Latino players who would follow him into the majors.

Gonzalez's career often paralleled that of Adolfo Luque, the "Pride of Havana." While Luque had a much longer and successful playing career, going 192–179 with a 3.24 and two World Series appearances, both men eventually returned to their native Cuba and enjoyed stellar second tenures as highly regarded managers. Hence, the Hemingway quote that begins this chapter.

"If, in addition to his accomplishments as a player, one considers Luque's impact as a manager in Cuba and Mexico, it is an injustice that he is not in the Hall of Fame in Cooperstown," writes Roberto Gonzalez Echevarria. "There are worse ballplayers and characters enshrined in that American temple."

Among today's managers, several appear destined for the ultimate recognition that eluded Luque. In large part, their success has to do with their ability to communicate in English and Spanish. Besides Peña in Kansas City, other managers who were bilingual, or at least able to talk Spanglish in the 2002 season, were the Cardinals' Tony La Russa, the Giants' Dusty Baker, the A's' Art Howe, the Tigers' Luis Pujols, the Blue Jays' Carlos Tosca, the Mariners' Lou Piniella, and the Angels' Mike Scioscia. Back when Peña was a player, the only managers who could converse in both languages were the Dodgers' Tommy Lasorda and La Russa. Lasorda learned Spanish while playing winter ball. La Russa, like Piniella and Tosca, was raised in the Tampa area. His mother was born in Tampa, but she was of Spanish descent and she and La Russa's father spoke Spanish at home. La Russa goes as far as to list Spanish as a prerequisite for managing in the big leagues. That he's bilingual has been helpful in his handling of shortstop Edgar Renteria, who's from Colombia, and budding superstar Albert Pujols, who moved from the Dominican Republic to the Kansas City area at the age of sixteen.

"If you sell French shoes in Times Square, you'd better have somebody that speaks French," says Omar Minaya, the first Latino general manager at the major-league level. "It's the same thing in baseball. If forty percent or more of the players that are in the game are Latino, you better have some people that speak Spanish."

"I'm not fluent. I speak Spanglish," says Scioscia, who picked it up while playing winter ball. "But I can converse and it can be an edge. What you want to have happen is to make the baseball terminology [in your clubhouse] as universal as you can."

Piniella says the bilingual trend in the modern era began with La Russa, and really took root with Felipe Alou's success in Montreal. Alou was the Expos manager from 1992 to 2001 and was National League manager of the year in 1994. Like Peña, he was raised in the Dominican Republic, and when he took the Montreal Expos to unexpected heights, often reassuring Latino prospects who reached the big leagues, the rest of the baseball world took notice. After the 2002 season ended, Alou told reporters that he didn't expect to return to the dugout soon, even though he wanted to. In surveying the game's recent hires, he saw that the tendency was for ball clubs to name younger, white managers. Yet only weeks after the World Series ended, Alou, like Cepeda before him, was heading home to the Bay Area. He had been named to succeed Dusty Baker as manager of the San Francisco Giants.

"I'm thrilled to go back where it all started for me," says Alou, who played for the Giants in the 1950s and 1960s. "Many times I never thought I would get back there."

While Alou was sixty-seven years old when he accepted the new post, the oldest manager named to run a team since a seventy-one-year-old Casey Stengel was brought on to manage the expansion New York Mets in 1961, Giants owner Peter Magowan maintains Alou has the makeup necessary to operate a modern ball club.

"It will be important for any manager who comes in here to deal with the different personalities, ages, and races that make up any organization, not just the Giants," he says.

"You know a fourth or a third of your roster are Spanish-speaking kids from the different Latin American countries, so it helps to communicate, and at the same time I think they feel more comfortable," Piniella told the *San Francisco Chronicle*. "You get to know them a little better that way. They feel more at ease and open up a little more."

Those who don't know the language often opt for an interpreter. Howe did when dealing with Tejada and his other Latin players. Rafael Bournigal and later Gil Heredia were his mouthpieces until he gained more confidence in a second tongue.

Yankees manager Joe Torre, who doesn't speak Spanish, cautioned that the choice of an interpreter might be one of the key signings a ball club makes. Often players from the Caribbean will pretend to understand English to avoid embarrassment.

"You need to make sure your message gets across," Torre tells me. "What they need to do in this situation and that situation. Then you have the beginnings of a relationship. One built on success. Then you can get to know them a little more, go from there."

If anything, Torre believed that the universal language of baseball, what Scioscia alluded to, can be easier with the Latino ballplayer than those from other lands like Japan or Korea.

"It's easier to communicate with the Latin player, even if they do need an interpreter, because they're closer to the game," Torre says. "Many of the things mean the same or are similar. With the Asian player, you try to use a phrase and it's not close to meaning the same thing."

While Latino players have been coming to this country to play ball longer than those from other lands, that doesn't mean language isn't an issue. Frank Robinson managed for ten years in the winter leagues. But he will admit that it didn't prepare him for managing the Montreal Expos, with their large percentage of Latino players. He found it especially frustrating in dealing with Vladimir Guerrero, arguably the best everyday player in the game. Over the course of the season, the manager spoke with his star player maybe ten times and always through an interpreter.

"I might do damage, so I leave it alone," he told Dan Le Batard, who writes for the *Miami Herald* and *ESPN Magazine*. "I can't teach him anything this way. I can't help him with the mental part of the game—slumps, approach, state of mind. It's awkward, frustrating. He would feel better, and I would feel better, if I could reach him, but I can't. He's on his own."

After pitcher Livan Hernandez defected from Cuba and signed with the Florida Marlins, he became so disoriented by his newfound freedom and prosperity, he almost didn't reach the major leagues, let alone become a World Series MVP. The drive-through window at the local Burger King became the place for most of his meals, and after he struggled at Triple A, the Marlins sent him down to Double A, where Carlos Tosca, another Cuban exile, was the manager.

"Basically I told [Livan] that I was there to help him," Tosca explains to me. "Obviously, we are both Cubans, which helped. We had our country, or our former country I should say, to talk about. I connected with him before I tried to discipline him or anything else. He felt that once the connection was made, both of us felt we could move forward and I could push him a bit. Get him to understand what he needed to do to get to the big leagues.

Tosca adds that Hernandez "didn't speak English at the time, so the Spanish really came in handy. I spoke to him almost entirely about life in general. What he liked about his new life here, what he didn't like, what he missed in Cuba. Those types of things before I even addressed any baseball issues.

"I just tried to get him to make the right choices. When you leave a country as poor as Cuba is and you're given that much money, who knows how it would affect any of us."

After managing in the Kansas City Royals' and Marlins' minor-league systems, Tosca came to Toronto as the third base coach. He was selected to head the Blue Jays after Buck Martinez was fired. During pregame batting practice, he'll try to check in with each of his players. Just a word or two, in English or Spanish or a combination of both.

"Being bilingual may help you more at the lower levels," says Tosca, who moved from Cuba at the age of eight. "By the time you get to Double A or Triple A, the majority of the Latin players can talk English. What is important is having an understanding of their culture and the way they operate. Being able to carry on conversations with them in Spanish or half in English can be more comfortable. For example, if I have conversation with Esteban Loaiza, half of it is in English and half of it is in Spanish."

Cleveland shortstop Omar Vizquel, who grew up in Venezuela, maintained that the relationship between player and manager is always better when they have a common language. There's only so much interpreters and teammates can do to bridge that gap.

"I was lucky—English came easy to me," Vizquel says. "I took five years in high school. I took another course after my high school career. So when you're talking with coaches, the manager, you know exactly what they're trying to tell you. It's easier for you to hang out with yourself. You don't have to rely on anybody else. If you're relying on a translator, he may not be saying the exact thing that you said. A translator has never played the game. So he puts it in his own words and sometimes things get lost.

"When you're here, this is the language. If you really want to climb levels, then it's a big key. You understand your surroundings. You understand all the plays. You have to know what is going on around you."

While Albert Pujols worked diligently on learning English throughout high school, he landed in a great baseball town in St. Louis with a manager who could help him in either language. Outside observers, like Minaya, claim that's a major reason why Pujols became the first player in major league history to hit .300 or better, with thirty home runs, 100 runs and 100 RBIs his first two seasons.

Le Batard, who is bilingual, says he's often surprised more newspapers don't require a working knowledge of Spanish for their reporters covering baseball teams. He calls Spanish "keys to the kingdom." While I'll never be as fluent as Le Batard or La

Russa, I know that a few words of Spanish can go a long way. Talk with an Anglo beat writer about Manny Ramirez and he'll probably tell you the Red Sox superstar is moody, not a good quote. But in the course of researching this book, I approached Ramirez in Spanish. In the Red Sox clubhouse, his locker is adjacent to that of Carlos Baerga, another Latino star. In essence, I was walking into their world, trying to converse in their native tongue.

To his credit, Ramirez heard me out as I asked if he had any time to talk. He smiled only slightly as I stumbled on *"Tiena tempo?"*—"Do you have time? Time to talk?" We began the interview in Spanish, slid into English, and finished in Spanish again.

"Manny is shy in English," Le Batard says, "but he can understand."

So part of coping with the language barrier is allowing yourself to look foolish at times. Over the years baseball has taught me that it will give you the answers, but you need to have enough courage to ask the questions. Even if that means carrying around a Spanish-English dictionary. Tony Peña wasn't concerned when some thought him a fool. If anything, he played along with his antics, his big smile. But behind that smile was a mind as keen as any in the game. It's what I learned by hanging with him for that three-game series in Chicago.

CATCHING A ROOKIE

On July 15, 1991, right-hander Mike Gardiner is fresh off the disabled list for a pulled rib cage, and before the game, Peña tells me his most important job tonight will be to "keep a close eye" on the rookie.

"If I see him flinch, start having trouble, I'll go right out there," Peña says. "I can't wait, even listen to him say there's no trouble. I want to make sure he doesn't hurt himself again."

It is a warm night on Chicago's South Side. That first hint of the dog days to come hangs in the air like a whisper. True to his word, from the first inning on, Peña tries to help the rookie out of trouble. When the White Sox' Robin Ventura and Dan Pasqua single, it brings up Carlton Fisk, Peña's catching counterpart and eventual Hall of Famer. On a 1-2 pitch, Gardiner attempts to get Fisk to chase a breaking ball in the dirt. Only Peña's flick of the glove keeps the ball from going to the backstop and costing the Red Sox a run.

"Nobody blocks the ball better," says Boston pitching coach Bill Fischer. "I've been in this game at the major-league level since '56, and nobody's been better at that part of the game than Tony."

Backup catcher John Marzano says Peña's defensive ability was remarkable, if again unorthodox. "Balls in the dirt, balls outside. Tony just picks them like he's on a ladder reaching for apples," Marzano explains. "It's a natural reaction for him. He has such great hands for it. I can't catch that way because it's impossible for most people.

"You're taught that when a ball's in the dirt, you're supposed to move your whole body in front of it to block it. But sometimes you can't move fast enough to do it by the book, and those balls you miss. Tony often will stop those balls with a flick of the glove. He catches balls in the dirt that way, which is next to impossible, but Tony does it all the time. The first couple of times you see it, you think he's lucky. But he does it so often, it's a real skill."

Later, Peña tells me that, growing up, he had no choice but to learn to stop errant throws in the dirt with a flick of his glove. The fields he played on were in awful shape. That many of the plays that are deemed unorthodox or too flashy at the major-league level were the only way to get things done on the sandlots he and other Latinos once called home.

"I always have fun playing the game," he says. "That will never end for me. But I also have great respect for the game. All Latinos do. People need to understand that just because they see us smile, make what some would call a flashy play, it doesn't mean we can't be serious, too."

In the end, this night isn't kind to Gardiner or Peña. After they escape the first-inning jam, things unravel in a hurry in the fifth inning. Frank Thomas drives a Gardiner fastball far over the center-field fence in the third inning and two innings later he gives the White Sox the lead for good when he blasts a Gardiner curveball out to left.

"I threw two stupid pitches and I'm the loser," Gardiner says later in the clubhouse. "That oh-two curveball to Thomas was the most idiotic pitch. Tony called it, but I didn't put in the place. I got way too much of the plate. I should have put it in the dirt, like Tony wanted. If I had, I betcha Thomas would have chased it. I'd been out of the inning."

Though his pitcher lost, Peña is satisfied with the outing.

"He didn't get hurt. He kept us in the game," Peña says. "It's something to build on. He may not believe it right this minute, but I do. And that's something I'm going to keep telling him. I'm going to tell him until he believes it."

THE JOURNEYMAN

Before the next game, Peña and Greg Harris, a slim right-hander who has pitched for eleven big-league seasons with seven teams, huddle in the Red Sox clubhouse. The White Sox' Frank Thomas has been feasting on any breaking pitch around the plate, like the 0-2 curveball Gardiner threw him the night before, so Peña devises a strategy. Against Thomas, the breaking stuff will be far off the plate, and then they will try and bust him inside with the fastball.

Thomas is the third batter up in the bottom of the first. Harris quickly gets ahead 0-2 when Thomas chases two pitches low and outside. After getting the two quick strikes, Peña signals for an inside fastball. After he flashes the sign to Harris, he opens his glove in the general location where he wants the pitch. As Harris goes into his delivery, Peña momentarily drops the glove down and then repositions it farther inside as the ball heads toward the plate. In doing so, he gives the umpire an optical illusion. It's called "the frame." With luck, Mike Reilly, the home-plate umpire, will remember where the glove originally was; not where Peña has set up with the sleight of hand that would make a pickpocket proud.

Peña doesn't have to move as Harris's fastball hits his glove with a pop. Even though Thomas jackknifes out of the way, due to Peña's frame the ball appears to come in over the inside corner, not an inch or two too far inside, as replays later reveal. Reilly calls strike three and Thomas is on his way to a 0-for-3 night and the Red Sox to a 2–0 victory.

THE HALL-OF-FAMER

There are no strategy sessions for the Red Sox before the deciding game at Comiskey. Their ace at that time, Roger Clemens, is due to take the mound.

"Nobody has a better idea of what he wants to do coming into a game than Roger," Peña says. "If a pitcher really wants to throw a pitch, I'm not going to stop him. They can throw whatever they want out there. It's when they're having trouble, then it's up to me to know how to help them.

"But with Roger there's a lot of agreement between us. I know how he thinks. He loves to go after hitters. Very, very aggressive. So sometimes when we're out there, it's magic. It's like we don't even need signals. I'll signal for a pitch, and it'll be just what he's thinking about throwing."

Tonight Clemens and Peña are once again on the same wavelength and if it wasn't for a misjudged fly ball to the outfield, the "Rocket" would have shut out Chicago before departing after the seventh inning. The Red Sox' bullpen allows the game to be tied at 2–2, but in the tenth inning Boston pushes two runs across against the White Sox' closer, Bobby Thigpen.

That brings Red Sox left-hander Tony Fossas to the mound to try and hold the lead. Only two nights before, in the game Gardiner had started and lost, Fossas had come in relief and promptly given up four earned runs. As soon as he reaches the mound, Peña is there to chat him up. Fossas barely gets a word in as Peña runs through the pitches he wants to use, how Fossas is ready for a good outing, how he is perfect for this situation, how he is going to pitch well tonight.

"I didn't want him to think too much," Peña later explains. "I sure didn't want him thinking about the last time he had pitched. So we got focused on what we had to do. That's the only place I wanted his head to be at.

"When I'm catching I have two personalities—hard guy and buddy. I have to know which one to use and when to use it with every pitcher I have."

Fossas proceeds to set down Chicago in order and the Red Sox win the game.

"If I'd had Tony as a catcher in the minors, I would have made the majors much earlier," says the Havana-born Fossas, who spent ten years rattling around Burlington, Tulsa, Edmonton, and Denver before reaching the big leagues. "He knows what you can throw and asks you to give it. Your best pitch may get hit, but Tony still believes in you. He wants to see that pitch again. I guess Tony's like E. F. Hutton. When he talks, every pitcher listens."

HEAVY ACCENT

One can learn a lot about baseball by listening to Tony Peña talk baseball. Unfortunately, fans of the Kansas City Royals didn't have the opportunity during Peña's first season as manager of that ball club. Although baseball has come a long way since the days of Minoso and Clemente (at the end of the 2002 season there were nine minority managers and Major League Baseball was trumpeting the fact that "more were in the pipeline"), sometimes an incident happens that reminds us how far we still have to go. As part of their pregame and sports talk show, many radio stations will routinely interview their home team manager. Invariably such segments focus on how the team is doing, what to expect in the upcoming game. As any player can tell you, Peña can provide insights as fine as anyone about how the game works. But soon after he was named the Royals' skipper, Kansas City's sports radio station, WHB-AM, announced that Peña wouldn't be a guest on its popular Kevin Kietzman Show because of his heavy accent.

"[It's] nothing personal against Tony," Kietzman told the *Kansas City Star*. "I like him. He's full of energy and enthusiasm. But the bottom line is I have to think about the show. That has to be my number-one priority. It is a difficult interview, to be honest. And it doesn't make for good radio.

"In no way do I think this is controversial. It's just that I do my show in English. My listeners speak English. I have to have a show that appeals to that audience. There are a lot of Spanish-speaking radio stations around that I'm sure wouldn't care to have me on because I don't speak very much Spanish."

To his credit, Peña refused to criticize WHB's decision in public. He told those in the Royals' front office that he believed the real problem was his deep voice, not his accent. Off the field, Peña took English classes and said he would continue to do so because it's "part of the job. . . . That's why I keep trying to get better. I'm trying to get better at everything, from my managerial skills to this. But I know that you can't please everybody. I learned that a long time ago."

SEVENTH INNING

DESPERATE ENOUGH TO LEAVE

"I am living at the center of a wound

still fresh."

◆ **OCTAVIO PAZ,** "Dawn"

choolchildren with red bandannas around their slender necks, military personnel in sharply creased brown uniforms, and aspiring doctors in white smocks crowd the balconies overlooking the courtyard. Everyone wants a glimpse. For below them stand thirty of Cuba's finest athletes: boxer Felix Savón, track star Ana Fidelia Quirot, the women's volleyball team, and Omar Linares, the best contemporary baseball player this island has ever produced.

Before the courtyard ceremony begins, I approach Alberto Juantorena, the man called the "Horse" after he stunned the world by winning the 400 and 800 meters at the 1976 Olympics in Montreal. After retiring, Juantorena rose to become Cuba's top sports official.

"An American," he exclaims. "How did you get in here, into this event?"

I shrug and await security. But Juantorena smiles like a used car salesman and starts to tell how me Cuba has guaranteed itself sporting glory forever. No matter that in recent months such top prospects as Livan Hernandez and Rey Ordonez had defected and Orlando "El Duque" Hernandez will soon follow. All of them quickly found places in the major leagues. Yet to hear Juantorena, there is no reason for worry. He and the Cuban powers that be have convinced the island's best, players like Linares, to continue to ignore the major leagues' siren call.

As La Premiacion del Atleta begins, the applause grows until Linares's name is finally called. He is one of the last to be honored. If he had ever bolted to the majors (the Yankees re-portedly offered him a $1 million signing bonus when such an amount meant something, and the Toronto Blue Jays tried to work out a deal where he would play games only in Canada), it would be a major blow to Cuban baseball, even its way of life. For years Linares has been a civic institution. For most of his ca-reer, he played in the Cuban league for his home province of Pinar del Rio. Visit him there and everyone knows where his home is. Often a Pied Piper crowd of kids will even lead you to his doorstep.

For Linares has been a wonder since his start: hitting .511 in his first amateur world championship at the age of fourteen, becoming the youngest player ever to play on a Cuban league team. By the age of eighteen, he was considered the best third baseman in amateur ball and one of the best in the world. In the 1989–90 season, he hit .425 in Cuba. He was nicknamed "El Niño" or "the Kid"—of course, the same moniker as Ted Williams.

I first met Linares in 1992, during an exhibition series be-tween the U.S. and Cuban Olympic teams. Even though the first of those three games wasn't scheduled to begin until 7:30 that evening, by noon the 40,000-seat stadium in Holguin, Cuba, was filled. The U.S. roster that day was loaded with players who would one day reach the major leagues—Nomar Garciaparra, Phil Nevin, Darren Dreifort, Jeffrey Hammonds, and Charles Johnson. None of them will ever forget that first game in Latin America. Neither will I.

In the long shadows of dusk, the foul poles glowed neon pink in the tropical twilight. The better to see if a long drive car-ries fair or foul, it was explained to us. The overflow crowd, spurred on by a salsa band and ringing cowbells, was impas-sioned and knowledgeable. Sacrifice bunts by the Cuban na-tional team were applauded with as much fervor as extra-base hits. "We are not just fans. We are baseball aficionados," one spectator told me, "and our players have come to understand that. To be inspired by that."

As I walked into the ballpark with Hammonds, he asked me what *Socialismo o Muerte* meant. The slogan was spread in red letters across the outfield fence. I told him that I believed it meant "socialism or death." Then I asked where he was playing that night.

"Right out there," he replied. "In that outfield."

There was no real press box, so we sat in the stands for those games. During the early innings, as I gazed out at Hammonds, an old man sat down next to me. I was at the end of the row and he sat on the step to my right.

"Tell me about the Minnesota Twins," he said.

This was in the off-season after that glorious team of Kirby Puckett and Kent Hrbek had upended the Atlanta Braves in one of the best World Series ever played. It's certainly ironic to reminisce about those games in light of Major League Baseball's efforts to eliminate that team and the Montreal Expos. But back in 1992, both the Twins and Expos were still viable franchises. Still, I told my visitor that it would be difficult for the Twins to repeat. They were getting older. The richer teams would sign away their younger stars.

"I know all that," the Cuban told me. "I need to know what they look like."

That's when I realized what a star-crossed land Cuba can be. In the United States we are bombarded with images. We may not know what the president or the hottest movie star is truly like or believes, but we sure know what they look like. In Cuba today, in the shadows among the columns, the newspapers still carry few photographs and fewer still have access to CNN or MSNBC.

So, in my tourist Spanish, I went around the diamond,

describing the 1991 Minnesota Twins to the old man beside me. It wasn't easy. Somebody like Puckett is difficult to describe in English, let alone in a second language. How do you tell somebody about a bowling ball of a man who always smiles and has a real tendency for the dramatic?

As I spoke, I gazed out toward the outfield. I tried to come up with the right words and I was still concerned for Hammonds, who wasn't having his best game.

When I finished, I turned back toward the old man. He had tears running down his face. He stood up and clasped me on the shoulder.

"Thank you," he said. "Now I know."

Then he disappeared back into the crowd that saw Linares lead the Cuban national team to a 16–1 victory. After the series, both teams flew back to Havana on the same plane. We landed in the early-morning hours and Linares's wife and family met him at the airport. She came to pick him up in a jet black Chevy, which could have been a contemporary of Minoso's Cadillac back during that victory parade into Havana. A few of us teased Linares about the wealth and fame that lay just ninety miles to the north. Can you say Corvette, Omar? Maybe a Porsche?

Linares only politely smiled at such suggestions. He maintained he didn't care about such things. No, instead he talked about the upcoming Olympics and how one day he hoped the Cuban team could play against major-leaguers instead of potential stars.

"It would be a series worth waiting for," he said. "We would get a chance to show how good a team we are."

With that he disappeared into the shadows of Havana.

WORTH WAITING FOR

Seven years later, Linares and the Cuban team got their chance. During spring training, a two-game exhibition series was arranged between the Cuban national squad and the Baltimore Orioles. One game would be played in Havana; another in Baltimore.

For batting practice in Cuba, the Orioles brought baseballs with more life than are usually seen on the island. In fact in the years immediately after the collapse of the Soviet Union, the Cuban leagues had difficulty keeping regulation balls in stock. Leather was scarce and a synthetic covering was used. This made it more difficult for pitchers to grip the ball. All of this tested the patience of the island's best hurlers. When the Cubans played in Atlanta during the 1996 games, more than a dozen pitchers, including the Hernandez brothers, had hurt their arms or had defected.

So, the buzz built as Oriole after Oriole drove baseballs far into the seats during warm-ups. The game itself began as a laugher for the big-league team as Baltimore gained a 2–0 lead. But with Castro, perhaps the ultimate team owner, in attendance alongside Commissioner Bud Selig and Orioles majority partner Peter Angelos, the Cubans made a game of it.

With two outs in the eighth inning, Linares tied the game with a single off Orioles reliever Mike Timlin. "For me, personally," he said later, "the moment was the game. The opportunity came, and I took it."

Two innings later, Linares had a chance to win the game outright, but he popped up with two on and two out. The next inning the Orioles edged ahead and hung on for the 3–2 victory.

Five weeks later, the teams met again in Camden Yards in Baltimore. Demonstrations, pro and con about the Cubans' appearance, were held on the sidewalk outside the classic-style ballpark. Meanwhile, Joe Cubas, the sports agent from Miami who had become as adept at spiriting Cuban prospects off the island as Joe Cambria once was, suggested that a half dozen stars could defect during the stay in "Charm City." None did. Castro and his baseball people had loaded the roster with veterans who were more likely to return home instead of causing an international incident. For instance, they kept German Mesa, perhaps the world's best defensive shortstop, off the roster for fear he would defect.

The Cubans came to Baltimore looking to make a statement, and that's what they did. Not only did Linares enjoy a pregame photo op with Cal Ripken, the Orioles' "Iron Man," he rapped out four hits as Team Cuba trounced the major-leaguers, 12–6. Still, the most memorable moment belonged to Andy Morales. His home run delivered the Cubans' final runs, and as the infielder rounded the bases he almost began to dance. He raised his arms in the air and nearly stumbled as he passed second base. His public demonstration was one of pure happiness—the kind usually reserved for the World Series, not an exhibition game.

"He was showing us up," several Orioles grumbled afterward in their clubhouse. "Did you see the way he was acting out there?"

When Team Cuba returned to Havana, they were feted like conquering heroes. Morales's home run was cited by Castro himself as a blow against gringo imperialism. But neither the Orioles' nor the Cuban party line fell anywhere close to the truth. What fans had seen was an athlete hitting a home run. Nothing more, nothing less. But to the man himself, such impromptu theatrics might have gotten him to thinking, to dreaming, about what life could be.

A year after that game in Camden Yards, Morales tried to defect. He and thirty-one others were picked up at sea only a few miles off Key West. In the wake of the Elian Gonzalez situation, U.S. officials were determined to curtail the lucrative smuggling market that exists off the Florida coast. Morales was sent back. Sixteen months later, he tried again and this time he made it.

So what makes one man run for the limelight, while another like Linares is happy to live out the best of his playing days in his own country? After seventeen years in Cuba's National Series League, Linares was allowed to play with the Chunichi Dragons in Japan. He was to be paid $4,000 a month, with much of that expected to go straight back to his government's coffers. Linares's legacy included more than 400 home runs and more than 2,000 hits, plus such strident words as "I would rather play for eleven million people than eleven million dollars."

But perhaps this once maybe it wasn't about the money. Consider Morales one last time. In the United States, we are truly blessed because we can compete against the best. Want to be the best stockbroker? Go to Wall Street. Itching to write a sequel to *Casablanca*? Look out, Hollywood.

If you play ball in Cuba, all you hear about is the major leagues. They know the names as well as we do—McGwire, Sosa, Griffey, Rodriguez. Scouts may label a Cuban star as of Triple A caliber. What's frustrating is that so rarely do the Cubans have the chance to show the best in the world what they can do. That's why the games against the Orioles were memorable for Morales and Linares and everybody in between.

Furthermore, that's what the Orioles never understood about that two-game exhibition series. For the Cubans, this was an opportunity they had been waiting for their entire lives. To prove they belonged.

Morales's father-in-law said he was "desperate" to get out of Cuba. Perhaps what was lost in the translation was that Morales was simply desperate to come to bat in a major-league park and swing for the fences again.

A ROOM WITH A VIEW

But what if you took the plunge? Left your country for the better life, a chance to play ball against the best in the world in the *Grandes Ligas*? Well, sometimes, it can be more than you ever bargained for.

The view from Livan Hernandez's condo balcony is as pretty as a picture. Or, better yet, a series of beautiful postcards that anyone would love to send back home. Play along for a minute. Hold out your hands with thumbs touching, in the old Hollywood director's pose, and imagine what this Cuban defector and then World Series MVP woke up to every morning.

Snap. In this shot the white-sand beach unfolds in the foreground and farther out, beyond the breakers of the Atlantic Ocean, cruise ships ply the turquoise-blue waters bound for exotic ports of call. Snap. Swing over a few steps and the picture becomes Biscayne Bay and the resort hotels and condominiums that rise like castles from a fairy tale north toward Fort Lauderdale, nearly fifteen miles away. What's that? We need a little caption copy to go along with these great images? Well, the famed Art Deco district is only a short drive down Collins Avenue. That part of town has long been home to entertainers and celebrities, from Jackie Gleason a generation ago, to Gloria Estefan today. If this was your view of the world, then no doubt you are living life large, my friend.

Now consider one last photo. Not a postcard, but a player's card—one of the series on his Cuban team that came out several years ago. In this picture, staring in from the mound, stands Hernandez. In this picture, he is eighteen years old. The card sits in the middle of the glass-topped table in the living room of Hernandez's high-rise condominium. The 1997 World Series MVP is asked to write the caption for this one. What is the difference between the kid on the card and the one who came to live amid some of the best postcard views that money can buy?

"I was skinnier," Hernandez jokes.

Then he falls silent. How do you explain how circumstance and good fortune can take a kid from the far side of nowhere and place him on top of the baseball world? And how does one approach the rest of a major-league career when the beginning must be a dream come true?

Livan Hernandez grew up on the Isla de Juventud, formerly the Isle of Pines. A six-hour trip by ferryboat from mainland Cuba, this is where Fidel Castro was sent to prison in 1953 after his first attempt at taking over the country. If Cuba remains light-years away from the United States in lifestyle and attitude, then Isla de Juventud might as well be the dark side of the moon. A year or so before he defected, Hernandez was considered a country hick in Havana. Then, in seemingly one fell swoop, he became the pride of South Florida. Even though Hernandez played many sports growing up, his talent for baseball soon attracted attention. At the age of nine he was identified as a prospect and was sent to a government sports initiation program. By thirteen, he was sent to a boarding school for budding sports stars, the ESPA, which loosely translates as the Advanced School for Athletic Perfection. Hernandez's father, Arnaldo, once pitched for the national team and of course his half-brother, Orlando, the great "El Duque," followed him to the United States and the major leagues. Yet, growing up, Hernandez didn't have much contact with either his father or his half-brother.

"My father was a good pitcher. He also played all the positions," Hernandez says. "But he didn't teach me much because my parents separated when I was very young."

"El Duque" was ten years older and was already on his way to becoming the winningest pitcher in Cuba when Livan was a schoolboy. Still, the game became Hernandez's salvation. If he was good enough, he could leave Isla de Juventud for the big island. Win enough games and maybe he could close the gap between himself and his father and half-brother.

"After my family, baseball is my first love," Hernandez tells Milton Jamail and me. We sit on the other side of the table in his condo. All of us are a bit uncomfortable because arguably the lines blurred for this pitcher at an early age. Long ago baseball became Hernandez's family, his first love.

Miami-based sports agent Joe Cubas has helped more than twenty Cuban stars defect. Many of his exploits could play in a James Bond movie. There was the time when he shepherded three defecting ballplayers by car through Mexico. Their journey took them through the heavily guarded Chiapas region. No matter that they had to sweet-talk their way past three checkpoints en route to safety.

No defection, though, was as harrowing for Cubas as the one involving Hernandez. By the age of seventeen, Hernandez was a member of the Cuban Junior team, and pitched a no-hitter at the world championships. Soon he was selected to the famed national team and was recognized as one of the top pitching prospects in the country. He traveled with the national team to Nicaragua and Japan, and it was during those trips that he decided to defect.

"There are a lot players in Cuba who are good," Hernandez explains that morning in his condo by the sea, "but they are fearful of the unknown. That's why they don't try to come (to the United States). But if you're a baseball player and you're the best, this is where you have to be. I knew the names. Players like Jose Canseco, Alex Fernandez, Frank Thomas, and Ken Griffey. You want to play against them."

In late September 1995, Hernandez got his chance to join them. Cubas remembers it being a blustery afternoon at

Monterrey Stadium in Mexico. The Cuban national team was practicing for a tournament that was to begin the next day. As Cubas watched from the stands through binoculars, one of his assistants, an attractive blonde, approached Hernandez with a pen and autograph book. Hernandez opened the book and saw a photo of Cubas, the one sports agent every Cuban ballplayer recognizes.

As Hernandez stared at the photo, the blonde slipped a piece of paper with Cubas's phone number at a local hotel into the pitcher's hand. Not only had Hernandez become good enough to make the national team; he had attracted the interest of the agent Cuban officials deride as "El Gordo," the Fat One. Later Hernandez called Cubas, telling him he was ready to defect that night. At one in the morning, Cubas was waiting in his car across the street from the hotel when he saw Hernandez. Carrying only a small duffel bag, the young pitcher stole past the Cuban officials in the lobby, who had fallen asleep.

When Hernandez reached the street, Cubas flashed his lights. In tears, Hernandez stepped off the curb and began to hurry across the street without looking. A passing car barely avoided hitting him.

"The car screeches and swerves, missing Livan by inches, and then speeds off," Cubas writes in a book proposal about his life. "We run into each other's arms like long-lost brothers and I throw him in the backseat of my rented car."

When asked about that night, Hernandez explains, "I just wasn't looking where I was going. That's all."

The phones in Hernandez's Miami Beach condo begin to chirp like a flock of mad birds. As we sit around the glass-topped table in his living room, they go off, one after another, interrupting any train of thought. Juan Iglesias, Hernandez's new agent, has just signed Canseco to a new contract and the various news organizations are checking in. Hernandez's cell phone rings about tee times at a local golf course later that afternoon. The house phone beckons for Livan's mother, Miram, who had stayed on since rejoining her son before game seven of the 1997 World Series.

While Cubas might be an expert on convincing Cuban ballplayers to defect, he has difficulty hanging on to his clients. Some leave because of his high fees. Others because he is invariably off to spirit another prospect away from Castro, the man he says he hates. Hernandez and Iglesias came together shortly after the prospect signed with the Florida Marlins. Hernandez spoke no English and didn't know a soul in this strange, new land of America.

"No family, nobody," Hernandez says. "Juan is still my best friend."

They make a curious pair. Hernandez stands at six foot two, with an easy grace for a man of his size and stature. The soft-spoken Iglesias appears to be one of those people willing to accept the weight of the world. He is easily eight inches shorter than his client, with slicked-back hair and a caterpillar mustache. As the phones continue to ring, Hernandez's answers to our questions—questions about Cuba and how this all came to be—become more clipped and strained. Iglesias sits motionless at the table, his head slightly bowed. He knows that Hernandez doesn't like to be questioned, to have his time monitored. It reminds him too much of Cuba.

A few years ago, CBS asked to follow Hernandez for the day. To see how the young defector was adjusting to life in paradise. After initially agreeing to the arrangement, Hernandez ended it by midday. People with cameras and microphones only follow those with something to hide, he told team officials. Iglesias knew as well as anybody that Hernandez's story, like any fairy tale or nightmare, will always be one of extremes.

For he is the phenom who came out of nowhere to become the youngest pitcher to start a World Series game since Dwight Gooden. The one who rode in team owner Wayne Huizenga's private jet to Miami after signing a professional contract. The one who pitched one of the greatest games in playoff history against Atlanta when he allowed only three hits and one walk while establishing a single-game National League Championship Series record for strikeouts.

"Livan hates it when I tell this story," Iglesias says. "But I drove him up to his first Marlins spring training camp. After that first day was over, Livan went into the clubhouse to change and he started to stuff his uniform and everything into a small bag to take home and wash. That's the only way he knew. I had to tell him leave it. Somebody else will wash the uniform and it will be waiting for you here tomorrow. He couldn't believe it."

Not that long ago Hernandez rode his bike, in uniform, to games in Cuba. In America he drives a jet-black Porsche Turbo. Three months after he was moved into the postseason rotation because of Alex Fernandez's torn rotator cuff, he was the grand marshal of the Orange Bowl parade. Soon afterward, he was honored at the ESPYs at Radio City Music Hall.

"This is the best baseball in the world," Hernandez says. "If you are a baseball player and you want to play at the highest level, this is where you have to be. You never know what the future holds. I came to this country for the baseball and the freedom."

Still, as any major-leaguer will tell you, professional baseball comes with a price tag called celebrity. Some simply accept it as part of the deal. Others rant and rave, and act more like children because of it. Some worry about how Hernandez so quickly gained a big-league attitude. When Hernandez was with the Florida Marlins, his first major-league team and where he enjoyed his most success, he saw his good friend Alex Fernandez batter his locker stall with a bat after a lousy start late last season. Weeks later, during the '97 World Series, Hernandez threw a temper tantrum of his own. In game one, he stormed into the dugout after being lifted, throwing his hat and glove against the wall and then turning over a cart holding the team's first aid equipment. Ironically, it was Fernandez who talked him down from that one.

Most foreign-born players have four to five years to adjust to life in the United States before reaching the major leagues. Hernandez had less than one season in the minor leagues, at Charlotte and Portland, Maine, before making his major-league debut.

"The way he performed in the World Series showed he can take the pressure on the mound. I have no doubt about that, and I don't think that will ever change," says Adolfo Salgueiro, who accompanied Hernandez to Triple A Charlotte in 1996 and became the manager of the Marlins' Hispanic marketing communications. "The part I'm not sure about is being a celebrity. Can he handle that?"

Maybe not. After going 9–3 in his rookie year and named the 1997 World Series MVP, Hernandez was eventually traded to the San Francisco Giants. As the 2002 season came to a close, his career record was .500. Still, he retained that uncanny ability to rise to the occasion in the postseason.

"I never lose in October," he said before taking the mound in game four of the 2002 National League Division Series. His Giants were on the verge of elimination—underdogs to the Atlanta Braves. Yet Hernandez once more resurrected the ghosts, carrying a no-hitter into the fifth and eventually becoming the winning pitcher in an 8–3 San Francisco victory.

"He was throwing eephus curveballs and eephus sliders," says Gary Sheffield, using the term Pittsburgh Pirates hurler

Rip Sewell first popularized in the 1940s to describe a pitch that takes a high, arching path to the plate. "Then he'd [throw] a fastball, so it made it look a lot faster than it really was."

What impressed Giants manager Dusty Baker was Hernandez's athletic ability. After the Braves put base runners on first and second in the fifth, the Cuban right-hander got pinch-hitter Darren Bragg to chop a grounder to first baseman J. T. Snow. Snow threw to second for the force, and Hernandez hustled over to first to take the relay throw and complete the double play.

"He knew we needed him," Baker said afterward, "and this enhances his reputation as a big-game pitcher."

Unfortunately, such magic didn't hold for Baker or Hernandez in the World Series. The Anaheim Angels became the first ball club to defeat Hernandez in the postseason and then defeated him again in the decisive game seven to capture the world championship.

Back in Miami, Hernandez's cell phone rings again. He paces back and forth as he talks, glancing back at the group at the table.

"He's late for golf," Iglesias says.

If anything can keep Hernandez from celebrity insanity, it might be golf. He broke 90 after only three months of playing. Clubs are usually found in his locker stall.

As Hernandez ends the call, he looks at his table of visitors as if he would like for them to disappear. Earlier in the day, there was discussion about Hernandez joining everybody for dinner. Yet the questions about Cubas and life back in Cuba haven't been to his liking.

"*No se,*" he has repeated when asked about Cubas, or when he realized he was a major-leaguer, or even something as innocent as what it was like to strike out fifteen Atlanta Braves in the biggest game of his life.

"No se," he repeated. "I don't know."

In other words, the English equivalent of "No comment" or "Leave me alone."

He smiles briefly, becoming the outgoing, gregarious guy who first endeared himself to everybody when he reached the majors for good. The kid who would talk to the media, even on the days he was scheduled to pitch. The rising superstar who roared like a lion when he struck out Fred McGriff in the NLCS. The World Series MVP who shouted, "I love you, Miami" after the Marlins won the championship.

But the joy soon fades from his face as he tries, one last time, to explain to us the distance between where he was a few years ago and the life he now leads.

"It was a rapid change," he agrees. "But you have to adjust, little by little. You have to understand what you are going through or you will go crazy.

"You miss your family, the food, everything. Then there is the solitude. The life on the streets is so much more different here. In Cuba you have your friends, and here you don't know anyone."

With that Hernandez says good-bye. Another round of golf awaits him.

THE ONE WHO LOST HIS WAY

A promising player like Hernandez frustrates fans and media alike because they've seen this act before. How quickly it can unravel upon the individual and, more important, the team. *Potential* may be the most damning word in our culture. It allows the observer to become judge. It also can be the most corrosive element in any troubled clubhouse.

Before the 1990 All-Star Game, I asked nine former All-Stars to pick the best player in the sport for USA Weekend magazine. The easy winner was Jose Canseco. Seven of them selected the brash outfielder, who then played for the Oakland A's. The only others to receive votes were Wade Boggs and Don Mattingly.

Originally from Havana, Canseco's family fled to the United States when Jose was a baby. His boyhood story strongly parallels that of Rafael Palmeiro. They both grew up in the Miami area, where they developed into promising ballplayers. Palmeiro played at Mississippi State before signing with the Chicago Cubs. Canseco, like Manny Ramirez, went right from high school to sign with a big-league club, the Oakland A's. After being the American League's top rookie in 1986, Canseco put together one of the best seasons ever two years later. He posted 42 home runs and 124 RBIs to lead the league. More important, he became the first player to hit more than 40 home runs and steal 40 bases in a season.

Brooks Robinson, the Hall of Fame third baseman, calls Canseco in his prime a combination of "Mantle, Mays, and Aaron."

"I don't rule anything out with this guy," Robinson told me in 1990. "Somebody could say he'll hit fifty home runs every season for the next ten years, and I wouldn't argue. His future is unbelievable."

Hall of Famer and television analyst Joe Morgan cited Canseco's "flair" and said that those early appearances at the plate were something to behold. "You can sense that everybody's stopped what they're doing just to watch him hit," Morgan said.

I covered the Oakland A's when Canseco, All-Star MVP Dave Parker, and a young rookie named Mark McGwire were in the same group for batting practice. There was the afternoon when a writer for Sports Illustrated arrived at the Oakland

Coliseum to do a story on the visiting Detroit Tigers. He took one look at the heart of the A's order and phoned his office back in New York. The assignment was changed to one about Oakland's "Bash Brothers."

"I start with power, then I look for who has the multiple ways of beating you," the late Willie Stargell once told me. "The only one who satisfies all that right now is Canseco."

There seemed to be nothing but blue skies for Canseco. He said that once Boggs and Kirby Puckett retired he had a legitimate shot at winning the Triple Crown in the American League. But, of course, the late 1980s and early 1990s proved to be Canseco's watershed years. He was traded to Texas in 1992 and hurt his arm in an ill-advised relief stint on the mound. His work ethic, especially in the outfield, faded and many remember a ball bouncing off his head and carrying over the fence for a home run more than any of the prodigious blasts he produced. Ex-teammate Dave Henderson says that Canseco "became bored with the game." It was too easy too soon for him. Others within the Oakland organization maintain that the Bash Brother was only concerned with how far he could hit a ball. He soon lost interest in working on his defense and base stealing. Even during his heyday, old-timers worried that Canseco's lifestyle— his brash demeanor and run-ins with the law for speeding and packing a gun—would eventually undermine his best efforts at the ballpark.

"Some things can't be avoided," Canseco says. "In the case of the gun, I'd choose the same action: I have my family to protect. The traffic tickets? Everyone gets tickets. If society can't handle it, too bad."

When he retired from the game with 462 career home runs—too few, the experts said, to land him in Cooperstown— Canseco threatened to blow the lid off baseball's steroid problem in a tell-all book. Once more he seemed only too ready to play to a public eager to believe in caricatures, especially when it comes to Latinos. Camilo Pascual, who signed Canseco out of high school to an A's contract, told Roberto Gonzalez Echevarria that Tony Oliva, not Canseco, was the greatest Cuban hitter who ever lived.

"Who am I to argue with Pascual?" Roberto Gonzalez Echevarria writes in *The Pride of Havana*. "But the numbers do not bear him out. While Canseco does not have Oliva's batting titles, and has hit for an average at least thirty points below his left-handed compatriot, he has more homers and RBIs. One could say that a Canseco with Oliva's level head could have accomplished more, but as a physical specimen, the big baby has no peer."

Canseco considers himself an entertainer, a rock star. He once told me that he couldn't understand the fuss about escalating players' salaries. After all, he and his peers didn't make as much as the top actors or singers. In many ways, Canseco is the ultimate baseball enigma. Long ago he decided that he could never live up to the expectations of the writers, fans, even his own teammates, so why bother? Life came with no guarantees. So, if that's the case, why not joke around? It sure beats the alternative.

Soon after the all-time greats ranked him the best in the game, I caught up with Oakland in Minneapolis. The year before, 1990, the A's had won 103 games and taken the American League West title, while the Minnesota Twins had finished last. A season later, the Twins were on an incredible roll—about to go from last to first. Meanwhile, the A's dynasty was beginning to crumble. On this weekend at the Metrodome, the A's had lost a tough series and any hope of winning their fourth consecutive divisional title.

One by one the Oakland players exited the visiting clubhouse in Minneapolis, glaring at the press. None of them was eager to discuss the latest defeat. One of the last players to leave that evening was Canseco. A few months earlier he had become tabloid fodder when he was photographed coming out of Madonna's West Side house in New York late one night. Soon afterward he had almost come to blows with a fan at Yankee Stadium who heckled him about his relationship with the Material Girl. Fed up with the press, Canseco had begun to carry a sign that stated he would talk with only the reporters he knew.

As Canseco stepped into the dark tunnel that ran from the A's clubhouse to the team bus, he slammed the door behind him. The noise echoed throughout the bowels of the Metrodome. Nobody said a word as Canseco stared down the assembly of television cameras and print media. But then, unpredictably, the A's star smiled and tilted his head curiously to one side.

"Just kidding," he said with a laugh and then strode off.

BROTHERS IN ARMS

After his half-brother defected, Orlando "El Duque" Hernandez was questioned by Cuban authorities about his relationship with Juan Ignacio Hernandez Nodar. In Cuba, one must always remember that one is being watched. On a 1997 trip to the island, I had hired a driver whom travel writer Tom Miller recommended.

"Be careful" was the last thing Miller told me before I left the country. While there is nothing more coveted in the country than the U.S. dollar (the problem became so epidemic that the Castro government had to accept it along with the Cuban peso as the official currency), the authorities don't want tourists and the natives mingling. In Cuba this policy is called "tourist apartheid" by the everyday people.

On our third day in Havana, Miller's driver dropped us off right in front of the Hotel Inglaterra. We had gotten to talking and somehow forgot that the most prudent plan was to disembark a few blocks away from the hotel. It was safer that way.

Plainclothesmen were upon us in a heartbeat. Milton Jamail and I tried to reason with them, tell them that it was our fault. The driver was an innocent victim. But the authorities told us to forget it as they surrounded our driver like jackals. In the end, the driver almost lost his car. He needed to find $300 in a few days to bribe the necessary officials. The next day we met far away from the hotel, and when the day was over I tipped him well.

"You know what I hope you use this for, right?" I said.

The driver only nodded and eventually retained his car.

Where baseball is played everywhere, El Duque's grievance was more dire than having to show Americans around town. In his case the authorities wanted to know about his relationship with Nodar, who was a player agent and of Cuban-American ancestry. Nodar had been arrested in Cuba with money sent by Livan Hernandez for his half-brother. To further complicate things, Nodar had once been employed by Cubas, the agent who maintains that the best way to hurt the Castro government is to spirit away every player he can from Team Cuba.

Nodar was sentenced to fifteen years in prison, and the day after that sentence was handed down, Hernandez, whom many regarded as the best Cuban pitcher since Dihigo, was banned from pitching again on the island. For the next seventeen months Hernandez lived in a cinder-block apartment a few blocks from Jose Martí International Airport in Havana. No matter that he had a 129–47 record in international play. In Cuba he might as well have died. He was relegated to playing third base in weekend pickup games. The authorities brought him in for frequent questioning and warned him that he would never be forgiven for meeting with the agent. And that he shouldn't hope for an exit visa either.

In 1997, on the eve of Pope John Paul II's visit to Cuba, Castro legalized Christmas. While the people in the streets didn't know what to make of this, few had the courage to hang holiday lights. For the world media, the pontiff's visit brought back memories of when he visited Poland almost two decades earlier. That visit had been one of the harbingers of the end of Communism in Eastern Europe. Amid such great expectations, Orlando Hernandez and seven others, including his girlfriend, Noris Bosch, and Albert Hernandez, another banned ballplayer of no relation, left Cuba by boat. A few weeks later they arrived at a detention center in the Bahamas. In between lay a tale that veered from the comic to the tragic and back again. So much so that Steve Fainaru and Ray Sanchez, in their book *The Duke of Havana,* labeled the escapees as "The Gang That Couldn't Shoot Straight."

Hernandez and the others were taken from Cuba by boat to Anguilla Cay, a small island in the Bahamas often used as a staging area for those being smuggled into the United States. At that point, they were supposed to transfer to another boat coming down from Miami. But the second boat had mechanical problems and, according to a story in *Sports Illustrated,* Hernandez and the others were stranded on Anguilla Cay for three days. Eventually they were picked up by a passing U.S. Coast Guard cutter and would have been taken back to Cuba, like Andy Morales, if they hadn't made it to Anguilla Cay. Reaching that small island technically put them on Bahamian soil and, more important, bought them time. Even though the Bahamas had a repatriation agreement with Cuba, soon after Hernandez and the others reached the Carmichael Road Detention Center outside of Nassau, Cubas was there, too. Within a week of the pitcher's arrival in the Bahamas, Cubas had negotiated a deal in which Hernandez gained political asylum in Costa Rica. That maneuver kept the right-hander from being included in Major League Baseball's amateur draft. After a public tryout, which more than fifty major-league scouts attended, Hernandez signed a four-year contract with the New York Yankees worth $6.6 million.

Hernandez's age remains a topic of debate. When he signed with the Yankees, he maintained that he was twenty-eight. The Yankees team doctor called him the best-conditioned athlete he had ever seen. But Jamail discovered his birthdate on his Cuban baseball card, which was put out by CubaDeportes, the marketing arm of the Cuban Sports Ministry. On it El Duque was thirty-two at the time of his defection. That number was later collaborated by his passport and divorce papers.

The well-seasoned prospect rose through the Yankees' system and made his major-league debut in June 1998. He replaced an injured David Cone and defeated Tampa Bay, 7–1. While the scouting reports had detailed his fastball (eighty-eight to ninety miles per hour with good movement), none had accounted for his high leg kick, his multiple release points, or his ability to think and adapt on the mound. Unlike his half-brother, who had defected at a tender age, El Duque had been tempered and schooled at the highest levels of the Cuban system. Back in Havana, the old-timers remembered Hernandez's Cuban league debut against Pinar del Rio. With the bases loaded and the score tied, Hernandez was sent in to face Luis Giraldo Casanova, who collected more than 300 home runs and 1,000 RBIs in his seventeen-year career. Casanova sent Hernandez's first pitch far over the left-center field wall.

"That moment made me a pitcher," Hernandez told Fainaru. "It taught me to respect *los grandes* [the great ones]."

While some players shy away from pressure, a sense of the historical, Hernandez often embraces it. By September, he was a cog in the Yankees' impressive rotation. The ball club won a record 114 regular-season games that year and many rank it among the top New York teams of all time. But in the 1998 American League Championship Series, the Yankees lost two of the first three games to Cleveland. With their season on the line, Hernandez took the mound and allowed just three hits in seven shutout innings.

What captivates us about sports is that it can break down into moments. Snippets of memory we can replay over and over in our minds. That game in Cleveland had two such plot points. The first came in the opening inning. With two out, the Indians had two men on. The sellout crowd of 44,981 was abuzz and the crescendo of those beating drums in tom-tom style had risen to above everything else. Cleveland first baseman Jim Thome was at the plate. He was enjoying a great postseason—reminiscent of the Indians' Sandy Alomar the year before when he almost single-handedly ousted the favored Yankees from the playoffs.

Thome worked the count to 3 and 1, and Hernandez had little choice but to come in with a fastball. It was a bit high, served right up for Thome, and the Cleveland slugger turned on the pitch, driving it hard to right field. On television, Bob Costas momentarily broke into his home run call. But in the moments leading up to that pitch, the wind had begun to blow in from the outfield seats. The ball rose majestically and then slowed to a stop. Yankee right fielder Paul O'Neill caught the ball just in front of the fence.

From then on Hernandez was in control until the sixth inning. In that inning, with one out, Omar Vizquel singled to center and Hernandez, trying to back David Justice off the plate, hit him in the right elbow. El Duque retired Manny Ramirez, who had 145 RBIs that season, with back-to-back sidearm fastballs. That brought Thome up again.

From a distance, the two protagonists—Hernandez and

Thome—could have been from another era. They both wore their stirrups high, covering much of the lower leg. Raised in Peoria, Illinois, the son of a Caterpillar Company foreman, Thome resembled a grizzled extra from the movie *The Natural,* while Hernandez could have been sent back in time to another grudge match between Habana and Almendares and never looked out of place.

In this bat, Hernandez initially worked the count in his favor, going 1 and 2. But Thome, unlike some sluggers, has a keen eye, and he let the next two go by. The count was now 3 and 2 and the crowd was abuzz once again. Hernandez came in with another fastball and Thome fouled it back. He was gaining the upper hand and El Duque seemed to sense it. Behind the plate, Yankee catcher Jorge Posada had signaled mostly for fastballs throughout the night, and the Indians were having a tough time catching up to them. But Posada knew that if they threw another to Thome, he would likely drive it out of the park. So, what to throw? Throughout the season Hernandez's best pitch was the curveball and Posada found himself leaning toward that. But as they ran through the signals, he was stunned when Hernandez wanted to go with a change-up. Back at the public audition in Costa Rica, with the fifty scouts in attendance, the consensus was that Hernandez needed another pitch. Something to go along with his impressive curveball and so-so fastball. Throughout the season the Yankees had been working on a change-up with him. The key to that pitch is to throw it with the same arm motion as the fastball, with the hope that it arrives at the plate eight to ten miles per hour slower. Even though Hernandez hadn't shown great control of the change, he wanted to throw it at the most pivotal moment of the Yankees' season.

Posada reluctantly agreed and went into his crouch. Thome peered out at the Yankee pitcher. He pointed his long black bat in Hernandez's direction. It's a timing device he uses before each pitch. Hernandez went into his windup and delivered the change. It was a borderline ugly pitch. Nowhere near as precise as the one Greg Maddux has made a name for himself throwing for year. But it did the job.

Expecting a fastball, Thome was out in front. He swung awkwardly at the slower offering and struck out. Hernandez jogged off the mound, pumping his fist. Even though the 1998 American League Championship Series had more innings to play, it was essentially over.

A few days later, with New York headed to the World Series, Hernandez sought out Jose Cardenal, then the Yankees' third base coach and former George Genovese prospect, in the celebration on the field. The two Cuban exiles embraced.

In a few years, when nagging injuries made Hernandez the topic of trade rumors, Cardenal would caution about how poorly this pitcher who loves the spotlight, especially in the postseason, would perform away from New York. El Duque had always taken pride in playing for two of the best teams ever—the New York Yankees and the (Havana) Industriales.

"If they trade him, it will break his heart," Cardenal told the *New York Times*. "I don't think he'll ever be the same if that happens."

That off-season Hernandez was sent to the Montreal Expos to play for Omar Minaya in a three-team deal.

EIGHTH INNING

THE NEW
IMMIGRANTS

"Choice is lost in the maze of generations."

◆ **CORMAC McCARTHY,** *Cities of the Plain*

pring training remains the period of hope and optimism in any baseball season. Much of this reputation may be undeserved, but the time remains something to relish, to revel in. Part of the romance of making rounds to the team camps in Florida and Arizona is that things become fuzzy around the edges. Stick around for a day or so, talk with enough managers, players, and coaches, and you can start to believe that they do. That if this young pitcher comes along, the rotation will have the depth that nearly every team covets. That if that free-agent acquisition has another good season left, then maybe the left side of the infield won't be as porous. That this team may be a contender.

In the Montreal Expos' camp in Jupiter, Florida, in the spring of 2002, there were no such daydreams, however. Only days after the Arizona Diamondbacks had defeated the New York Yankees in a riveting World Series that went the full seven games, baseball's powers had announced that two teams would be eliminated before the start of the next season. One of them would be the Expos. While the other team slated for contraction, the Minnesota Twins, saw its fans, stadium authority, and legislators fight the proposal in the courts and on Capitol Hill, the Expos seemed to have few in their corner. The first-ever major-league team located outside the United States, hailed at its inception as a new chapter in the history of the national pastime, the globalization of the game, was living on borrowed time. Its former ownership group, led by Jeffrey Loria, had purchased the Florida Marlins. When Loria pulled up stakes, he took his staff with him. That left Major League Baseball in charge of the Expos. The team had become a ward of the state.

"We'll make the best of things," said Omar Minaya, whom MLB had appointed as the team's new general manager. "We'll be better than a lot of people think."

One of the first moves Minaya made in Jupiter was take what remained of the office staff out to dinner. That was considered so unusual by the employees that some had tears in their eyes.

"They're the little people," Minaya told Paul White of *USA Today Baseball Weekly*. "They're the people who stayed behind. Maybe that's the Latin in me."

To make a trade, Minaya couldn't add to his payroll. Financially, any move had to be a wash—perfectly balanced when it came to money. Privately, rival GMs said they wouldn't be surprised if the entire season went by without the Expos' making a single move to improve their ball club.

That Minaya's appointment made him the first Latino ever to guide a major-league club seemed oddly fitting for those who closely follow baseball. After all, no Latinos, even the great Roberto Clemente, were named to MLB's All-Century Team. With Minaya in charge of a team whose days were seemingly numbered allowed baseball to claim progress when it came to minority hiring, even if the first post for a Latino GM afforded little opportunity to get the job done.

As spring training opened and Minaya met with the media under the hot Florida sun, he refused to acknowledge any bias or conspiracy or competitive disadvantage. He said he relinquished his position as assistant general manager for the New York Mets because it was important to demonstrate that a Latino could perform as a GM. No matter that besides putting together his big-league roster he needed to hire twenty-seven minor-league coaches and managers, as well as everybody from equipment manager to janitors, before the season began.

"I was comfortable in New York," says Minaya, who first gained a reputation as a scout for the Texas Rangers in the 1980s, signing Sosa, Rich Aurilia and Juan Gonzalez. "I had a great position with the Mets. But when this opportunity came along, I knew I had to do it. Simply to prove that somebody with my background could.

"If there was a selfish reason in me taking the job, it is to send a message to minorities that if you set a goal, you can reach it. From now on, when you go to winter meetings and see all those people looking for jobs and you see more minorities, I hope you think of me."

Almost in an effort to prove the skeptics wrong, Minaya made three trades with three different ball clubs before the Expos broke camp in 2002. He brought in veterans Andres Galarraga, Jose Canseco, and my old friend Lance Johnson. Galarraga was the only one still with the team by midseason. Still, the moves got the attention of his team.

"From the first day in camp, he and [manager Frank] Robinson have laid it all out for us," says Gold Glove shortstop Orlando Cabrera. "Omar even said if anybody was too uncomfortable with the situation he'd do what he could to move them to another team. Nobody asked to. That's a reflection of him and Robinson. This may not be the best situation for a team, but for a player it's okay—it's much more than okay, because you can trust them.

"We're kind of on a mission here. Who knows where we'll be next season. But, in a way that's not important. The only thing we can worry about is playing ball."

Cabrera first met Minaya almost a decade ago at a tryout in his native Colombia.

"From what I remember he didn't like me at all," says Cabrera, who grew up using an Omar Vizquel–model glove. "He didn't think I could play at this level."

The shortstop laughs and then adds, "But he proved he can change his mind. Not a lot of GMs are that honest with themselves. That makes him the kind of person a lot of guys would love to play for."

Minaya says he didn't mind if the players adopted an "us versus them" mentality.

"That could be good," he told the media in those first days of spring in Florida. "I sincerely believe we have a good team. That we can contend."

Few believed him.

When Omar Minaya was a boy, he watched games from the upper deck of Shea Stadium. He and his father would go four or five times a year, always to see the San Francisco Giants or Pittsburgh Pirates.

"You tended to be more of a National League guy back then if you were Latino or Jewish or black," he says. "That's because they had much more of the earlier stars—Clemente, Cepeda, Marichal, and Mays. The guys I wanted to watch. So my dad and I would go to Shea, but we never really cared for the Mets."

Born in the Dominican Republic, Minaya grew up in Queens, New York. He earned All-American honors as a catcher. His number 21, worn in honor of Roberto Clemente, was retired by Newton High School in Elmhurst, Queens, and after graduation he was selected by the Oakland A's in the fourteenth round of the 1978 free-agent draft. The A's saw that he had good speed and converted him to an outfielder. But even as early as Class A ball, Minaya was honest enough with himself to realize that he didn't have the chops to play in the majors. Already others hit for better power than he did. Others threw the ball with more zip than he did from the outfield. Baseball was his first love, so he decided that he would find another place for himself in the sport. He could always coach. If he was determined, perhaps even a job in the front office. After playing in the minor leagues for the A's and Seattle Mariners, he became a top scout and rose to become director of professional and international scouting with the Texas Rangers before moving on to become the number-two man with the Mets.

Despite his background, Minaya never landed any of the general managerial jobs he interviewed for. Several teams told him that he needed to be better "organizationally." To this day he still doesn't know what that means.

"And, frankly, I don't care," he tells me. "I've got a job to do here with Montreal."

Minaya may have been born in the Dominican Republic, the island of Sosa and Gonzalez, but he was raised in America. On the walls of his new office in Montreal, he hung portraits of two other trailblazers—Jackie Robinson and Felipe Alou. He often wore a blue baseball cap with an M on it. It was the same style that Robinson wore in the minor leagues with the Montreal Royals. Throughout much of the last century baseball traveled throughout the Caribbean and down through Central America to be embraced by Venezuela and Colombia. But in recent years the game has made a U-turn and returned to American shores. A generation ago, the prominent Latino stars were like migrant workers. They played in the United States during the season and then returned home for the rest of the year. The only ones who weren't allowed such flexibility were the Cubans because of Castro's revolution and the embargo that began between the island of columns and the United States. As the number of Latinos at the major- and minor-league levels rose, as the number of Latino superstars increased, a new phenomenon took root. Instead of being migrant workers, sometimes dismissed as such, most began to live in this land. For many it was a natural transition. Their parents had come to this land and, like Minaya, they had been raised in the United States. They were comfortable with its language and culture. Yet they still held on to their link with the old country.

"Past and present," Minaya says. "That's one of the great things about baseball. You always have both."

"FIREWORKS"

On a hot day in early July in Philadelphia, Minaya holds court in the visitors' dugout. Thanks to his wheeling and dealing, and the cell phone that never remains silent for long, Minaya has transformed his ward of the state into the most talked-about team in baseball. Days before, he had shocked the sports world by trading first baseman Lee Stevens and three prospects to Cleveland for All-Star pitcher Bartolo Colón, journeyman Tim Drew, and cash. The money was as significant as obtaining Colón, a hard-throwing right-hander who rates among the top pitchers in the game, because it reveals the lengths Minaya will go to get something done in his first opportunity as a general manager. Because he couldn't add to his team's $37 million payroll, he convinced the Indians to make up the difference— $925,000.

"To get a guy like Colón is a no-brainer," Minaya says. "A trade like this sends a message to baseball that the Montreal Expos aren't just playing this season, we're in it competing to win.

"You start with pitching, you end with pitching. When you get a chance to obtain a Bartolo Colón, one of the best young arms around, you just have to take him. As far as prospects, what we had to give up, I've been around the game for almost twenty years and I've seen a lot of prospects that are in Double A, Triple A, and at the end of the day they just aren't major-leaguers."

With that, Minaya's cell phone rings again and he breaks into a wide smile when he recognizes the incoming number.

"This is getting good," he says.

After telling the caller that he will call him back in a moment, not to do anything until they talked again, Minaya heads for the clubhouse. At the end of the bench sits Montreal manager Frank Robinson. He was the first one Minaya had huddled with when he arrived at the stadium an hour earlier from Harrisburg, Pennsylvania, site of the Expos' Double A team.

"We going to see you after the game?" Robinson asks.

"Don't think so," Minaya says. "I'm going home to New Jersey. Sleep in my own bed for once."

"Too bad," Robinson says, nodding at Veterans Stadium's simmering AstroTurf surface. "They're going to have fireworks after the game. Should be something."

Minaya chuckles and then heads up the hallway and some privacy, eager to return that call.

Within days, the rookie GM would confound the baseball world again. This time he obtained outfielder Cliff Floyd from Florida in a package deal that sent relief pitcher Graeme Lloyd and right-handed starting pitcher Carl Pavano to Florida. As in the Colón deal, the key was Minaya obtaining cash—roughly $1 million this time—to balance his books. For a few weeks in July, the buzz in baseball was about the Montreal Expos—the team that the game had tried to put out of existence. Montreal scouts were in New York scouting Yankee right-hander Orlando "El Duque" Hernandez. Even though the Expos trailed the first-place Atlanta Braves by 10½ games at that juncture, Minaya was intent on putting together a contender. With Vladimir Guerrero and Jose Vidro leading the way, it could have been a Latino All-Star squad. The kind of team that could put real pressure on the Braves or the Los Angeles Dodgers or San Francisco Giants for the National League wild card.

"I don't understand these trades," Braves closer John Smoltz told the *Washington Post.* "Now they're [adding key players] because baseball owns them?"

Colón adds, "I was really happy when I found out I had been traded to Montreal. . . . I'm going to a good organization to play for a Latin GM on a good ball club that has a good chance of winning."

Unfortunately for Minaya, those hot days in July would be the team's high-water mark. The Expos finished the 2002 season above .500, a mark of 83–79, but they somehow lost fifteen of their next twenty-four games with Colón in uniform as they fell from contention for the divisional crown. Floyd was soon dealt away to Boston, and once again Montreal was a team with few prospects and huge questions about its future.

Inside the Montreal clubhouse, the Latino All-Star approach had unforeseen ramifications. Robinson, who prides himself on being an "old school" manager, declared that his players were too passive about losing. After the bullpen gave up eight ninth-inning runs against the Phillies, the *Montreal Gazette* reported that Robinson stood in front of the team and tore off his jersey and threatened to resign. Robinson later denied the report. But the Expos' team chemistry soon went from bad to worse. Pitcher Tony Armas Jr. left the mound before Robinson arrived, a major breach of baseball protocol, and then argued in the dugout with his manager. The double-play combination of Gold Glove shortstop Orlando Cabrera and All-Star second baseman Jose Vidro unraveled as they barely spoke to each other after their wives had had an argument.

"The [Latino] guys hang together, bound by language and a common sense of displacement," *Gazette* beat writer Stephanie Myles wrote. "Most of them can speak English. But there's a gap in understanding with the Americans, cultural more than anything, that makes it a challenge for the team to bond as one and for Robinson to get his message across without seeming unduly harsh."

Despite the fireworks on and off the field, the Expos finished on a high note. Although they failed to reach the playoffs for the twenty-first consecutive year (they finished first in 1994, but that postseason was canceled because of a labor dispute), more than 25,000 fans attended the final game of the season at Olympic Stadium to see Guerrero and Al Oliver, the old and the new, embrace. Behind the scenes, Major League Baseball tried to determine where the team would play the next season. Several groups in the Washington, D.C., area were interested in having the ball club move down there. In addition, there was talk about the Expos playing some of their home games in San Juan, Puerto Rico. Perhaps an All-Star Latino team could draw a crowd there.

To the surprise of many, Robinson strongly suggested that he would like to return as manager—if the team's payroll wasn't cut too drastically.

"I'm satisfied with our solid finish, but I'm not altogether satisfied with our season," he said at an end-of-the-season press conference. "There were several areas that, if this team is kept together, it won't take much to make it a contender. I have to know I'm wanted."

Minaya ended the 2002 season with a team payroll of $37 million. To bring back the same roster next spring, it would need to be raised to $55 million. Still, he turned down Larry Lucchino's inquiries about becoming the Red Sox' new general manager.

"In a way, I'm the captain of this ship," Minaya explains. "It wouldn't be right to leave now."

GRAB A BAT

If Minaya had jumped ship before the 2003 season and become Boston's next GM, he would have headed up in a ball club with two of the most recognizable Latinos in the game: Manny Ramirez and Nomar Garciaparra. Both are All-Star hitters and quiet in the clubhouse. But the perceptions of both, among the fans, media, and those they share the Red Sox clubhouse with, couldn't be more different.

Ramirez can drive his teammates crazy. In his autobiography, Omar Vizquel recalls how he once saw Ramirez hunt through the bat rack and use a half-dozen different pieces of lumber during BP. He doesn't seem to care that much about familiarity, either. Teammates have seen him go four for four in a game using four different bats. That's a far cry from Rod Carew, who cherished his specific models so much that he would lock them away in a closet next to the sauna in the Twins' clubhouse.

"I baby my bats—they're how I make my living," Carew once said. "I think the heat from sauna bakes out the bad or weak wood in a bat."

Don't look for any such tender loving care from Ramirez. When he was in Cleveland, teammate Sandy Alomar got upset with him because Ramirez kept taking and breaking his bats.

"The stuff in your locker was never safe when Manny was around," Vizquel says. "He'd wear other people's shoes. He'd put on other people's T-shirts, socks, and underwear. He used bullpen catcher Dan Williams's pants. His favorite place in the clubhouse was the locker that had a tag reading, NO NAME. It was where the clubhouse guys put stuff when they couldn't fig-ure out whom it belonged to."

When asked about his ways, Ramirez smiles sheepishly.

"It works for me," he says. "You don't argue with what works."

Indeed, it does, as Ramirez became the first player since Joe DiMaggio to average more than an RBI per game in consecutive seasons at the major-league level. When he left Cleveland, where he was protected in the batting order and not expected to be a team leader in the clubhouse because the Indians had Jim Thome and Omar Vizquel, and signed with Boston, many pre-dicted the increased media scrutiny and fans' expectations would get to him. But in the first season of an eight-year, $160 million contract, Ramirez hit .306 and drove in 125 runs, as Garciaparra was injured for much of the season. The next year he led the league with a .349 batting average.

"I'm always trying to make adjustments," Ramirez says. He and Roberto Alomar are known for studying videotapes of their plate appearances for hours. "Every year is different. That's what some guys never understand. You always have to change things or they will start to get you out too much."

When Ramirez was twelve years old, his family moved from the Dominican Republic to the Washington Heights section of New York City. It was a rough neighborhood. Gangs ruled the streets after dark and Ramirez passed drug dealers on his way to school. Baseball kept him out of trouble, but he wasn't a star right away. On his Little League teams, he often batted last. Into junior high Ramirez began to work on his game. He would prac-tice with his school team during the week and play sandlot games on the weekends in Brooklyn. At George Washington High School, he became the star—alternating between third base and center field. The *New York Times* did a series about his high school team and television crews found their way uptown.

During his senior year, Martinez hit .643 and was named the best high school player in the city. He was inducted into the city's Public Schools Athletic Hall of Fame alongside Bobby Thomson, Shawon Dunston, John Franco, and basketball's Nate "Tiny" Archibald. Selected by Cleveland in the first round of the draft, Ramirez began his professional career in the Appalachian Rookie League with Burlington. The next year he had at least one RBI in seven consecutive games at Class A Kinston, but he hit .278 and bruised his left hand.

"When I was kid starting out, I was never a very good hitter," he tells me. "It wasn't like now. I even remember my first full year in the minor leagues I didn't do very good. I wasn't hitting at all. But then in the second half, I went off. I'm still not sure what it was exactly, except that I learned I couldn't count on one thing. Again, it's about making adjustments. Knowing you're going to have to change because the pitches you're getting are going to change."

At Triple A Charlotte, manager Charlie Manuel, who would later become batting coach and then manager for the Cleveland Indians, saw Ramirez's swing and decided to "leave him alone." Ramirez, like Sosa, has the ability to leave a bad day at the ballpark. Not take it home with him.

"He's one of the best hitters alive," says Carlos Baerga. "He's a guy that can go for 0 for 4 three nights in a row and he can come back and drive in fourteen runs in a week."

Still, Ramirez's nonchalance, his reluctance to run out every play, do rub some baseball people the wrong way. After he quit on a tapper back to the mound in a late-season game against Tampa Bay, the Red Sox nation worked itself into a frenzy. Manager Grady Little eventually said that he should have benched Ramirez. As it was, the RBI machine apologized to his teammates. But that fell far short of satisfying everyone.

"The Sox are paying Manny a guaranteed twenty million per

172 ◆ TIM WENDEL

season . . . ," wrote *Boston Globe* columnist Dan Shaughnessy. "This makes him untradeable and unaccountable. They have to be careful not to embarrass him. Fines mean nothing. There's no indication that a bench would bother Ramirez; he's the guy who went to [Triple A] Pawtucket for rehab and never wanted to leave."

For his part, Ramirez takes such criticism in stride.

"I knew this could be a tough place to play," he says. "[But] I make my off-season home here. I may go back to the Dominican Republic for a few weeks, but I live in the States now. I work out here in Boston year-round. It's just the way things came to be."

OLD AND NEW

When the Red Sox take batting practice, Luis Tiant will usually hit ground balls to All-Star shortstop Nomar Garciaparra. Tiant was born and raised in Marianao, Cuba. His father, Luis Sr., played in the old Cuban and U.S. Negro leagues for two decades. In 1959, at the age of eighteen, as his homeland was being rocked by Castro's revolution, Luis Jr. left home to play for Mexico City. His first year of professional ball was a failure, as he won just five games and his ERA was 5.92. Still, Tiant hung on to his dream of reaching the big leagues because of the example set by his father and Orestes Minoso.

"Minoso was my idol," Tiant tells me. "He was the first one to stand up for black Cubans. Guys like myself. You see somebody like that make it and you have some hope. You start to believe that maybe one day you can reach the big leagues, too."

Tiant posted seventeen victories the next year in Mexico and twelve more in 1961, and at the end of that season the Cleveland Indians purchased his contract for $35,000. While he was on his way to gaining a place at baseball's highest level, Tiant, like many Cubans at that time, was forced into becoming an immigrant to this country. He was married in Mexico in August 1961 and planned to return to Marianao afterward. But he received word from his parents that the political situation in Cuba had gotten worse and that if he returned home, he probably wouldn't be allowed to leave. It would be another fourteen years before Tiant would see his parents again.

In the Indians' organization, the right-hander with the unorthodox delivery didn't turn heads as did fireballer Sam McDowell, but Tiant eventually joined "Sudden Sam" in Cleveland in 1964. To make room for the young Cuban, the Indians cut Tommy John. In his first game on the mound for Cleveland, Tiant shut out Whitey Ford and the New York Yankees. In 1968, the so-called year of the pitcher, he went 21 and 9 with a league-best 1.60 ERA. Although he ranked just behind Detroit's Denny McLain, who went 31 and 6, in the estimation of many players Tiant was the better pitcher. Tiant's exaggerated delivery, his multiple release points, prompted Indians manager Alvin Dark to tell the press that it was only a matter of time before Tiant hurt his arm. Of course, Dark was the same manager who drove Orlando Cepeda to distraction in San Francisco.

That off-season the Indians ordered Tiant not to play winter ball, even though he had done so for the previous decade. In 1969, he lost a league-worst twenty games and he wouldn't win twenty again until four years later, after he had been traded to the Minnesota Twins and then signed by Boston.

Dark calls Tiant "the classic Cuban pitcher. . . . He has every pitch in the book and throws them from every angle, and in 1968 won twenty-one games for the Indians. But he pitched 258 innings, the most he'd ever pitched, and the next year he lost twenty games and couldn't blacken your eye with the ball.

"We traded him in 1970. In 1971, he was spinning his wheels in the minors. But he came around. He had a strong, mature body [he was already in his thirties then], and he had so many ways to get you out. In 1973, he won twenty games for the Red Sox, and twenty-two the next year."

Tiant became a crowd favorite in Boston, a harbinger of what was to come with Pedro Martinez. Between 1973 and 1976, he won eighty-one games for the Red Sox, and after nineteen years in the majors, eight with Boston, Tiant retired in 1982. He now works as analyst for the Red Sox' Spanish radio affiliate. Before games Tiant can usually be found in the team clubhouse. He still has a locker stall and a jersey that he puts on to hit infield grounders in BP.

"It's good to keep a hand in," Tiant says. "Keeps you young. But you want to know the real reason? It's to help him," he says, nodding in Garciaparra's direction, whose locker is nearby. "His makeup is more American than Latin. He went to school here, college here. His parents spoke Spanish at home. His Spanish may not be that good, but he gets by. I talk to him in Spanish almost every day. I do that because he reminds me of the old ones—Clemente, Cepeda, Minoso. He acts the same every day. He doesn't change. Whether he does good or bad, he's the same. Some of these other guys? I don't know what's the matter with them. These guys are making all this money now, but you don't see the fun, the sense of being a team, that existed in the old days.

"Nomar could fit in with the old times. He could have played on those Cuban winter ball teams—Almendares, Havana—because he has class. No matter how much they were making back then, it didn't matter. How they played was the most important thing. That's the way it is with this kid. That's what makes him one of the best around."

Garciaparra's father, Ramon, was born in Mexico and was a big baseball fan. After he married, he and his wife, Sylvia, moved to Whittier in Southern California, where they ran a print shop and became Dodger fans because of Fernando Valenzuela. By the age of six, Garciaparra was already turning heads on the neighborhood sandlots. Even though he excelled at basketball and soccer and could kick a sixty-yard field goal on the football field, baseball remained his first love.

"My dad coached me in it," he says. "Baseball's always been number one with me."

Garciaparra went on to play at Georgia Tech. While he weighed only 135 pounds when he arrived on campus, there was no doubt he was a player. He hit .363 his freshman year. In the summer of 1992, Miami coach Ron Fraser was in charge of the Olympic team. A freshman had never played for Team USA before. But after seeing Garciaparra in action, Fraser asked him to attend the walk-on camp. Garciaparra not only made the team, he also played that exhibition series in Cuba, and by the time the Barcelona Games began he had taken over at short-stop.

He did the same thing once he joined the Red Sox after two years at Georgia Tech. Garciaparra was just the sixth unanimous choice as the American League Rookie of the Year, following Carlton Fisk, Sandy Alomar Jr., Tim Salmon, Mark McGwire, and Derek Jeter. His 365 total bases eclipsed Ted Williams's rookie record and made the Hall-of-Famer a permanent fan and confidant. In 2000, Garciaparra hit .372—the highest average by a Red Sox player since Williams's .388 in 1957. After Williams's death, Garciaparra kneeled and bowed his head in tribute at a ceremony at Fenway Park.

Day after day, Tiant and Garciaparra go up the field together.

"We'll talk in Spanish," Tiant says. "It's good to have that. He'll never lose that link with where he's come from. The ones who've come before."

Garciaparra adds, "I don't speak Spanish fluently, but at the same time it doesn't mean that I don't know my culture. I still know everything about it because I grew up in it. How many people can say they're true Americans? Everybody is something and an American. They are this, and then of that descent. It's pride thing. It's what makes this country special. We can share that with everybody else."

NINTH INNING

THE NEW CAPITAL
OF IT ALL

"Spanish, labyrinthine in nature, has at least

four conjugations to address the past; the lone

future tense is hardly used. One can portray a

past even in multiple ways, but when it comes

to one of tomorrow, a speaker in Buenos Aires,

Lima, Mexico City, and Caracas has little

choice. The fact is symptomatic: Hispanics,

unable to recover from history, are obsessed

with memory. English, on the other hand, is

exact."

◆ **ILAN STAVANS,** *Growing Up Latino*

Y ou can tell the team leaders by their lockers. They are the ones with the best view of the televisions. If there's an empty stall to be had, it could well be located next to theirs, so they can stack the boxes of extra spikes, the new gloves or another box of bats that arrived today. Most ballplayers only have stools or padded folding chairs to sit upon. The stars have chairs that border on thrones. When Ken Griffey Jr. played in Seattle, he had a Barcalounger. One of his favorite jokes was to invite visitors to have a seat. Tilt them back and get them nice and comfy and then tell them to get out. Didn't they realize it was time for him to suit up for another game?

In the Red Sox dressing room, the team's major Latino stars—Nomar Garciaparra, Manny Ramirez, and Pedro Martinez—hold places of distinction. Garciaparra is the closest to the door, just across from the coaches and his good friend Luis Tiant. Ramirez's station is back in the corner, near the training room, where he can have animated conversations with fellow Latino Carlos Baerga and longtime coach Johnny Pesky. Almost in the center of the room, at the head of the row of lockers for the pitching staff, is where Pedro Martinez holds court. He sits in an office chair of imitation leather. It may not be as gaudy as Griffey's, but it's close. Not only is Martinez the biggest leader on a team of stars, he also is a spokesman for his country, the Dominican Republic. He and Sammy Sosa have shared that mantle for several seasons now. The latter ranks as one of the best hitters in the game, while Martinez remains one of the best pitchers in the American League and only the fourth pitcher in the junior circuit since 1967 to win the Cy Young award in consecutive seasons (Roger Clemens, Jim Palmer, and Denny McLain are the others). Many contend he should have won his fourth Cy Young in 2002. As it was, Martinez finished second to Barry Zito of the Oakland A's, despite leading the league in ERA, strikeouts, and winning percentage.

"I have been here long enough to understand a lot of things that people don't think I understand," Martinez said the day of the announcement. "After looking around me and seeing that the top ten players are from the Dominican Republic—think about Alex Rodriguez, Vladimir [Guerrero], [Alfonso] Soriano, Manny Ramirez, Sammy Sosa—not everything can go to the Dominican."

Ask Martinez about baseball in his homeland and he leans back in his clubhouse chair and gets a faraway look in his eyes.

"What you have to remember is that so much has changed there," says the pitcher who dedicated his first Cy Young to countryman Juan Marichal. "Maybe the best place to start is to always remember that we weren't the ones who invented this game. We just play it. We play it the way we were taught."

Any life is a miracle. But it may be especially so for those who become baseball players from the Dominican Republic. For any of them the route to the majors is a labyrinth; so arbitrary and Byzantine that one soon learns that the only hope is to play with joy. Revel in the moments and pray that the baseball gods look favorably upon the endeavor. There are few paths to any success in the Dominican Republic. The island seemingly has armed security guards on every corner in large part because that's a job in a society where there are so few jobs. Alan Klein, professor of sociology-anthropology at Northeastern University and the author of *Sugarball: The American Game, the*

Dominican Dream, estimates that 30 percent of the people in Martinez's country "are unemployed or underemployed."

Martinez nods in agreement with that figure.

"The sport is big in the Dominican Republic because there are no more paths with the same opportunities," he says. "Maybe that makes us hungrier to play. To do well. All I know is that we need this game more than most people do."

If it hadn't been for Castro's revolution in Cuba, many doubt if the Dominican Republic would have become the top supplier of baseball talent outside U.S. borders. Politics and an embargo kept major-league fans from ever enjoying the likes of such Cuban greats as Omar Linares and Victor Mesa. Yet the Dominican Republic soon filled that talent vacuum. Since the early 1960s, when Castro declared that baseball should be only an amateur game, one town in the Dominican Republic—San Pedro de Macoris—has sent such stars as Tony Fernandez, George Bell, Pedro Guerrero, Manny Lee, Joaquin Andujar, and Sammy Sosa to the major leagues.

"San Pedro de Macoris, the whole of the Dominican Republic—that's the capital of baseball now," says Expos third baseman Fernando Tatis. He, too, grew up beginning play as a shortstop and dreaming of one day reaching the major leagues. "Baseball is the only thing we really love," he says. "It's like power for us. It's a passion. We grew up watching those guys play—Pedro Guerrero, Alfredo Griffin, George Bell, Tony Fernandez. When we watch those people, how could we not love baseball? When I was a little kid, I knew I had to be like those guys. You follow your heroes. Anybody does."

Yet to follow one's heroes, to travel the path to *El Norte* and the major leagues, is filled with pitfalls and obstacles. And when you begin to understand how far such players have come, how fortunate and skilled they must have been to arrive at any clubhouse, whether they sit in the big chair or not, the word *miracle* just doesn't do the whole process justice.

THE GAME FROM THE WEST

The Dominican Republic shares the island that Columbus called Hispaniola with Haiti. The Dominican Republic isn't a large nation, barely half the size of Indiana or Illinois. Yet it currently has produced 10 percent of today's major-leaguers.

Baseball was introduced to the Dominican side of the island late in 1891. Once again the Cubans were the game's apostles. The Aloma brothers had moved to the island from neighboring Cuba and taught their new countrymen the game. Ironically, the game never caught on in Haiti, which to this day remains much more enthusiastic about soccer. The Aloma brothers were industrious and soon formed two local teams. The Cerveceria squad was named after a local brewery, and the Cauto club after a river back home in Cuba, according to Klein. The two teams played in Santo Domingo, the country's capital.

Soon this new sport became interwoven with the island's major industry—sugarcane. The cash crop was introduced from the Canary Islands in 1505, and its production requires vast plantations and refineries located in the midst of the countryside. To pass the time, amateur baseball teams formed as part of the community activities surrounding the harvest and production of the cane. Hence, the name "sugarball."

Even though two professional teams, Licey and Escogido, soon formed, early on Dominican baseball was considered inferior to the game played in Cuba, Puerto Rico and Panama. By the 1920s, though, Dominican players had become skilled enough to earn roster spots in those lands. By the next decade, players from the Cuban and Negro leagues were playing in the Dominican Republic, too. But it took the country's dictator, Rafael Trujillo, to focus more attention on baseball. To bolster his power base, Trujillo decided to merge the capital teams into the Ciudad Trujillo Dragons, who battled Estrellas Orientales and Santiago for the championship. Satchel Paige, Josh Gibson, and James "Cool Papa" Bell were just a few of the Negro League stars who headed south to play for the big money offered by Trujillo. In fact, the Negro Leagues suspended play for a time that season because so many players had gone to the Dominican Republic. Cubans and Americans dominated rosters and, in the end, Trujillo's Dragons won. But the endeavor left fans and politicians exhausted. That memorable season of 1937 derailed professional baseball in the Dominican Republic nearly two decades, according to Klein. Instead the game's focus fell back to the amateurs playing in various parts of the island. Rivalries referred to as "wildball" developed between such refinery towns as La Paja, Quisqueya, and San Pedro de Macoris. For there the game was played with a particular passion and hustle. Eventually, this style of play would be known as *beisbol romantico*.

RIPPLING OUT

Always hustling, taking the extra base, on offense and defense striving to make things happen. To some, that's *beisbol romantico*. In *Sugarball*, Klein tells how Roger Maris and other U.S. ballplayers who played winter ball in the Caribbean rarely won over the local fans if they didn't hustle. Today the local rivalries remain as intense as they ever were. During a recent Licey-

Escogido game, fans waved flags and blew whistles in support of their team. Thousands of blue-clad Licey fans went as far as to chant "Move bitch, get out of the way" from Ludacris's rap song when their ball club scored. Any ballplayer who views Dominican winterball as simply a way to get in shape for the next major-league season is likely to be overwhelmed and certainly less appreciated by the local fans.

"You have to have pride when you put the uniform on," Baerga says. "That's something we're taught from such a young age—to play hard. It doesn't matter if you're Puerto Rican or Dominican or whatever. You cannot play this game just for the money. If you're doing that, you might as well retire."

Still, in the Dominican Republic, *beisbol romantico* can extend even further. Talk with Sammy Sosa or Fernando Tatis or Pedro Martinez about being a star from this country and they will soon regale a listener with what it's like to return to the Dominican Republic in the off-season. Few conquering heroes ever had it so good. In the years leading up to his home run chase with Mark McGwire, Sosa would return to the old neighborhood field in San Pedro de Macoris. There, in front of his friends and kids who dream about growing up to be a big-leaguer like him, he would work out. It's almost as if he needed their respect and acceptance before he ventured north to play another season in the major leagues.

"Here in the United States, ballplayers aren't part of a neighborhood anymore," Tatis explains. "But back in the Dominican Republic you can walk a few blocks and you'll see somebody who's playing or used to play in the majors. You walk some more and there's somebody else. It's not that unusual to see ballplayers, to be able to talk to them. They're still a part of where they came from."

This connection can lead to far different perceptions, depending upon where a fan is from. In this country, pitcher

Joaquin Andujar, who once referred to himself as "one tough Dominican," is best remembered for his temper tantrums, the most notable being his meltdown in the 1985 World Series, when he and manager Whitey Herzog were ejected for complaining about the umpiring. But back in the Dominican Republic, Andujar is known for his charitable acts—the money and equipment that he's donated to various neighborhood teams.

"They give back," says Philadelphia Phillies manager Larry Bowa. "No wonder they're heroes down there. The players coming up can play [baseball] twelve months out of the year in places like the Dominican Republic. They have the weather, the fields; now they have the equipment from Sammy Sosa and others donating stuff over there. This is just going to keep growing."

When shipments of new baseballs arrive at the academies that dot the island, coaches and players often gather in the afternoon shade to separate out the old ones. The balls that have become too lumpy, their seams too worn, to be used for professional batting practice anymore are placed in cardboard boxes and given away to Dominican youth teams.

"It's the only way we know," explains Hector de la Cruz, who once played in the Blue Jays' system and is now a minor-league coach. "We all know how much a baseball can mean to a kid because we were once that kid."

While the Dominican Republic and other Latin countries have plenty of kids eager to play in the major leagues, there are not as many opportunities for them. The United States Department of Labor restricts the number of foreign-born baseball players allowed to enter the country. At the minor-league level, each major-league team is allotted an average of thirty-five temporary work visas per season, according to Milton Jamail. Those who reach the majors are allowed to work in this country under a federal provision reserved for those with "extraordinary ability in sciences, arts, education, business, and athletics." Prospects from the Dominican Republic compete against those from around the world for these few slots at playing the great American game.

"This quota imposed by the U.S. government is the greatest single factor limiting the participation of foreign-born players— the majority of whom are from the Dominican Republic—in organized baseball in the United States," Jamail writes in *Baseball as America.*

"I believe it's harder for Latinos to get a job in the major leagues," Baerga says. "When you get a job up here, you don't want it for just one year. So it's all about playing hard. You want to keep it."

GETTING THE CHANCE

For almost every Dominican, there's a moment when, if fate had gone the other way, he probably wouldn't have reached the major leagues. For Sosa, it was agreeing to take another bus ride to another tryout when he was tired and the weekend was at hand. If he hadn't been there to show Texas Rangers scouts Amado Dinzey and Omar Minaya his stuff, one of the greatest home run hitters of all-time could still be in San Pedro de Macoris.

For Miguel Tejada this moment came when he signed with the Oakland Athletics at the age of seventeen. Tejada had been born in Bani, an impoverished town in the Dominican Republic. A hurricane destroyed what passed for the family home when he was three, and for next five years the family lived in homeless shelters. After signing with the A's, Tejada was sent to the ball club's baseball academy in the Dominican jungle. At such places, prospects are grilled in baseball fundamentals, and classes in English are held. Just as important at the academies, players enjoy three square meals a day, often for the first time in their lives. Cuba and the Dominican Republic are often compared to each other when it comes to baseball in the Caribbean. One was where the game began; the other has risen to prominence. But when it comes down to life's basics, there's little comparison.

"Cubans, even the poor Cubans, are better fed than most Dominicans," Minaya says.

In the Dominican Republic, a dozen or so families dominate the island's economy. Below this ruling aristocracy lies a small middle class, leaving much of the nation in poverty. With gasoline prices and electrical rates soaring (it costs $400 a month to air-condition an American-sized apartment), baseball is a rare opportunity at a better life.

"We're sick for baseball," explains a taxi driver in Santo Domingo. His vehicle's top speed may be thirty miles per hour and the doors are held to the rusting frame by bent rebar rods. "It is our only game."

For many it's their only chance.

The Dominican Republic has been placing players in the majors since 1956 with Ozzie Virgil Sr., who played all the positions in the majors except for pitcher and center field. He was followed by Rico Carty, Sosa, and Martinez—all products of the country's amateur system. In recent years that old path to the majors has been overwhelmed by the academy system. The Los Angeles Dodgers and Toronto Blue Jays were among the first to embrace this system and the rest of baseball soon followed. Down a deeply rutted dirt road off the major highway connecting the Dominican capital with San Pedro de Macoris stands one of the many baseball academies. Four fields, with an observation tower in the middle, have been carved out of the bush and acres of sugarcane. By 8:30 in the morning, prospects for the Arizona Diamondbacks are already working out. Coaches will drill them on the game's basics and throw batting practice for several hours before half of the group—twenty to twenty-five players—will travel by bus to play another academy team nearby.

On this morning, Junior Noboa chats with several visitors, including former Cleveland Indians player Enrique Wilson, in the shade of the first base dugout. Born in the Dominican Republic, Noboa went on to play eight years in the major leagues for six different teams. After his playing career was over, he returned home to the Dominican Republic and followed the lead of other ex-major-leaguers by opening a baseball academy. Today he runs the Diamondbacks' operation with his father, Milciades Sr.

"Ten years ago, I was telling anybody who would listen that the Dominican Republic and Latino players would soon become the majority in the major leagues," says Noboa, who is dressed in a polo shirt and Eddie Bauer jeans. "What I said is coming true. Just look out there. That's the future of the game."

On the emerald field, the academy's pecking order is as finely delineated as rank at an army base. Those out of uniform, wearing T-shirts or a jersey from home, are here for a day or so. If they attract the attention of Noboa or one of his coaches they will be given a thirty-day tryout. At the Diamondbacks' academy, they will be issued a purple jersey. If they continue to excel, they will be signed to a contract and then awarded a black-mesh jersey. But with the crowded visa situation and only so many jobs in the minor and then the major leagues, few will ever make a big-league roster.

"This is the base of the baseball pyramid," Jamail says.

If one or two prospects pan out a year, the entire process pays for itself. Those in baseball justify this "boatload mentality" because they're giving kids who would otherwise be stuck in poverty a chance. But as Marcos Breton points out, "All but a few of those brought to the U.S. are released without ever playing major-league ball. Most of these discarded Latino players stay in the U.S. as undocumented immigrants rather than return as 'failures' to a country that offers them little future. The lives these young men lead are often dangerous, destitute, and sad. Many go to New York because they have friends and family in what is the largest concentration of Dominicans in the United States."

Klein says that "underwriting the whole thing is devastating poverty in the Dominican Republic. I've never been in a country where there's no correlation between education and employment. That means if you have two semesters to go as a doctor, there's a fifty-fifty chance that you'll bail out. It doesn't mean that much to get that degree. As long as you have that happening at that level, you can imagine what's going on at the level of the poor and underemployed. Nobody goes to school. They start practicing baseball as soon as they can. It's seen as the only way out.

"I listen to [Major League Baseball] say how they're giving guys opportunities and all that. They're giving individuals opportunities. But really it's a Third World country. They're making hay out of the fact that it's a Third World country. I don't expect them to solve the problems of the Dominican Republic, but I expect them to be aware of them."

Tejada, of course, was one of the fortunate few. Despite his being able to speak little English, he was good enough to be sent north out of the academy, and he quickly advanced through the A's minor-league system—from Medford, Oregon, to Modesto, California, to Huntsville, Alabama. Tejada reached the A's for good less than five years after he signed. A meteoric rise that even he has difficulty comprehending.

"Everyone wants to know: 'How am I doing?'" he told *USA Today Baseball Weekly* as the 2002 regular-season raced to its conclusion. "'How do we keep winning? Are you going to make the playoffs? Who's going to win the MVP?' Everything.

"Sometimes, it can be so much, but never too much. People don't like it, but I like it. I like people recognizing me and calling me. You see, for me, this is a dream come true. Nobody back home can believe this. They remember how I used to be, how I had nothing. So they can't believe this is happening."

Tejada would pace Oakland to twenty consecutive victories, often on the strength of his late-inning heroics. It would be the longest winning streak in American League history and the fourth-longest in major-league history. Days before the MVP award was to be awarded, Tejada decided that he wouldn't fly to Oakland for the announcement. Instead, he would remain in the Dominican Republic. "This is where my people are," he explained to baseball officials. On the day of the award, Tejada easily outdistanced another shortstop of Dominican descent, the Rangers' Alex Rodriguez. The streets of Santo Domingo were filled with well-wishers as the A's shortstop made his way into the capital from his hometown of Bani, forty miles away. Tejada became the third Dominican to win an MVP award, joining Bell in 1987 and Sosa in 1998.

"And I don't think anybody thought we could have a good year after we lost Jason Giambi," Tejada says. "But I don't think it's a miracle.

"If you want to know what that is, ask the people back home [in the Dominican Republic]. Ask them if they thought this could happen to anyone. They'll tell you they never thought I could make it. They said I was too poor. Too small. They said I should be working and was wasting my time in baseball. Now look at me. Maybe that's the miracle."

LAND OF THE RISING SUN

If the path from the Dominican barrios to the major leagues weren't treacherous enough, one must remember that this is a world with few rules. "To live in a world without grays, where all decisions were final: Balls and strikes, safe and out, the game won or lost beyond question or appeal," novelist Eric Rolfe Greenberg once wrote. That is certainly one of baseball's attractions on the field. But there is no such consistency when one is trying to move from poverty to prosperity, especially in the Dominican Republic. Alfonso Soriano knows.

He, too, grew up wanting to be a shortstop from San Pedro de Macoris. Outside of his hometown, a large billboard proudly proclaims, Welcome to San Pedro de Macoris, The City Which Has Given the Most Major Leaguers to the World. While several of Soriano's friends were scouted as early as sixth grade, he was nicknamed "Mule" because he was so slow. In addition, he was deemed too skinny and awkward at the plate to be of use to any team. By his mid-teens, Soriano had begun to fill out, but he was still a far cry from the player he would eventually become. Desperate to sign with anyone, Soriano visited a baseball academy operated by the Hiroshima Carp of Japan's Eastern League. Dominican talent has become so coveted that major-league teams aren't the only organizations flocking to its shores. The Carp offered him a contract, and Soriano accepted. His pay was less than $500 a month. In Japan, batting practice began at nine in the morning and routinely went on until dark. His homeland was a fifteen-hour plane flight away, but what bothered Soriano more than the distance was the lack of emotion in the Japanese game. He remembers that nobody really smiled. He learned Japanese through television and radio and those times when his teammates would try and talk with him. After his second season in Hiroshima, Soriano got into a salary dispute that almost ended his hopes of one day playing in the major leagues. The Carp told him they would raise his salary to $40,000 a year—a pittance of what he might make in the United States. The case went to an arbitration panel and Soriano had to plea his case with his attorney out of the room. To no one's surprise, the Japanese arbitrators ruled against him.

In search of a loophole out of Japan, Soriano decided to try the route that eventually led pitcher Hideo Nomo to the major leagues. He would retire. Only then would Japanese baseball have no say in his professional future. In response, the Carp management sent letters to the thirty major-league clubs in America, warning them if any entered into negotiations with Soriano they would be sued. In addition, Carp representatives visited Soriano and his mother back in the Dominican Republic, trying to strong-arm him into returning to Japan.

"I was very scared," Soriano told the New York *Daily News*, "because they told me if I left, I wouldn't be able to play in the U.S. or Japan."

Even though the suit in Japan was eventually settled, many teams had moved on. Even when MLB ruled him a free agent after a two-month investigation, there wasn't much interest in him. Soriano moved to Los Angeles and played in a recreation league on the weekends, while his agent scrambled to arrange workouts with various clubs. The delay cost Soriano much of the 1998 season. But once teams took a look at him, what was a bear market became a full-fledged auction. At the Cubs' training facility in Arizona, his batting display caused everyone to stop and take notice. In the end, Soriano signed with the New York Yankees—a $3.1 million, four-year deal. Still, it took the Yankees a while to realize what they had. Several teams, including the Blue Jays and Angels, asked for him in subsequent trades.

"You hear that talk," Soriano says. "But I couldn't control that. I wanted to stay with the Yankees. It's where I wanted to be and it's all worked out."

Indeed, it has. After spending 1996–97 in Japan, Soriano played what was left of the '98 season in the Arizona Fall League. The next year he made up for lost time, jumping from Double A–Norwich to Triple A–Columbus and reaching the parent club as a September call-up. His first major-league hit was a game-ending solo homer off Tampa Bay's Norm Charlton. In 2000, splitting time between Triple A and the majors, Soriano was rated one of the best prospects in baseball. That was quite an accomplishment, as he was only finishing his second season of baseball in America.

The following year, Soriano took over for the error-prone Chuck Knoblauch at second base and set a Yankee rookie record for stolen bases (forty-three) and hit eighteen home runs. Only one other rookie—Tommie Agee in 1966—has ever put up better numbers in those two categories in his first season. In the postseason, Soriano became the first rookie to hit a game-ending home run. Japan and the threat of being forced to play there again was far enough behind him that Soriano could be more reflective about the time he spent there.

"In some ways my time there reminded me of the Dominican Republic because they played hard. It was disciplined," he tells me. "There were certain things you needed to do and you did them. You did them as a team. I see that now."

In short order, Soriano had earned a place in the majors. Still, nobody expected that he would soon be putting up numbers that would impress the game's greats and call some surprising comparisons to mind. One of those comparisons is with all-time home run leader Hank Aaron.

Aaron's office at Atlanta's Turner Field looks out over left field, the area in so many ballparks where his home runs landed.

In the age before weight lifting and steroids, Aaron became the all-time home run king because of his quick wrists and strong forearms. During the Mark McGwire–Sammy Sosa home run chase in 1998, Aaron was as amazed as anyone by their exploits. But one thing he couldn't understand was why these sluggers and so many who followed them tried to hit every home run to the moon.

"A home run's a home run," he says. "They all count the same. So why not let your wrists, your swing, do the work? How far a guy can hit the ball never impressed me. What I like is consistency at the plate."

Aaron, like Cepeda and others from that generation, developed strong forearms by squeezing a grip device several hundred times a day. Soriano limits his weight lifting to dumbbells and still is able to swing a 34½-ounce bat, one of the heaviest in the game. But it's in Soriano's swing that so many see flashes of the past.

"I can't believe how much [he and Aaron] resemble each other," Yankees television analyst Jim Kaat, who pitched in the same era as the all-time home run king, told the *New York Times*. "It's the speed in their wrists, how they swing, even how they stand at the plate. When I look at Alfonso, it's like I'm looking at a young Hank."

Soriano reminded Luis Sojo of another new Latino star—Alex Rodriguez. Coming into the majors, they "both wanted to learn about the game, ask questions, learn about the team," Sojo says. "They both had basically the same body when they came in. And Sori's going to get bigger and bigger. He's going to put up unbelievable numbers."

Soriano certainly put up some incredible statistics in his second full season in the major leagues as he fell one home run short of equaling Jose Canseco's feat of forty home runs and forty stolen bases. Only Rodriguez and Barry Bonds have duplicated Canseco's epic season. Though disappointed to finish the season with thirty-nine home runs, Soriano could take solace in the fact that he had a better season statistically than such legendary second basemen as Jackie Robinson, Ryne Sandberg, or Joe Morgan.

"With what he showed this year," teammate Mariano Rivera says, "who knows what he can eventually do."

"I used to tell people once that he's going to be a forty-forty guy," adds teammate Jason Giambi. "Now, I'm thinking, fifty-fifty."

"SHY IN ANY LANGUAGE"

Alfonso Soriano wasn't the only Dominican chasing forty-forty during the 2002 season. To the north, often playing in front of only a few thousand fans a night, Vladimir Guerrero of the Montreal Expos was putting together a season for the ages, too. Heading into the final weekend of the season, he had surpassed forty stolen bases. He only needed one more home run to join the forty-forty club.

Even though a respectable crowd of 25,178 attended the final game at Olympic Stadium and at Andres Galarraga's suggestion the team put Guerrero's 3½-year-old son, Vladimir Jr., on the bench, this budding superstar also came up empty. On his fifth and final trip to the plate for the season, first base umpire Alfonso Marquez ruled that Guerrero had failed to check his swing on a ball in the dirt. As the boos and plastic beer cups cascaded down, manager Frank Robinson went out to argue the call. In the opposition dugout, Cincinnati Reds manager Bob Boone resisted the urge to go out and argue on Guerrero's behalf.

"Even if he did swing, there's no call in that situation," Galarraga told the *Montreal Gazette*. "The worst part was that [the umpire] was Latin, too."

So, Guerrero joined Soriano and Barry Bonds's father, Bobby, as members of the thirty-nine home runs–forty steals club. Certainly not as prestigious as forty-forty, but the future was certainly bright for the two newcomers.

"When Vladimir learns to stay away from those pitches in the dirt, like Sammy Sosa did, who knows what he'll do," says Omar Minaya. "It could be fifty, sixty, seventy home runs in a season."

The Expos battled back to finish the 2002 season with a winning record and while the team's future was very much in doubt, Guerrero's wasn't. He had already joined Ted Williams, Joe DiMaggio, and Jimmie Foxx as the only players in baseball history with thirty home runs, 100 RBIs and a .300 batting average in three consecutive years before the age of twenty-five.

"You guys should get a satellite dish," Robinson told reporters throughout the second half of the season, "because he's something."

From Nizao Bani, a small town west of Santo Domingo, Guerrero had to quit school by his teens and go to work. The Dodgers invited him to their Dominican academy because his older brother, Wilton, was turning some heads. But after eight weeks at that academy, the Dodgers decided Vladimir was too slow a player with too big a swing. The Texas Rangers were the next to give him a look, but they also passed. Almost as a last resort, Guerrero caught a ride on the back of a motorcycle to an Expos' tryout. He pulled his groin running to first base in his initial bat, but between that one time at the plate and shagging flies in the outfield, Montreal scout Fred Ferreira had seen enough to offer Guerrero a contract. In fact, another Dominican ballplayer, Jhonathan Leyba, remembers that the Expos were so impressed with Guerrero's arm that they had him pitch at their academy before returning him to right field.

Within three years, the Dominican whom nobody wanted had reached the majors. Early in his career the Expos asked Guerrero to list his hobbies. According to *Sports Illustrated,* he gave a one-word answer: *"Pelotero"*—Spanish for ballplayer.

"Baseball has attained such importance to players like me, those from the Dominican Republic, because it's the world," Guerrero tells me. "It's there for you growing up, but it's also what you can become, where you can go. It's the world that you can reach, if you are fortunate and good and work hard. You must understand that it's always baseball. That's where it begins and ends."

When Manny Acta joined the Expos as their third base coach, Guerrero was the one he really wanted to get to know. He'd seen the highlights. The player who could throw out the potential winning run at the plate and golf a ball in the dirt over the outfield fence. Acta, like Guerrero, Soriano and Tejada, was born and raised in the Dominican Republic. These new players, how they can swing the bat, mean everything to him because they have elevated the island's reputation. It wasn't that long ago that the Dominican Republic was known for producing stellar pitchers and singles hitters. Sluggers were few and far between.

Acta was eager to talk with the Expos' superstar. Recommend that he do endorsements, be more outgoing, let the world know about Dominican greatness. What he discovered was a guy who was "shy in any language." A *pelotero* happy to play in a baseball backwater like Montreal, a city in which he could walk down the street and often go unrecognized.

"Vlad knows outside of baseball that he could be making millions in endorsements," Acta says. "He just turns them down. Money is not his biggest thing. He wants to be a private guy, and I now have a lot of respect for that. I was one of the guys telling him how much bigger he could be in the game. But he told me he wanted to be recognized for his achievements, what he did on the field, not for how many endorsements he had. That impressed me. It taught me something, too."

After batting practice, Guerrero will rarely sign autographs. He's too shy. But day after day he'll sit in front of his locker and doggedly go through his fan mail. Two times as the 2002 season came to a close, Robinson tried to give him a chance to bask in the adulation. The manager substituted for him late in games, but the young superstar ran off the field before many fans could scramble to their feet and give him a standing ovation. Finally, it was left to another ballplayer to keep Guerrero in one spot so he could acknowledge the cheers.

On that last homestand of the season (which some thought could be the Expos' final one in Montreal), Guerrero didn't reach forty-forty, but he did set a team single-season record with his 205th hit. Al Oliver, who set the record in 1982, was in town for old-timer activities. With Guerrero standing on first base and the scoreboard telling everyone the news, Oliver came down out of the stands, shook hands with Guerrero and then gave him a big hug.

Later, when the game was over, many of the Expos players threw baseballs and their caps into the stands, and some took a moment to say a few words into a microphone that had been set up on the field. Befitting his temperament, Guerrero had only one word for everything that had happened that season, perhaps for everything that had led him from the Dominican Republic to this new land of the major leagues.

"*Merci*," he told the Montreal faithful.

THE $252 MILLION MAN

For many U.S. sports fans, Alex Rodriguez aka "A-Rod" would seem to be as American a sports hero as Michael Jordan or Michael Vick.

"But, deep down, I'm a Dominican," Rodriguez stresses. "I grew up in Miami, but my roots are Dominican. That's what my parents were from. That's where my loyalty is."

Questions about loyalty, when it's the best time to stay or go, dog Alex Rodriguez, arguably the best player in the game. He says it shouldn't surprise anyone that team clubhouses, from the major leagues on to rookie ball, are in flux because of the increasing number of Latinos playing the game. In winterball, Rodriguez remembers how the Americans would hang out together; the Latinos would do the same.

"It's human nature," he says. "The language situation doesn't mean that anybody is inferior or superior to anybody else. It doesn't mean that somebody doesn't like anybody else. They're facilitated by hanging out with each other. When I went to winter ball, we had nine to ten Americans, and they hung out with the other Americans. I don't think the Americans were prejudiced toward the Latins, they just felt more comfortable with each other. I'm one of the few guys who can be comfortable with both sides."

That's a major reason why many in baseball believe that the All-Star shortstop could be the key component in the game's renaissance. Let the attorneys for the owners and players talk about becoming partners for the good of the game. Let the commissioner predict that one day America's pastime will be the biggest global game, followed eagerly from Tokyo to San Juan. It will be at the game's core, in the clubhouse, where such a sea change must first happen.

As the 2002 season came to a close, many baseball fans were divided about Rodriguez. For some he was the poster boy for a new era, photogenic, articulate in English and Spanish, putting up numbers at shortstop that not even Cal Ripken or Ernie Banks could ever imagine. But for others he was the current example of everything that had gone wrong with the game. In signing a $252 million, ten-year deal with the Texas Rangers he had made a pact with the devil. Just another example of a greedy ballplayer who put dollar signs above the chance to play for world championships and stay in a city that cherished him.

Late in the 2002 season, with the Rangers nearly twenty-five games out of first place in the American League West, Rodriguez continued to push himself hard, as if he were trying to prove to anyone who would watch and listen that he wasn't in it just for the money. He finished the season with a .300 batting average, fifty-seven home runs, and 143 RBIs. More than one general manager called him the best player in the game, destined to become one of the best of all time. He became just the fifth player in baseball history to post back-to-back fifty–home run seasons and the first who was neither an outfielder nor a first baseman to do so. On his birthday that season, he had won the game with a grand slam in the tenth inning. He had already homered earlier in that same game. Afterward, in a rare display of emotion for him, Rodriguez told USA Today Baseball Weekly, "I want people to look at my career and look at this year and that year and that year and not be able to tell when my free-agent year was. The last thing I ever want to do is have a good first year, a bad next year, then an okay last year, then a great year."

Being consistent was the last thing Rodriguez could take pride in as his team again fell out of contention.

"I love the game," he says. "That's what people don't understand. That's what keeps me going. I wish we were winning, but we will. Each day, every day I take pride in playing this game. Seeing how well I can do."

Rodriguez was born in New York City on July 27, 1975. His parents owned a shoe store in Manhattan and the family lived in the rooms behind it. His father had played amateur baseball in the Dominican Republic and soon taught his youngest the game. Both of his parents were from the Dominican Republic, and when Rodriguez was four years old, the family returned to the island and moved into a house a block from the beach in Santo Domingo. It was supposed to be their dream home and the move was to be permanent. Yet when the economy slowed, the Rodriguez family had to sell their home near the beach and return to the United States, this time to a small rental in Miami. Rodriguez was eight when the family returned, and he struggled in school because he had spoken mostly Spanish back in the Dominican Republic. It was baseball that kept him going. Day after day he would sit under a tree near his school, Everglades Elementary, and watch the local youth team practice. One day the regular catcher didn't show, so the coach, Juan Diego Arteaga, asked if Rodriguez could play the position. Rodriguez told him sure, even though he had never played catcher before. Arteaga saw that Rodriguez had plenty of potential and asked him to join the team. J. D. Arteaga would become Rodriguez's best friend and Juan Arteaga a second father. Soon after Rodriguez joined the local team, his father left to work in New York. He never returned.

"I thirsted for Dad for so long," Rodriguez writes in his autobiography. "I have not seen him since. I can count on one hand the times I've talked to my father by phone since he left, I still don't understand how a parent could abandon a family."

Through the Arteaga family, Rodriguez became a regular at the Boys and Girls Clubs of Miami. There he came under the tutelage of Eddy Rodriguez. He was no relation but had coached such players as Jose Canseco, Danny Tartabull, Alex Fernandez, and Rafael Palmeiro. At Westminster Christian High School in Miami, Rodriguez excelled at football and basketball, too. He earned All-State football honors as a quarterback and set several school passing records. His peers in that sport were high school rivals Brian Griese (University of Michigan and the Denver Broncos) and Danny Kanell (Florida State, Atlanta Falcons, and New York Giants), and Rodriguez maintains that he would have at least become a backup in the NFL if he'd stuck with that sport.

In June 1993, the Seattle Mariners made Rodriguez the first pick overall in the free-agent draft. Even though Rodriguez wasn't happy about going that far away from home, he made the parent club for good the following year, joining Tony La Russa and Robin Yount as the only eighteen-year-olds to play shortstop in the majors. Rodriguez and Seattle were never a natural fit. In the beginning he took a backseat to such established stars as Randy Johnson, Edgar Martinez, and Ken Griffey Jr. When the Mariners moved from the Kingdome to Safeco Field, where it was more difficult to hit home runs, Rodriguez and the other sluggers weren't happy. Privately, Rodriguez predicted that Safeco would "be the worst hitting park in the history of the game." Because he had made the majors so young, Rodriguez was eligible for free agency only three months after his twenty-fifth birthday. It's unusual for a marquee player to be able to sign with any team as he's entering the prime of his career. Rodriguez said that winning was his only concern. He talked with the Atlanta Braves and the New York Mets and publicly didn't rule out staying in Seattle.

"I love Seattle," he said at the time. "It is one of my favorite cities in the world. The people here have been incredible toward me. But the only question I'm asking is one: Can we win? That's the only thing—a ring."

That's why when he signed with Texas—a team that had reached the postseason only three times and won just one such game—it left many scratching their heads. After playing in the shadow of Griffey and others in Seattle, Rodriguez was determined to go to a team where there would be no doubt that he was the leader.

"He's the man here," says Rafael Palmeiro as he gazes across the Rangers clubhouse at Rodriguez's locker. "We rise and fall with him. He's a tremendous talent and he's proving to be a great leader, too."

Rodriguez jokes that before he came to the Rangers, which has a large Latino contingent and history, he had to brush up on his Spanish.

"I was losing it," he says. "But here, with the Rangers, I might forget to speak English because we speak so much Spanish. Baseball for us Latinos is like a cult, it's a religion for us. Latinos are big on being unified, and when they get unified, all they do is watch baseball. It will always be the thing that brings us together."

As far as his signing with the Rangers, whether he feels like a marked man, Rodriguez replies, "I feel a great responsibility to turn around this team. Anybody who wants to criticize, all I ask them to do is to watch me play. How I play every day.

"As for our sport, I believe we're on the verge of something big. Being Dominican will always be my ethnic group. I'll always identify with that no matter what happens. But every ethnic group is going to have to contribute to the rise of baseball. We're a global sport. The sooner we all realize that, the bigger the impact baseball can have in the future."

Rodriguez has also realized the enormous clout his celebrity and his net worth can have upon the places he treasured in his youth. Growing up, the All-Star shortstop used to sneak into the University of Miami baseball stadium. Days after the 2002 regular season ended, Rodriguez attended a ceremony at which it was announced that he was giving $3.9 million to help with the facility's renovation.

"This is my Yankee Stadium," he says, "my Candlestick Park, my Dodger Stadium."

After the ceremony, despite the topic being money and how many millions he was worth today, Rodriguez was all smiles. As it was when Orestes Minoso slid across home plate at the old Comiskey Park or when Roberto Clemente was named the World Series MVP or those times when Sammy Sosa jumps into the air after sending another ball soaring over the ivy-covered walls at Wrigley Field, this snapshot of a grinning Rodriguez is another example of the ballplayers who have become the new face of baseball. Their heritage may date back to the turn of the century, to lands that many Americans aren't familiar with, but their legacy has only just begun, and one can only imagine what the future holds.

THE LATINO ALL-CENTURY TEAM

When Major League Baseball came out with its All-Century Team, no Latino star made the cut. Roberto Clemente was the Latino who came the closest, finishing tenth—46,805 votes behind Pete Rose. The All-Century Team was chosen by the fans during the second half of the 1999 season and consisted of two players at each infield position, two catchers, six pitchers and nine outfielders.

A special panel was named to compensate for oversights in the fan voting and it added five players to the team—shortstop Honus Wagner, outfielder Stan Musial, and pitchers Lefty Grove, Christy Mathewson, and Warren Spahn. All are in the Hall of Fame, so it's hard to argue with those additional choices. Still, as I researched this book three seasons after the All-Century Team was announced, it was interesting to hear how controversial that assemblage of players still was. Orlando Cepeda couldn't understand why a place for Clemente wasn't found. Orestes Minoso couldn't believe that none of the legendary Latino shortstops, past or present, had made it, and declared that the next All-Century Team would be dominated by the likes of Sammy Sosa and Fernando Valenzuela. After talking with them, I couldn't help thinking that there should be a Latino All-Century Team. But who could help me put one together?

I thought it was only fitting to turn to Omar Minaya for his thoughts. As the first Latino general manager in Major League Baseball, Minaya certainly had the background and knowledge to do the job. What surprised me was how excited he became with the idea.

"You have to start with Alex Rodriguez" was his first reaction. "Either him or Vladimir Guerrero."

Minaya and his friend, Lou Melendez, Major League Baseball's vice president for international operations, were seated at a table in the dining room at Veterans Stadium. On the field below, Minaya's Montreal Expos would soon take the field against the Philadelphia Phillies. Together, the two of them scrutinized a list of the all-time Latino All-Stars I had put before them.

"It's a good start," Minaya said, in the same way that Tony Peña once told me I had a good fastball. "But it needs some work. Where's Davey Concepcion? You're going to need to load up at short. You've got no choice. That's the position of choice for a lot of Latins. The toughest place to play and where so many excel."

So allowances have been made on the Latino All-Century team as proposed by Minaya. While most positions go three deep, at shortstop we went with a half-dozen. It's difficult enough to determine who should have been the 2002 American League MVP—Alex Rodriguez or Miguel Tejada—without the possibility of leaving one of them off this star-studded squad.

Minaya looked over the list with Melendez's help. He got out a pen and began to rearrange things. He added players and debated with Melendez about where to play others. To open up more room at first base, Tony Pérez was moved to third, where he played a great deal early in his career.

"That also helps shore up that position," Minaya said. "Too many Latinos end up playing short anyway."

As the Phillies took the field, the opening pitch only minutes away, Minaya slid the list back across the tabletop to me.

"That's a team I'd pay to see," he said. "The book should have a list like this. Let people know how many great Latin players there's been."

"With more on the way," Melendez added.

Chosen by Omar Minaya and Tim Wendel

FIRST BASE
Vic Power
Orlando Cepeda
Rafael Palmeiro

SECOND BASE
Rod Carew
Roberto Alomar
Alfonso Soriano

SHORTSTOP
Luis Aparicio
Dave Concepcion
Omar Vizquel
Alex Rodriguez
Nomar Garciaparra
Miguel Tejada

THIRD BASE
Vinny Castilla
Tony Pérez

CATCHER
Manny Sanguillen
Tony Peña
Ivan Rodriguez

OUTFIELD
Orestes "Minnie" Minoso
Roberto Clemente
Tony Oliva
Jose Canseco
Sammy Sosa
Juan Gonzalez
Bernie Williams
Manny Ramirez
Vladimir Guerrero

STARTING PITCHERS
Dolf Luque
Camilo Pascual
Juan Marichal
Luis Tiant
Fernando Valenzuela
Pedro Martinez

RELIEF PITCHERS
Willie Hernandez
Mariano Rivera

BENCH
Martin Dihigo
Julio Franco
Jose Vidro

VIC POWER

Victor Pellot Power Pove (*born Victor Felipe Pellot Pove*)

BATS: Right **THROWS:** Right
HEIGHT: 5' 11" **WEIGHT:** 195 lbs.
DEBUT: April 13, 1954 **POSITION:** First Base
BORN: November 1, 1927, in Arecibo, Puerto Rico

◆ All-Star in 1955, 1956, 1959, and 1960
◆ Led American League in triples in 1958
◆ Gold-Glove winner 1958–1964
◆ Top 10 MVP in 1955

BATTING

Year	Tm	G	AB	R	H	2B	3B	HR	RBI	SB	BB	SO	BA
1954	PHA	127	462	36	118	17	5	8	38	2	19	19	.255
1955	KCA	147	596	91	190	34	10	19	76	0	35	27	.319
1956	KCA	127	530	77	164	21	5	14	63	2	24	16	.309
1957	KCA	129	467	48	121	15	1	14	42	3	19	21	.259
1958	KCA	52	205	35	62	13	4	4	27	1	7	3	.302
	CLE	93	385	63	122	24	6	12	53	2	13	11	.317
	TOT	145	590	98	184	37	10	16	80	3	20	14	.312
1959	CLE	147	595	102	172	31	6	10	60	9	40	22	.289
1960	CLE	147	580	69	167	26	3	10	84	9	24	20	.288
1961	CLE	147	563	64	151	34	4	5	63	4	38	16	.268
1962	MIN	144	611	80	177	28	2	16	63	7	22	35	.290
1963	MIN	138	541	65	146	28	2	10	52	3	22	24	.270
1964	MIN	19	45	6	10	2	0	0	1	0	1	3	.222
	LAA	68	221	17	55	6	0	3	13	1	8	14	.249
	PHI	18	48	1	10	4	0	0	3	0	2	3	.208
	TOT	87	266	23	65	8	0	3	14	1	9	17	.244
	TOT	105	314	24	75	12	0	3	17	1	11	20	.239
1965	CAL	124	197	11	51	7	1	1	20	2	5	13	.259
12 Seasons		1627	6046	765	1716	290	49	126	658	45	279	247	.284
Career High		147	611	102	190	37	10	19	84	9	40	35	.319

ORLANDO CEPEDA

Orlando Manuel Cepeda Penne (*Cha Cha or Baby Bull*)

BATS: Right **THROWS:** Right
HEIGHT: 6'2" **WEIGHT:** 210 lbs.
DEBUT: April 15, 1958 **POSITION:** First Base
BORN: September 17, 1937, in Ponce, Puerto Rico

◆ All-Star in 1959, 1960, 1961, 1962, 1963, 1964, and 1967
◆ Led National League in home runs in 1961
◆ Led National League in RBIs in 1961 and 1967
◆ Elected into the National Baseball Hall of Fame in 1999

BATTING

Year	Tm	G	AB	R	H	2B	3B	HR	RBI	SB	BB	SO	BA
1958	SFG	148	603	88	188	38	4	25	96	15	29	84	.312
1959	SFG	151	605	92	192	35	4	27	105	23	33	100	.317
1960	SFG	151	569	81	169	36	3	24	96	15	34	91	.297
1961	SFG	152	585	105	182	28	4	46	142	12	39	91	.311
1962	SFG	162	625	105	191	26	1	35	114	10	37	97	.306
1963	SFG	156	579	100	183	33	4	34	97	8	37	70	.316
1964	SFG	142	529	75	161	27	2	31	97	9	43	83	.304
1965	SFG	33	34	1	6	1	0	1	5	0	3	9	.176
1966	SFG	19	49	5	14	2	0	3	15	0	4	11	.286
	STL	123	452	65	137	24	0	17	58	9	34	68	.303
	TOT	142	501	70	151	26	0	20	73	9	38	79	.301
1967	STL	151	563	91	183	37	0	25	111	11	62	75	.325
1968	STL	157	600	71	149	26	2	16	73	8	43	96	.248
1969	ATL	154	573	74	147	28	2	22	88	12	55	76	.257
1970	ATL	148	567	87	173	33	0	34	111	6	47	75	.305
1971	ATL	71	250	31	69	10	1	14	44	3	22	29	.276
1972	ATL	28	84	6	25	3	0	4	9	0	7	17	.298
	OAK	3	3	0	0	0	0	0	0	0	0	0	.000
	TOT	31	87	6	25	3	0	4	9	0	7	17	.287
1973	BOS	142	550	51	159	25	0	20	86	0	50	81	.289
1974	KCR	33	107	3	23	5	0	1	18	1	9	16	.215
17 Seasons		2124	7927	1131	2351	417	27	379	1365	142	588	1169	.297
Career High		162	625	105	192	38	4	46	142	23	62	100	.325

RAFAEL PALMEIRO

Rafael Palmeiro Corrales

BATS: Left **THROWS:** Left
HEIGHT: 6'0" **WEIGHT:** 188 lbs
DEBUT: September 8, 1986 **POSITION:** First Base
BORN: September 24, 1964, in Havana, Cuba

◆ All-Star 1988, 1991, 1998, and 1999
◆ Gold-Glove winner 1997–1999
◆ Led American League in hits in 1990
◆ Led American League in doubles in 1991
◆ Led American League in runs in 1993

BATTING

Year	Tm	G	AB	R	H	2B	3B	HR	RBI	SB	BB	SO	BA
1986	CHC	22	73	9	18	4	0	3	12	1	4	6	.247
1987	CHC	84	221	32	61	15	1	14	30	2	20	26	.276
1988	CHC	152	580	75	178	41	5	8	53	12	38	34	.307
1989	TEX	156	559	76	154	23	4	8	64	4	63	48	.275
1990	TEX	154	598	72	191	35	6	14	89	3	40	59	.319
1991	TEX	159	631	115	203	49	3	26	88	4	68	72	.322
1992	TEX	159	608	84	163	27	4	22	85	2	72	83	.268
1993	TEX	160	597	124	176	40	2	37	105	22	73	85	.295
1994	BAL	111	436	82	139	32	0	23	76	7	54	63	.319
1995	BAL	143	554	89	172	30	2	39	104	3	62	65	.310
1996	BAL	162	626	110	181	40	2	39	142	8	95	96	.289
1997	BAL	158	614	95	156	24	2	38	110	5	67	109	.254
1998	BAL	162	619	98	183	36	1	43	121	11	79	91	.296
1999	TEX	158	565	96	183	30	1	47	148	2	97	69	.324
2000	TEX	158	565	102	163	29	3	39	120	2	103	77	.288
2001	TEX	160	600	98	164	33	0	47	123	1	101	90	.273
16 Seasons		2258	8446	1357	2485	488	36	447	1470	89	1036	1073	.294
Career High		162	631	124	203	49	6	47	148	22	103	109	.324

ROD CAREW

Rodney Cline Carew

BATS: Left **THROWS:** Right
HEIGHT: 6' 0" **WEIGHT:** 182 lbs.
DEBUT: April 11, 1967 **POSITION:** Second Base
BORN: October 1, 1945, in Gatun, Canal Zone, Panama

◆ American League Rookie of the Year 1967
◆ Led American League in batting average in 1969,
1972–1975, 1977, and 1978
◆ Led American League in hits in 1973, 1974,
and 1977
◆ American League MVP 1977
◆ Led American League in triples in 1973 and 1977
◆ Elected into the National Baseball Hall of Fame
in 1991

BATTING

Year	Tm	G	AB	R	H	2B	3B	HR	RBI	SB	BB	SO	BA
1967	MIN	137	514	66	150	22	7	8	51	5	37	91	.292
1968	MIN	127	461	46	126	27	2	1	42	12	26	71	.273
1969	MIN	123	458	79	152	30	4	8	56	19	37	72	.332
1970	MIN	51	191	27	70	12	3	4	28	4	11	28	.366
1971	MIN	147	577	88	177	16	10	2	48	6	45	81	.307
1972	MIN	142	535	61	170	21	6	0	51	12	43	60	.318
1973	MIN	149	580	98	203	30	11	6	62	41	62	55	.350
1974	MIN	153	599	86	218	30	5	3	55	38	74	49	.364
1975	MIN	143	535	89	192	24	4	14	80	35	64	40	.359
1976	MIN	156	605	97	200	29	12	9	90	49	67	52	.331
1977	MIN	155	616	128	239	38	16	14	100	23	69	55	.388
1978	MIN	152	564	85	188	26	10	5	70	27	78	62	.333
1979	CAL	110	409	78	130	15	3	3	44	18	73	46	.318
1980	CAL	144	540	74	179	34	7	3	59	23	59	38	.331
1981	CAL	93	364	57	111	17	1	2	21	16	45	45	.305
1982	CAL	138	523	88	167	25	5	3	44	10	67	49	.319
1983	CAL	129	472	66	160	24	2	2	44	6	57	48	.339
1984	CAL	93	329	42	97	8	1	3	31	4	40	39	.295
1985	CAL	127	443	69	124	17	3	2	39	5	64	47	.280
19 Seasons		2469	9315	1424	3053	445	112	92	1015	353	1018	1028	.328
Career High		156	616	128	239	38	16	14	100	49	78	91	.388

ROBERTO ALOMAR

Roberto Alomar Velazquez

BATS: Both **THROWS:** Right
HEIGHT: 6' 0" **WEIGHT:** 185 lbs.
DEBUT: April 22, 1988 **POSITION:** Second Base
BORN: February 5, 1968, in Ponce, Puerto Rico

◆ All-Star in 1990–2001
◆ Top 10 MVP in 1991, 1992, 1993, 1999, and 2001
◆ Led American League in runs in 1999
◆ Gold-Glove winner in 1991, 1992–1996, 1998–2001

BATTING

Year	Tm	G	AB	R	H	2B	3B	HR	RBI	SB	BB	SO	BA
1988	SDP	143	545	84	145	24	6	9	41	24	47	83	.266
1989	SDP	158	623	82	184	27	1	7	56	42	53	76	.295
1990	SDP	147	586	80	168	27	5	6	60	24	48	72	.287
1991	TOR	161	637	88	188	41	11	9	69	53	57	86	.295
1992	TOR	152	571	105	177	27	8	8	76	49	87	52	.310
1993	TOR	153	589	109	192	35	6	17	93	55	80	67	.326
1994	TOR	107	392	78	120	25	4	8	38	19	51	41	.306
1995	TOR	130	517	71	155	24	7	13	66	30	47	45	.300
1996	BAL	153	588	132	193	43	4	22	94	17	90	65	.328
1997	BAL	112	412	64	137	23	2	14	60	9	40	43	.333
1998	BAL	147	588	86	166	36	1	14	56	18	59	70	.282
1999	CLE	159	563	138	182	40	3	24	120	37	99	96	.323
2000	CLE	155	610	111	189	40	2	19	89	39	64	82	.310
2001	CLE	157	575	113	193	34	12	20	100	30	80	71	.336
14 Seasons		2034	7796	1341	2389	446	72	190	1018	446	902	949	.306
Career High		161	637	138	193	43	12	24	120	55	99	96	.336

ALFONSO SORIANO

Alfonso Guilleard Soriano

BATS: Right **THROWS:** Right
HEIGHT: 6' 1" **WEIGHT:** 180 lbs.
DEBUT: September 14, 1999 **POSITION:** Second Base
BORN: January 7, 1978, in San Pedro de Macoris,
Dominican Republic

◆ First second baseman to steal more than 30 bases
  and hit 30 home runs in same season (2002)
◆ Holds New York Yankees rookie mark for stolen
  bases
◆ All-Star in 2002

BATTING

Year	Tm	G	AB	R	H	2B	3B	HR	RBI	SB	BB	SO	BA
1999	NYY	9	8	2	1	0	0	1	1	0	3	0	.125
2000	NYY	22	50	5	9	3	0	2	3	1	15	2	.180
2001	NYY	158	574	77	154	34	3	18	73	29	125	43	.268
2002	NYY	156	696	128	209	51	2	39	102	23	157	41	.300
4 Seasons		345	1328	212	373	88	5	60	179	53	300	86	.281
Career High		158	696	128	209	51	3	39	102	29	157	43	.300

LUIS APARICIO

Luis Ernesto Aparicio Montiel (Little Louie)

BATS: Right **THROWS:** Right
HEIGHT: 5' 9" **WEIGHT:** 160 lbs.
DEBUT: April 17, 1956 **POSITION:** Shortstop
BORN: April 29, 1934, in Maracaibo, Venezuela

◆ All-Star 1958–1964 and 1970–1972
◆ Led American League in stolen bases 1956–1964
◆ Led American League in at bats in 1966
◆ Gold-Glove winner 1958–1962, 1964, 1966, 1968, and 1970

BATTING

Year	Tm	G	AB	R	H	2B	3B	HR	RBI	SB	BB	SO	BA
1956	CHW	152	533	69	142	19	6	3	56	21	34	63	.266
1957	CHW	143	575	82	148	22	6	3	41	28	52	55	.257
1958	CHW	145	557	76	148	20	9	2	40	29	35	38	.266
1959	CHW	152	612	98	157	18	5	6	51	56	53	40	.257
1960	CHW	153	600	86	166	20	7	2	61	51	43	39	.277
1961	CHW	156	625	90	170	24	4	6	45	53	38	33	.272
1962	CHW	153	581	72	140	23	5	7	40	31	32	36	.241
1963	BAL	146	601	73	150	18	8	5	45	40	36	35	.250
1964	BAL	146	578	93	154	20	3	10	37	57	49	51	.266
1965	BAL	144	564	67	127	20	10	8	40	26	46	56	.225
1966	BAL	151	659	97	182	25	8	6	41	25	33	42	.276
1967	BAL	134	546	55	127	22	5	4	31	18	29	44	.233
1968	CHW	155	622	55	164	24	4	4	36	17	33	43	.264
1969	CHW	156	599	77	168	24	5	5	51	24	66	29	.280
1970	CHW	146	552	86	173	29	3	5	43	8	53	34	.313
1971	BOS	125	491	56	114	23	0	4	45	6	35	43	.232
1972	BOS	110	436	47	112	26	3	3	39	3	26	28	.257
1973	BOS	132	499	56	135	17	1	0	49	13	43	33	.271
18 Seasons		2599	10230	1335	2677	394	92	83	791	736	506	742	.262
Career High		156	659	98	182	29	10	10	61	57	66	63	.313

DAVE CONCEPCION

David Ismael Concepcion Benitez

BATS: Right **THROWS:** Right
HEIGHT: 6' 1" **WEIGHT:** 180 lbs.
DEBUT: April 6, 1970 **POSITION:** Shortstop
BORN: June 17, 1948, in Aragua, Venezuela

◆ All-Star in 1973, 1975–1982
◆ Gold-Glove winner 1974–1979 and 1982
◆ MVP in 1982
◆ Top 10 National League MVP in 1979 and 1981

BATTING

Year	Tm	G	AB	R	H	2B	3B	HR	RBI	SB	BB	SO	BA
1970	CIN	101	265	38	69	6	3	1	19	10	23	45	.260
1971	CIN	130	327	24	67	4	4	1	20	9	18	51	.205
1972	CIN	119	378	40	79	13	2	2	29	13	32	65	.209
1973	CIN	89	328	39	94	18	3	8	46	22	21	55	.287
1974	CIN	160	594	70	167	25	1	14	82	41	44	79	.281
1975	CIN	140	507	62	139	23	1	5	49	33	39	51	.274
1976	CIN	152	576	74	162	28	7	9	69	21	49	68	.281
1977	CIN	156	572	59	155	26	3	8	64	29	46	77	.271
1978	CIN	153	565	75	170	33	4	6	67	23	51	83	.301
1979	CIN	149	590	91	166	25	3	16	84	19	64	73	.281
1980	CIN	156	622	72	162	31	8	5	77	12	37	107	.260
1981	CIN	106	421	57	129	28	0	5	67	4	37	61	.306
1982	CIN	147	572	48	164	25	4	5	53	13	45	61	.287
1983	CIN	143	528	54	123	22	0	1	47	14	56	81	.233
1984	CIN	154	531	46	130	26	1	4	58	22	52	72	.245
1985	CIN	155	560	59	141	19	2	7	48	16	50	67	.252
1986	CIN	90	311	42	81	13	2	3	30	13	26	43	.260
1987	CIN	104	279	32	89	15	0	1	33	4	28	24	.319
1988	CIN	84	197	11	39	9	0	0	8	3	18	23	.198
19 Seasons		2488	8723	993	2326	389	48	101	950	321	736	1186	.267
Career High		160	622	91	170	33	8	16	84	41	64	107	.319

OMAR VIZQUEL

Omar Enrique Vizquel Gonzalez

BATS: Both **THROWS:** Right
HEIGHT: 5' 9" **WEIGHT:** 165 lbs.
DEBUT: April 3, 1989 **POSITION:** Shortstop
BORN: April 24, 1967, in Caracas, Venezuela

◆ All-Star 1998, 1999, and 2002
◆ Gold-Glove winner 1993–2001
◆ Led American League in sacrifice hits in 1997 and 1999

BATTING

Year	Tm	G	AB	R	H	2B	3B	HR	RBI	SB	BB	SO	BA
1989	SEA	143	387	45	85	7	3	1	20	1	28	40	.220
1990	SEA	81	255	19	63	3	2	2	18	4	18	22	.247
1991	SEA	142	426	42	98	16	4	1	41	7	45	37	.230
1992	SEA	136	483	49	142	20	4	0	21	15	32	38	.294
1993	SEA	158	560	68	143	14	2	2	31	12	50	71	.255
1994	CLE	69	286	39	78	10	1	1	33	13	23	23	.273
1995	CLE	136	542	87	144	28	0	6	56	29	59	59	.266
1996	CLE	151	542	98	161	36	1	9	64	35	56	42	.297
1997	CLE	153	565	89	158	23	6	5	49	43	57	58	.280
1998	CLE	151	576	86	166	30	6	2	50	37	62	64	.288
1999	CLE	144	574	112	191	36	4	5	66	42	65	50	.333
2000	CLE	156	613	101	176	27	3	7	66	22	87	72	.287
2001	CLE	155	611	84	156	26	8	2	50	13	61	72	.255
13 Seasons		1775	6420	919	1761	276	44	43	565	273	643	648	.274
Career High		158	613	112	191	36	8	9	66	43	87	72	.333

ALEX RODRIGUEZ

Alexander Emmanuel Rodriguez

BATS: Right **THROWS:** Right
HEIGHT: 6' 3" **WEIGHT:** 190 lbs.
DEBUT: July 8, 1994 **POSITION:** Shortstop
BORN: July 27, 1975, in New York, NY

◆ All-Star 1996, 1997, 1998, 2000–2002
◆ Led American League in runs in 1996 and 2002
◆ Led American League in doubles in 1996
◆ Led American League in hits in 1998
◆ Led American League in home runs in 2001
◆ Gold-Glove winner in 2002

BATTING

Year	Tm	G	AB	R	H	2B	3B	HR	RBI	SB	BB	SO	BA
1994	SEA	17	54	4	11	0	0	0	2	3	3	20	.204
1995	SEA	48	142	15	33	6	2	5	19	4	6	42	.232
1996	SEA	146	601	141	215	54	1	36	123	15	59	104	.358
1997	SEA	141	587	100	176	40	3	23	84	29	41	99	.300
1998	SEA	161	686	123	213	35	5	42	124	46	45	121	.310
1999	SEA	129	502	110	143	25	0	42	111	21	56	109	.285
2000	SEA	148	554	134	175	34	2	41	132	15	100	121	.316
2001	TEX	162	632	133	201	34	1	52	135	18	75	131	.318
8 Seasons		952	3758	760	1167	228	14	241	730	151	385	747	.311
Career High		162	686	141	215	54	5	52	135	46	100	131	.358

NOMAR GARCIAPARRA

Anthony Nomar Garciaparra

BATS: Right **THROWS:** Right
HEIGHT: 6' 0" **WEIGHT:** 165 lbs.
DEBUT: August 31, 1996 **POSITION:** Shortstop
BORN: July 23, 1973, in Whittier, CA

◆ All-Star 1997, 1999, 2000, and 2002
◆ Led American League in hits in 1997
◆ Led American League in triples in 1997
◆ Led American League in batting average in 1999 and 2000

BATTING

Year	Tm	G	AB	R	H	2B	3B	HR	RBI	SB	BB	SO	BA
1996	BOS	24	87	11	21	2	3	4	16	5	4	14	.241
1997	BOS	153	684	122	209	44	11	30	98	22	35	92	.306
1998	BOS	143	604	111	195	37	8	35	122	12	33	62	.323
1999	BOS	135	532	103	190	42	4	27	104	14	51	39	.357
2000	BOS	140	529	104	197	51	3	21	96	5	61	50	.372
2001	BOS	21	83	13	24	3	0	4	8	0	7	9	.289
6 Seasons		616	2519	464	836	179	29	121	444	58	191	266	.332
Career High		153	684	122	209	51	11	35	122	22	61	92	.372

MIGUEL TEJADA

Miguel Odalis Tejada Martinez

BATS: Right **THROWS:** Right
HEIGHT: 5' 10" **WEIGHT:** 170 lbs.
DEBUT: August 27, 1997 **POSITION:** Shortstop
BORN: May 25, 1976, in Bani, D.R.

◆ Led American League in games played in 2001
◆ Top 10 leader in at bats in 2001
◆ Top 10 leader in runs in 2001
◆ American League MVP and All-Star in 2002

BATTING

Year	Tm	G	AB	R	H	2B	3B	HR	RBI	SB	BB	SO	BA
1997	OAK	26	99	10	20	3	2	2	10	2	2	22	.202
1998	OAK	105	365	53	85	20	1	11	45	5	28	86	.233
1999	OAK	159	593	93	149	33	4	21	84	8	57	94	.251
2000	OAK	160	607	105	167	32	1	30	115	6	66	102	.275
2001	OAK	162	622	107	166	31	3	31	113	11	43	89	.267
5 Seasons		612	2286	368	587	119	11	95	367	32	196	393	.257
Career High		162	622	107	167	33	4	31	115	11	66	102	.275

TONY PEREZ

Atanasio Perez Rigal

BATS: Right **THROWS:** Right
HEIGHT: 6' 2" **WEIGHT:** 205 lbs.
DEBUT: July 26, 1964 **POSITION:** First and Third Base
BORN: May 14, 1942, in Ciego de Avila, Cuba

◆ All-Star in 1967–1970 and 1974–1976
◆ National League MVP in 1967, 1969, 1970 and 1973
◆ Top 10 in home runs in 1967, 1969, 1970, 1973, 1974, and 1980

BATTING

Year	Tm	G	AB	R	H	2B	3B	HR	RBI	SB	BB	SO	BA
1964	CIN	12	25	1	2	1	0	0	1	0	3	9	.080
1965	CIN	104	281	40	73	14	4	12	47	0	21	67	.260
1966	CIN	99	257	68	10	4	4	39	1	1	14	44	.265
1967	CIN	156	600	78	174	28	7	26	102	0	33	102	.290
1968	CIN	160	625	93	176	25	7	18	92	3	51	92	.282
1969	CIN	160	629	103	185	31	2	37	122	4	63	131	.294
1970	CIN	158	587	107	186	28	6	40	129	8	83	134	.317
1971	CIN	158	609	72	164	22	3	25	91	4	51	120	.269
1972	CIN	136	515	64	146	33	7	21	90	4	55	121	.283
1973	CIN	151	564	73	177	33	3	27	101	3	74	117	.314
1974	CIN	158	596	81	158	28	2	28	101	1	61	112	.265
1975	CIN	137	511	74	144	28	3	20	109	1	54	101	.282
1976	CIN	139	527	77	137	32	6	19	91	10	50	88	.260
1977	MON	154	559	71	158	32	6	19	91	4	63	111	.283
1978	MON	148	544	63	158	38	3	14	78	2	38	104	.290
1979	MON	132	489	58	132	29	4	13	73	2	38	82	.270
1980	BOS	151	585	73	161	31	3	25	105	1	41	93	.275
1981	BOS	84	306	35	77	11	3	9	39	0	27	66	.252
1982	BOS	69	196	18	51	14	2	6	31	0	19	48	.260
1983	PHI	91	253	18	61	11	2	6	43	1	28	57	.241
1984	CIN	71	137	9	33	6	1	2	15	0	11	21	.241
1985	CIN	72	183	25	60	8	0	6	33	0	22	22	.328
1986	CIN	77	200	14	51	12	1	2	29	0	25	25	.255
23 Seasons		2777	9778	1272	2732	505	79	379	1652	49	925	1867	.279
Career High		160	629	107	186	38	7	40	129	10	83	134	.317

VINNY CASTILLA

Vinicio Castilla Soria

BATS: Right **THROWS:** Right
HEIGHT: 6' 1" **WEIGHT:** 185 lbs.
DEBUT: September 1, 1991 **POSITION:** Third Base
BORN: July 4, 1967, in Oaxaca, Mexico

◆ All-Star in 1995 and 1998
◆ Top 10 in batting average in 1995 and 1998
◆ Top 10 in hits 1995–1998
◆ Top 10 in home runs 1995–1998

BATTING

Year	Tm	G	AB	R	H	2B	3B	HR	RBI	SB	BB	SO	BA
1991	ATL	12	5	1	1	0	0	0	0	0	0	2	.200
1992	ATL	9	16	1	4	1	0	0	1	0	1	4	.250
1993	COL	105	337	36	86	9	7	9	30	2	13	45	.255
1994	COL	52	130	16	43	11	1	3	18	2	7	23	.331
1995	COL	139	527	82	163	34	2	32	90	2	30	87	.309
1996	COL	160	629	97	191	34	0	40	113	7	35	88	.304
1997	COL	159	612	94	186	25	2	40	113	2	44	108	.304
1998	COL	162	645	108	206	28	4	46	144	5	40	89	.319
1999	COL	158	615	83	169	24	1	33	102	2	53	75	.275
2000	TBD	85	331	22	73	9	1	6	42	1	14	41	.221
2001	TBD	24	93	7	20	6	0	2	9	0	3	22	.215
	HOU	122	445	62	120	28	1	23	82	1	32	86	.270
	TOT	146	538	69	140	34	1	25	91	1	35	108	.260
11 Seasons		1187	4385	609	1262	209	19	234	744	24	272	670	.288
Career High		162	645	108	206	34	7	46	144	7	53	108	.319

MANNY SANGUILLEN

Manuel De Jesus Sanguillen Magan

BATS: Right **THROWS:** Right
HEIGHT: 6' 0" **WEIGHT:** 193 lbs.
DEBUT: July 23, 1967 **POSITION:** Catcher
BORN: March 21, 1944, in Colon, Panama

◆ All-Star in 1971, 1972, and 1975
◆ Top 10 American League MVP in 1971
◆ Top 10 batting average in 1970, 1971, and 1975

BATTING

Year	Tm	G	AB	R	H	2B	3B	HR	RBI	SB	BB	SO	BA
1967	PIT	30	96	6	26	4	0	0	8	0	4	12	.271
1969	PIT	129	459	62	139	21	6	5	57	8	12	48	.303
1970	PIT	128	486	63	158	19	9	7	61	2	17	45	.325
1971	PIT	138	533	60	170	26	5	7	81	6	19	32	.319
1972	PIT	136	520	55	155	18	8	7	71	1	21	38	.298
1973	PIT	149	589	64	166	26	7	12	65	2	17	29	.282
1974	PIT	151	596	77	171	21	4	7	68	2	21	27	.287
1975	PIT	133	481	60	158	24	4	9	58	5	48	31	.328
1976	PIT	114	389	52	113	16	6	2	36	2	28	18	.290
1977	OAK	152	571	42	157	17	5	6	58	2	22	35	.275
1978	PIT	85	220	15	58	5	1	3	16	2	9	10	.264
1979	PIT	56	74	8	17	5	2	0	4	0	2	5	.230
1980	PIT	47	48	2	12	3	0	0	2	3	3	1	.250
13 Seasons		1448	5062	566	1500	205	57	65	585	35	223	331	.296
Career High		152	596	77	171	26	9	12	81	8	48	48	.328

TONY PEÑA

Antonio Francisco Peña Padilla

BATS: Right **THROWS:** Right
HEIGHT: 6' 0" **WEIGHT:** 181 lbs.
DEBUT: September 1, 1980 **POSITION:** Catcher
BORN: June 4, 1957, in Montecristi, Dominican
Republic

◆ All-Star 1982, 1984–1986, and 1989
◆ National League Gold-Glove winner 1983–1985
  and 1991
◆ Top 10 batting average in 1982 and 1983

BATTING

Year	Tm	G	AB	R	H	2B	3B	HR	RBI	SB	BB	SO	BA
1980	P I T	8	21	1	9	1	1	0	1	0	0	4	.429
1981	P I T	66	210	16	63	9	1	2	17	1	8	23	.300
1982	P I T	138	497	53	147	28	4	11	63	2	17	57	.296
1983	P I T	151	542	51	163	22	3	15	70	6	31	73	.301
1984	P I T	147	546	77	156	27	2	15	78	12	36	79	.286
1985	P I T	147	546	53	136	27	2	10	59	12	29	67	.249
1986	P I T	144	510	56	147	26	2	10	52	9	53	69	.288
1987	S T L	116	384	40	82	13	4	5	44	6	36	54	.214
1988	S T L	149	505	55	133	23	1	10	51	6	33	60	.263
1989	S T L	141	424	36	110	17	2	4	37	5	35	33	.259
1990	B O S	143	491	62	129	19	1	7	56	8	43	71	.263
1991	B O S	141	464	45	107	23	2	5	48	8	37	53	.231
1992	B O S	133	410	39	99	21	1	1	38	3	24	61	.241
1993	B O S	126	304	20	55	11	0	4	19	1	25	46	.181
1994	C L E	40	112	18	33	8	1	2	10	0	9	11	.295
1995	C L E	91	263	25	69	15	0	5	28	1	14	44	.262
1996	C L E	67	174	14	34	4	0	1	27	0	15	25	.195
1997	CHW	31	67	4	11	1	0	0	8	0	8	13	.164
	HOU	9	19	2	4	3	0	0	2	0	2	3	.211
	TOT	40	86	6	15	4	0	0	10	0	10	16	.174
18 Seasons		1988	6489	667	1687	298	27	107	708	80	455	846	.260
Career High		151	546	77	163	28	4	15	78	12	53	79	.301

IVAN RODRIGUEZ

Ivan Rodriguez Torres *(Pudge or I-Rod)*

BATS: Right **THROWS:** Right
HEIGHT: 5' 9" **WEIGHT:** 205 lbs.
DEBUT: June 20, 1991 **POSITION:** Catcher
BORN: November 30, 1971, in Vega Baja, Puerto Rico

◆ All-Star 1992–2001
◆ American League Gold-Glove winner 1992–2000
◆ American League MVP 1999

BATTING

Year	Tm	G	AB	R	H	2B	3B	HR	RBI	SB	BB	SO	BA
1991	TEX	88	280	24	74	16	0	3	27	0	5	42	.264
1992	TEX	123	420	39	109	16	1	8	37	0	24	73	.260
1993	TEX	137	473	56	129	28	4	10	66	8	29	70	.273
1994	TEX	99	363	56	108	19	1	16	57	6	31	42	.298
1995	TEX	130	492	56	149	32	2	12	67	0	16	48	.303
1996	TEX	153	639	116	192	47	3	19	86	5	38	55	.300
1997	TEX	150	597	98	187	34	4	20	77	7	38	89	.313
1998	TEX	145	579	88	186	40	4	21	91	9	32	88	.321
1999	TEX	144	600	116	199	29	1	35	113	25	24	64	.332
2000	TEX	91	363	66	126	27	4	27	83	5	19	48	.347
2001	TEX	111	442	70	136	24	2	25	65	10	23	73	.308
11 Seasons		1371	5248	785	1595	312	26	196	769	75	279	692	.304
Career High		153	639	116	199	47	4	35	113	25	38	89	.347

MINNIE MINOSO

Saturnino Orestes Armas Minoso Arrieta

BATS: Right **THROWS:** Right
HEIGHT: 5' 10" **WEIGHT:** 175 lbs.
DEBUT: April 19, 1949 **POSITION:** Third Base and Left Field
BORN: November 29, 1922, in Havana, Cuba

◆ All-Star 1951–1954, 1957, 1959, and 1960
◆ American League Top 10 MVP in 1951, 1953,
   1954, 1957, and 1960
◆ Hit leader in 1960

BATTING

Year	Tm	G	AB	R	H	2B	3B	HR	RBI	SB	BB	SO	BA
1949	C L E	9	16	2	3	0	0	1	1	0	2	2	.188
1951	C L E	8	14	3	6	2	0	0	2	0	1	1	.429
	CHW	138	516	109	167	32	14	10	74	31	71	41	.324
	T O T	146	530	112	173	34	14	10	76	31	72	42	.326
1952	CHW	147	569	96	160	24	9	13	61	22	71	46	.281
1953	CHW	151	556	104	174	24	8	15	104	25	74	43	.313
1954	CHW	153	568	119	182	29	18	19	116	18	77	46	.320
1955	CHW	139	517	79	149	26	7	10	70	19	76	43	.288
1956	CHW	151	545	106	172	29	11	21	88	12	86	40	.316
1957	CHW	153	568	96	176	36	5	12	103	18	79	54	.310
1958	C L E	149	556	94	168	25	2	24	80	14	59	53	.302
1959	C L E	148	570	92	172	32	0	21	92	8	54	46	.302
1960	CHW	154	591	89	184	32	4	20	105	17	52	63	.311
1961	CHW	152	540	91	151	28	3	14	82	9	67	46	.280
1962	S T L	39	97	14	19	5	0	1	10	4	7	17	.196
1963	WSA	109	315	38	72	12	2	4	30	8	33	38	.229
1964	CHW	30	31	4	7	0	0	1	5	0	5	3	.226
1976	CHW	3	8	0	1	0	0	0	0	0	0	2	.125
1980	CHW	2	2	0	0	0	0	0	0	0	0	0	.000
17 Seasons		1835	6579	1136	1963	336	83	186	1023	205	814	584	.298
Career High		154	591	119	184	36	18	24	116	31	86	63	.326

ROBERTO CLEMENTE

Roberto Clemente Walker (*Arriba*)

BATS: Right **THROWS:** Right
HEIGHT: 5' 11" **WEIGHT:** 175 lbs.
DEBUT: April 17, 1955 **POSITION:** Right Field
BORN: August 18, 1934, in Carolina, Puerto Rico
DIED: December 31, 1972, in San Juan, Puerto Rico

◆ All-Star 1960–1967 and 1969–1972
◆ National League MVP 1966
◆ Led National League in batting average in 1961, 1964, 1965, and 1967
◆ Led National League in hits in 1964 and 1967
◆ Led National League in triples in 1969

BATTING

Year	Tm	G	AB	R	H	2B	3B	HR	RBI	SB	BB	SO	BA
1955	PIT	124	474	48	121	23	11	5	47	2	18	60	.255
1956	PIT	147	543	66	169	30	7	7	60	6	13	58	.311
1957	PIT	111	451	42	114	17	7	4	30	0	23	45	.253
1958	PIT	140	519	69	150	24	10	6	50	8	31	41	.289
1959	PIT	105	432	60	128	17	7	4	50	2	15	51	.296
1960	PIT	144	570	89	179	22	6	16	94	4	39	72	.314
1961	PIT	146	572	100	201	30	10	23	89	4	35	59	.351
1962	PIT	144	538	95	168	28	9	10	74	6	35	73	.312
1963	PIT	152	600	77	192	23	8	17	76	12	31	64	.320
1964	PIT	155	622	95	211	40	7	12	87	5	51	87	.339
1965	PIT	152	589	91	194	21	14	10	65	8	43	78	.329
1966	PIT	154	638	105	202	31	11	29	119	7	46	109	.317
1967	PIT	147	585	103	209	26	10	23	110	9	41	103	.357
1968	PIT	132	502	74	146	18	12	18	57	2	51	77	.291
1969	PIT	138	507	87	175	20	12	19	91	4	56	73	.345
1970	PIT	108	412	65	145	22	10	14	60	3	38	66	.352
1971	PIT	132	522	82	178	29	8	13	86	1	26	65	.341
1972	PIT	102	378	68	118	19	7	10	60	0	29	49	.312
18 Seasons		2433	9454	1416	3000	440	166	240	1305	83	621	1230	.317
Career High		155	638	105	211	40	14	29	119	12	56	109	.357

TONY OLIVA

Pedro Oliva Lopez

BATS: Left **THROWS:** Right
HEIGHT: 6' 2" **WEIGHT:** 190 lbs.
DEBUT: September 9, 1962 **POSITION:** Right Field
BORN: July 20, 1940, in Pinar Del Rio, Cuba

◆ All-Star 1964–1970
◆ Top 10 MVP in 1964–1966 and 1970–1971
◆ Led both leagues in batting average in 1964 and 1965
◆ Hit leader 1964–1966 and 1969–1970

BATTING

Year	Tm	G	AB	R	H	2B	3B	HR	RBI	SB	BB	SO	BA
1962	MIN	9	9	3	4	1	0	0	3	0	3	2	.444
1963	MIN	7	7	0	3	0	0	0	1	0	0	2	.429
1964	MIN	161	672	109	217	43	9	32	94	12	34	68	.323
1965	MIN	149	576	107	185	40	5	16	98	19	55	64	.321
1966	MIN	159	622	99	191	32	7	25	87	13	42	72	.307
1967	MIN	146	557	76	161	34	6	17	83	11	44	61	.289
1968	MIN	128	470	54	136	24	5	18	68	10	45	61	.289
1969	MIN	153	637	97	197	39	4	24	101	10	45	66	.309
1970	MIN	157	628	96	204	36	7	23	107	5	38	67	.325
1971	MIN	126	487	73	164	30	3	22	81	4	25	44	.337
1972	MIN	10	28	1	9	1	0	0	1	0	2	5	.321
1973	MIN	146	571	63	166	20	0	16	92	2	45	44	.291
1974	MIN	127	459	43	131	16	2	13	57	0	27	31	.285
1975	MIN	131	455	46	123	10	0	13	58	0	41	45	.270
1976	MIN	67	123	3	26	3	0	1	16	0	2	13	.211
15 Seasons		1676	6301	870	1917	329	48	220	947	86	448	645	.304
Career High		161	672	109	217	43	9	32	107	19	55	72	.337

JOSE CANSECO

Jose Canseco Capas Jr.

BATS: Right **THROWS:** Right
HEIGHT: 6' 4" **WEIGHT:** 240 lbs.
DEBUT: September 2, 1985 **POSITION:** Right and Left Field
BORN: July 2, 1964, in Havana, Cuba

◆ All-Star in 1986, 1988–1990, 1992, and 1999
◆ American League MVP 1988
◆ Home run leader in 1988 and 1991
◆ RBI leader in 1988

BATTING

Year	Tm	G	AB	R	H	2B	3B	HR	RBI	SB	BB	SO	BA
1985	OAK	29	96	16	29	3	0	5	13	1	4	31	.302
1986	OAK	157	600	85	144	29	1	33	117	15	65	175	.240
1987	OAK	159	630	81	162	35	3	31	113	15	50	157	.257
1988	OAK	158	610	120	187	34	0	42	124	40	178	128	.307
1989	OAK	65	227	40	61	9	1	17	57	6	23	69	.269
1990	OAK	131	481	83	132	14	2	37	101	19	72	158	.274
1991	OAK	154	572	115	152	32	1	44	122	26	78	152	.266
1992	OAK	97	366	66	90	11	0	22	72	5	48	104	.246
	TEX	22	73	8	17	4	0	4	15	1	15	24	.233
	TOT	119	439	74	107	15	0	26	87	6	63	128	.244
1993	TEX	60	231	30	59	14	1	10	46	6	16	62	.255
1994	TEX	111	429	88	121	19	2	31	90	15	69	114	.282
1995	BOS	102	396	64	121	25	1	24	81	4	42	93	.306
1996	BOS	96	360	68	104	22	1	28	82	3	63	82	.289
1997	OAK	108	388	56	91	19	0	23	74	8	51	122	.235
1998	TOR	151	583	98	138	26	0	46	107	29	65	159	.237
1999	TBD	113	430	75	120	18	1	34	95	3	58	135	.279
2000	TBD	61	218	31	56	15	0	9	30	2	41	65	.257
	NYY	37	111	16	27	3	0	6	19	0	23	37	.243
	TOT	98	329	47	83	18	0	15	49	2	64	102	.252
2001	CHW	76	256	46	66	8	0	16	49	2	45	75	.258
17 Seasons		1887	7057	1186	1877	340	14	462	1407	200	906	1942	.266
Career High		159	630	120	187	35	3	46	124	40	78	175	.307

SAMMY SOSA

Samuel Peralta Sosa

BATS: Right **THROWS:** Right
HEIGHT: 6' 0" **WEIGHT:** 185 lbs.
DEBUT: June 16, 1989 **POSITION:** Right Field
BORN: November 12, 1968, in San Pedro de Macoris, Dominican Republic

◆ All-Star in 1995 and 1998–2002
◆ National League MVP 1998
◆ Top 10 in home runs 1993–2001
◆ Leader in runs in 1998 and 2001
◆ Leader in home runs in 2001

BATTING

Year	Tm	G	AB	R	H	2B	3B	HR	RBI	SB	BB	SO	BA
1989	TEX	25	84	8	20	3	0	1	3	0	0	20	.238
	CHW	33	99	19	27	5	0	3	10	7	11	27	.273
	TOT	58	183	27	47	8	0	4	13	7	11	47	.257
1990	CHW	153	532	72	124	26	10	15	70	32	33	150	.233
1991	CHW	116	316	39	64	10	1	10	33	13	14	98	.203
1992	CHC	67	262	41	68	7	2	8	25	15	19	63	.260
1993	CHC	159	598	92	156	25	5	33	93	36	38	135	.261
1994	CHC	105	426	59	128	17	6	25	70	22	25	92	.300
1995	CHC	144	564	89	151	17	3	36	119	34	58	134	.268
1996	CHC	124	498	84	136	21	2	40	100	18	34	134	.273
1997	CHC	162	642	90	161	31	4	36	119	22	45	174	.251
1998	CHC	159	643	134	198	20	0	66	158	18	73	171	.308
1999	CHC	162	625	114	180	24	2	63	141	7	78	171	.288
2000	CHC	156	604	106	193	38	1	50	138	7	91	168	.320
2001	CHC	160	577	146	189	34	5	64	160	0	116	153	.328
13 Seasons		1725	6470	1093	1795	278	41	450	1239	231	635	1690	.277
Career High		162	643	146	198	38	10	66	160	36	116	174	.328

JUAN GONZALEZ

Juan Alberto Gonzalez Vazquez

BATS: Right **THROWS:** Right
HEIGHT: 6' 3" **WEIGHT:** 210 lbs.
DEBUT: September 1, 1989 **POSITION:** Right Field
BORN: October 16, 1969, in Vega Baja, Puerto Rico

◆ All-Star in 1993, 1998, and 2001
◆ American League MVP in 1996 and 1998
◆ Leader in home runs in 1992 and 1993
◆ Leader in RBIs in 1998

BATTING

Year	Tm	G	AB	R	H	2B	3B	HR	RBI	SB	BB	SO	BA
1989	TEX	24	60	6	9	3	0	1	7	0	6	17	.150
1990	TEX	25	90	11	26	7	1	4	12	0	2	18	.289
1991	TEX	142	545	78	144	34	1	27	102	4	42	118	.264
1992	TEX	155	584	77	152	24	2	43	109	0	35	143	.260
1993	TEX	140	536	105	166	33	1	46	118	4	37	99	.310
1994	TEX	107	422	57	116	18	4	19	85	6	30	66	.275
1995	TEX	90	352	57	104	20	2	27	82	0	17	66	.295
1996	TEX	134	541	89	170	33	2	47	144	2	45	82	.314
1997	TEX	133	533	87	158	24	3	42	131	0	33	107	.296
1998	TEX	154	606	110	193	50	2	45	157	2	46	126	.318
1999	TEX	144	562	114	183	36	1	39	128	3	51	105	.326
2000	DET	115	461	69	133	30	2	22	67	1	32	84	.289
2001	CLE	140	532	97	173	34	1	35	140	1	41	94	.325
13 Seasons		1503	5824	957	1727	346	22	397	1282	23	417	1125	.297
Career High		155	606	114	193	50	4	47	157	6	51	143	.326

BERNIE WILLIAMS

Bernabe Williams Figueroa

BATS: Both **THROWS:** Right
HEIGHT: 6' 2" **WEIGHT:** 205 lbs.
DEBUT: July 7, 1991 **POSITION:** Center Field
BORN: September 13, 1968, in San Juan, Puerto Rico

◆ All-Star in 1997, 1999, 2000, and 2001
◆ American League Gold-Glove winner 1997–2000
◆ Led American League in batting average in 1998

BATTING

Year	Tm	G	AB	R	H	2B	3B	HR	RBI	SB	BB	SO	BA
1991	NYY	85	320	43	76	19	4	3	34	10	48	57	.238
1992	NYY	62	261	39	73	14	2	5	26	7	29	36	.280
1993	NYY	139	567	67	152	31	4	12	68	9	53	106	.268
1994	NYY	108	408	80	118	29	1	12	57	16	61	54	.289
1995	NYY	144	563	93	173	29	9	18	82	8	75	98	.307
1996	NYY	143	551	108	168	26	7	29	102	17	82	72	.305
1997	NYY	129	509	107	167	35	6	21	100	15	73	80	.328
1998	NYY	128	499	101	169	30	5	26	97	15	74	81	.339
1999	NYY	158	591	116	202	28	6	25	115	9	100	95	.342
2000	NYY	141	537	108	165	37	6	30	121	13	71	84	.307
2001	NYY	146	540	102	166	38	0	26	94	11	78	67	.307
11 Seasons		1383	5346	964	1629	316	50	207	896	130	744	830	.305
Career High		158	591	116	202	38	9	30	121	17	100	106	.342

MANNY RAMIREZ

Manuel Aristides Ramirez Onelcida

BATS: Right **THROWS:** Right
HEIGHT: 6' 0" **WEIGHT:** 190 lbs.
DEBUT: September 2, 1993 **POSITION:** Right Field
BORN: May 30, 1972, in Santo Domingo, Dominican
Republic

◆ All-Star 1995 and 1998–2002
◆ Top 10 American League MVP 1998–2001
◆ Top 10 batting average in 1997, 1999, and 2000

BATTING

Year	Tm	G	AB	R	H	2B	3B	HR	RBI	SB	BB	SO	BA
1993	CLE	22	53	5	9	1	0	2	5	0	2	8	.170
1994	CLE	91	290	51	78	22	0	17	60	4	42	72	.269
1995	CLE	137	484	85	149	26	1	31	107	6	75	112	.308
1996	CLE	152	550	94	170	45	3	33	112	8	85	104	.309
1997	CLE	150	561	99	184	40	0	26	88	2	79	115	.328
1998	CLE	150	571	108	168	35	2	45	145	5	76	121	.294
1999	CLE	147	522	131	174	34	3	44	165	2	96	131	.333
2000	CLE	118	439	92	154	34	2	38	122	1	86	117	.351
2001	BOS	142	529	93	162	33	2	41	125	0	81	147	.306
9 Seasons		1109	3999	758	1248	270	13	277	929	28	622	927	.312
Career High		152	571	131	184	45	3	45	165	8	96	147	.351

VLADIMIR GUERRERO

Vladimir Alvino Guerrero

BATS: Right **THROWS:** Right
HEIGHT: 6' 2" **WEIGHT:** 210 lbs.
DEBUT: September 19, 1996 **POSITION:** Right Field
BORN: February 9, 1976, in Nizao, Dominican Republic

◆ All-Star 1999–2000 and 2002
◆ Top 10 National League MVP in 2000
◆ Top 10 batting average in 1998 and 2000

BATTING

Year	Tm	G	AB	R	H	2B	3B	HR	RBI	SB	BB	SO	BA
1996	MON	9	27	2	5	0	0	1	1	0	0	3	.185
1997	MON	90	325	44	98	22	2	11	40	3	19	39	.302
1998	MON	159	623	108	202	37	7	38	109	11	42	95	.324
1999	MON	160	610	102	193	37	5	42	131	14	55	62	.316
2000	MON	154	571	101	197	28	11	44	123	9	58	74	.345
2001	MON	159	599	107	184	45	4	34	108	37	60	88	.307
6 Seasons		731	2755	464	879	169	29	170	512	74	234	361	.319
Career High		160	623	108	202	45	11	44	131	37	60	95	.345

DOLF LUQUE

Adolfo Domingo De Guzman Luque (*The Pride Of Havana*)

BATS: Right **THROWS:** Right
HEIGHT: 5' 7" **WEIGHT:** 160 lbs.
DEBUT: May 20, 1914 **POSITION:** Pitcher
BORN: August 4, 1890, in Havana, Cuba
DIED: July 3, 1957, in Havana, Cuba

◆ ERA leader in 1923 and 1925
◆ Win leader in 1923
◆ Shutout leader in 1921, 1923, and 1925
◆ Top 10 in saves in 1919, 1921, 1932, 1933, and 1934

PITCHING

Year	Tm	W	L	G	SV	IP	H	ER	HR	BB	SO	ERA
1914	BSN	0	1	2	0	8.7	5	4	0	4	1	4.15
1915	BSN	0	0	2	0	5.0	6	2	0	4	3	3.60
1918	CIN	6	3	12	0	83.0	84	35	1	32	26	3.80
1919	CIN	10	3	30	3	106.0	89	31	2	36	40	2.63
1920	CIN	13	9	37	1	207.7	168	58	5	60	72	2.51
1921	CIN	17	19	41	3	304.0	318	114	13	64	102	3.38
1922	CIN	13	23	39	0	261.0	266	96	7	72	79	3.31
1923	CIN	27	8	41	2	322.0	279	69	2	88	151	1.93
1924	CIN	10	15	31	0	219.3	229	77	5	53	86	3.16
1925	CIN	16	18	36	0	291.0	263	85	7	78	140	2.63
1926	CIN	13	16	34	0	233.7	231	89	7	77	83	3.43
1927	CIN	13	12	29	0	230.7	225	82	10	56	76	3.20
1928	CIN	11	10	33	1	234.3	254	93	12	84	72	3.57
1929	CIN	5	16	32	0	176.0	213	88	7	56	43	4.50
1930	BRO	14	8	31	2	199.0	221	95	18	58	62	4.30
1931	BRO	7	6	19	0	102.7	122	52	6	27	25	4.56
1932	NYG	6	7	38	5	110.0	128	49	4	32	32	4.01
1933	NYG	8	2	35	4	80.3	75	24	4	19	23	2.69
1934	NYG	4	3	26	7	42.3	54	18	3	17	12	3.83
1935	NYG	1	0	2	0	3.7	1	0	0	1	2	0.00
Career High		27	23	41	7	322.0	318	114	18	88	151	1.93

CAMILO PASCUAL

Camilo Alberto Pascual Lus (*Camile or Little Potato*)

BATS: Right **THROWS:** Right
HEIGHT: 5' 11" **WEIGHT:** 185 lbs.
DEBUT: April 15, 1954 **POSITION:** Pitcher
BORN: January 20, 1934, in Havana, Cuba

◆ All-Star 1959–1962 and 1964
◆ Pitched most strikeouts 1961–1963
◆ Leader in shutouts in 1959, 1961, and 1962

PITCHING

Year	Tm	W	L	G	SV	IP	H	ER	HR	BB	SO	ERA
1954	WSH	4	7	48	3	119.3	126	56	7	61	60	4.22
1955	WSH	2	12	43	3	129.0	158	88	5	70	82	6.14
1956	WSH	6	18	39	2	188.7	194	123	33	89	162	5.87
1957	WSH	8	17	29	0	175.7	168	80	11	76	113	4.10
1958	WSH	8	12	31	0	177.3	166	62	14	60	146	3.15
1959	WSH	17	10	32	0	238.7	202	70	10	69	185	2.64
1960	WSH	12	8	26	2	151.7	139	51	11	53	143	3.03
1961	MIN	15	16	35	0	252.3	205	97	26	100	221	3.46
1962	MIN	20	11	34	0	257.7	236	95	25	59	206	3.32
1963	MIN	21	9	31	0	248.3	205	68	21	81	202	2.46
1964	MIN	15	12	36	0	267.3	245	98	30	98	213	3.30
1965	MIN	9	3	27	0	156.0	126	58	12	63	96	3.35
1966	MIN	8	6	21	0	103.0	113	56	9	30	56	4.89
1967	WSA	2	10	28	0	164.7	147	60	15	43	106	3.28
1968	WSA	13	12	31	0	201.0	181	60	11	59	111	2.69
1969	CIN	0	0	5	0	7.3	14	7	2	4	3	8.59
1970	LAD	0	0	10	0	14.0	12	.4	2	5	8	2.57
1971	CLE	2	2	9	10	23.1	17	8	0	11	20	3.09
Career High		21	18	48	3	267.3	245	123	33	100	221	2.46

JUAN MARICHAL

Juan Antonio Marichal Sanchez
(Manito, Dominican Dandy or Mar)

BATS: Right **THROWS:** Right
HEIGHT: 6' 0" **WEIGHT:** 185 lbs.
DEBUT: July 19, 1960 **POSITION:** Pitcher
BORN: October 20, 1937, in Laguna Verde, Dominican
Republic

◆ All-Star 1962–1971
◆ Top 10 National League MVP in 1971
◆ ERA leader in 1969
◆ Pitched most innings in 1963 and 1968
◆ Leader in shutouts in 1965 and 1969

PITCHING

Year	Tm	W	L	G	SV	IP	H	ER	HR	BB	SO	ERA
1960	SFG	6	2	11	0	81.3	59	24	5	28	58	2.66
1961	SFG	13	10	29	0	185.0	183	80	24	48	124	3.89
1962	SFG	18	11	37	1	262.7	233	98	34	90	153	3.36
1963	SFG	25	8	41	0	321.3	259	86	27	61	248	2.41
1964	SFG	21	8	33	0	269.0	241	74	18	52	206	2.48
1965	SFG	22	13	39	1	295.3	224	70	27	46	240	2.13
1966	SFG	25	6	37	0	307.3	228	76	32	36	222	2.23
1967	SFG	14	10	26	0	202.3	195	62	20	42	166	2.76
1968	SFG	26	9	38	0	326.0	295	88	21	46	218	2.43
1969	SFG	21	11	37	0	299.7	244	70	15	54	205	2.10
1970	SFG	12	10	34	0	242.7	269	111	28	48	123	4.12
1971	SFG	18	11	37	0	279.0	244	91	27	56	159	2.94
1972	SFG	6	16	25	0	165.0	176	68	15	46	72	3.71
1973	SFG	11	15	34	0	207.3	231	88	22	37	87	3.82
1974	BOS	5	1	11	0	57.3	61	31	3	14	21	4.87
1975	LAD	0	1	2	0	6.0	11	9	2	5	1	13.50
Career High		26	16	41	1	326.0	295	111	34	90	248	2.10

LUIS TIANT

Luis Clemente Tiant Vega

BATS: Right **THROWS:** Right
HEIGHT: 5' 11" **WEIGHT:** 190 lbs.
DEBUT: July 19, 1964 **POSITION:** Pitcher
BORN: November 23, 1940, in Marianao, Cuba

◆ All-Star in 1968, 1974, and 1976
◆ Top 10 American League MVP in 1968 and 1972
◆ ERA leader in 1968 and 1972
◆ Leader in shutouts in 1966, 1968, and 1974

PITCHING

Year	Tm	W	L	G	SV	IP	H	ER	HR	BB	SO	ERA
1964	CLE	10	4	19	1	127.0	94	40	13	47	105	2.83
1965	CLE	11	11	41	1	196.3	166	77	20	66	152	3.53
1966	CLE	12	11	46	8	155.0	121	48	16	50	145	2.79
1967	CLE	12	9	33	2	213.7	177	65	24	67	219	2.74
1968	CLE	21	9	34	0	258.3	152	46	16	73	264	1.60
1969	CLE	9	20	38	0	249.7	229	103	37	129	156	3.71
1970	MIN	7	3	18	0	92.7	84	35	12	41	50	3.40
1971	BOS	1	7	21	0	72.3	73	39	8	32	59	4.85
1972	BOS	15	6	43	3	179.0	128	38	7	65	123	1.91
1973	BOS	20	13	35	0	272.0	217	101	32	78	206	3.34
1974	BOS	22	13	38	0	311.3	281	101	21	82	176	2.92
1975	BOS	18	14	35	0	260.0	262	116	25	72	142	4.02
1976	BOS	21	12	38	0	279.0	274	95	25	64	131	3.06
1977	BOS	12	8	32	0	188.7	210	95	26	51	124	4.53
1978	BOS	13	8	32	0	212.3	185	78	26	57	114	3.31
1979	NYY	13	8	30	0	195.7	190	85	22	53	104	3.91
1980	NYY	8	9	25	0	136.3	139	74	10	50	84	4.89
1981	PIT	2	5	9	0	57.3	54	25	3	19	32	3.92
1982	CAL	2	2	6	0	29.7	39	19	3	8	30	5.76
Career High		22	20	46	8	311.3	281	116	37	129	264	1.60

FERNANDO VALENZUELA

Fernando Valenzuela Anguamea

BATS: Left **THROWS:** Left
HEIGHT: 5' 11" **WEIGHT:** 195 lbs.
DEBUT: September 15, 1980 **POSITION:** Pitcher
BORN: November 1, 1960, in Navajoa, Mexico

◆ All-Star 1981–1986
◆ National League Cy Young Award winner in 1981
◆ Pitched most innings in 1981
◆ Leader in shutouts in 1981

PITCHING

Year	Tm	W	L	G	SV	IP	H	ER	HR	BB	SO	ERA
1980	LAD	2	0	10	1	17.7	8	0	0	5	16	0.00
1981	LAD	13	7	25	0	192.3	140	53	11	61	180	2.48
1982	LAD	19	13	37	0	285.0	247	91	13	83	199	2.87
1983	LAD	15	10	35	0	257.0	245	107	16	99	189	3.75
1984	LAD	12	17	34	0	261.0	218	88	14	106	240	3.03
1985	LAD	17	10	35	0	272.3	211	74	14	101	208	2.45
1986	LAD	21	11	34	0	269.3	226	94	18	85	242	3.14
1987	LAD	14	14	34	0	251.0	254	111	25	124	190	3.98
1988	LAD	5	8	23	1	142.3	142	67	11	76	64	4.24
1989	LAD	10	13	31	0	196.7	185	75	11	98	116	3.43
1990	LAD	13	13	33	0	204.0	223	104	19	77	115	4.59
1991	CAL	0	2	2	0	6.7	14	9	3	3	5	12.15
1993	BAL	8	10	32	0	178.7	179	98	18	79	78	4.94
1994	PHI	1	2	8	0	45.0	42	15	8	7	19	3.00
1995	SDP	8	3	29	0	90.3	101	50	16	34	57	4.98
1996	SDP	13	8	33	0	171.7	177	69	17	67	95	3.62
1997	SDP	2	8	13	0	66.3	84	35	10	32	51	4.75
	STL	0	4	5	0	22.7	22	14	2	14	10	5.56
	TOT	2	12	18	0	89.0	106	49	12	46	61	4.95
Career High		21	17	37	1	285.0	254	111	25	124	242	2.45

PEDRO MARTINEZ

Pedro Jaime Martinez

BATS: Right **THROWS:** Right
HEIGHT: 5' 11" **WEIGHT:** 170 lbs.
DEBUT: September 24 1992 **POSITION:** Pitcher
BORN: October 25, 1971, in Manoguayabo, Dominican
Republic

◆ All-Star 1996–2000 and 2002
◆ National League Cy Young Award winner in 1997
◆ American League Cy Young Award winner in 1999
   and 2000
◆ ERA leader in 1997, 1999, and 2000
◆ Pitched most strikeouts in 1999 and 2000

PITCHING

Year	Tm	W	L	G	SV	IP	H	ER	HR	BB	SO	ERA
1992	L A D	0	1	2	0	8.0	6	2	0	1	8	2.25
1993	L A D	10	5	65	2	107.0	76	31	5	57	119	2.61
1994	MON	11	5	24	1	144.7	115	55	11	45	142	3.42
1995	MON	14	10	30	0	194.7	158	76	21	66	174	3.51
1996	MON	13	10	33	0	216.7	189	89	19	70	222	3.70
1997	MON	17	8	31	0	241.3	158	51	16	67	305	1.90
1998	B O S	19	7	33	0	233.7	188	75	26	67	251	2.89
1999	B O S	23	4	31	0	213.3	160	49	9	37	313	2.07
2000	B O S	18	6	29	0	217.0	128	42	17	32	284	1.74
2001	B O S	7	3	18	0	116.7	84	31	5	25	163	2.39
Career High		23	10	65	2	241.3	189	89	26	70	313	1.74

WILLIE HERNANDEZ

Guillermo Hernandez Villanueva (*played as Guillermo*)

BATS: Left **THROWS:** Left
HEIGHT: 6' 3" **WEIGHT:** 180 lbs.
DEBUT: April 9, 1977 **POSITION:** Pitcher
BORN: November 14, 1954, in Aguada, Puerto Rico

◆ All-Star 1984–1986
◆ American League Cy Young Award winner in 1984
◆ American League MVP in 1984

PITCHING

Year	Tm	W	L	G	SV	IP	H	ER	HR	BB	SO	ERA
1977	CHC	8	7	67	4	110.0	94	37	11	28	78	3.03
1978	CHC	8	2	54	3	59.7	57	25	6	35	38	3.77
1979	CHC	4	4	51	0	79.0	85	44	8	39	53	5.01
1980	CHC	1	9	53	0	108.3	115	53	8	45	75	4.40
1981	CHC	0	0	12	2	13.7	14	6	0	8	13	3.95
1982	CHC	4	6	75	10	75.0	74	25	3	24	54	3.00
1983	CHC	1	0	11	1	19.7	16	7	0	6	18	3.20
	PHI	8	4	63	7	95.7	93	35	9	26	75	3.29
	TOT	9	4	74	8	115.3	109	42	9	32	93	3.27
1984	DET	9	3	80	32	140.3	96	30	6	36	112	1.92
1985	DET	8	10	74	31	106.7	82	32	13	14	76	2.70
1986	DET	8	7	64	24	88.7	87	35	13	21	77	3.55
1987	DET	3	4	45	8	49.0	53	20	8	20	30	3.67
1988	DET	6	5	63	10	67.7	50	23	8	31	59	3.06
1989	DET	2	2	32	15	31.3	36	20	4	16	30	5.74
Career High		9	10	80	32	140.3	115	53	13	45	112	1.92

MARIANO RIVERA

BATS: Right **THROWS:** Right
HEIGHT: 6' 2" **WEIGHT:** 170 lbs.
DEBUT: May 23, 1995 **POSITION:** Pitcher
BORN: November 29, 1969, in Panama City, Panama

◆ All-Star in 1997 and 1999–2002
◆ Top 10 Cy Young Award winner in 1996 and 1999
◆ Leader in saves in 1999 and 2001

PITCHING

Year	Tm	W	L	G	SV	IP	H	ER	HR	BB	SO	ERA
1995	NYY	5	3	19	0	67.0	71	41	11	30	51	5.51
1996	NYY	8	3	61	5	107.7	73	25	1	34	130	2.09
1997	NYY	6	4	66	43	71.7	65	15	5	20	68	1.88
1998	NYY	3	0	54	36	61.3	48	13	3	17	36	1.91
1999	NYY	4	3	66	45	69.0	43	14	2	18	52	1.83
2000	NYY	7	4	66	36	75.7	58	24	4	25	58	2.85
2001	NYY	4	6	71	50	80.7	61	21	5	12	83	2.34
Career High		8	6	71	50	107.7	73	41	11	34	130	1.83

MARTIN DIHIGO

HEIGHT: 6' 1" **WEIGHT:** 190 lbs.
DEBUT: 1923
BORN: May 25, 1905, in Matanzas, Cuba
DIED: May 22, 1971, in Cienfuegos, Cuba

◆ Played all nine positions
◆ Threw no-hitters in three countries—Mexico, Puerto Rico, and Venezuela
◆ Elected into National Baseball Hall of Fame in 1977
◆ Inducted into Mexican, Venezuelan, and Cuban Halls of Fame

BATTING

Year	Tm	G	AB	H	2B	3B	HR	SB	BA
1923	Cuban Stars	17	63	17	1	1	0	1	.270
1924	Cuban Stars	52	190	47	8	3	3	4	.247
1925	Cuban Stars	41	149	45	7	1	2	3	.302
1926	Cuban Stars	21	76	32	5	0	8	3	.421
1927	Cuban Stars	52	190	47	8	3	3	4	.247
1928	Grays	N/A							
1929	PHI Hildales	68	207	77	8	1	13	7	.372
1930	Stars of Cuba	24	98	40	5	3	7	0	.408
1931	BAL Black Sox and PHI Hildales								
1931	Total	50	193	51	1	3	2	0	.264
1932	Did not play	N/A							
1933	Venezuela	N/A							
1934	Did not play	N/A							
1935	NY Cubans	38	120	37	8	4	7	5	.308
1936	NY Cubans	33	93	31	6	1	10	2	.333
1937	Latin America	N/A							
1938	Latin America	N/A							
1939	Latin America	N/A							
1940	Latin America	N/A							
1944	Latin America								
1945	NY Cubans	7	20	1	0	0	0	0	.050
Career High		68	207	77	8	4	13	7	.421

JULIO FRANCO

Julio Cesar Franco

BATS: Right **THROWS:** Right
HEIGHT: 6' 1" **WEIGHT:** 188 lbs.
DEBUT: April 23, 1982 **POSITION:** Second Base
and Shortstop
BORN: August 23, 1958, in San Pedro de Macoris,
Dominican Republic

◆ All-Star 1989–1991
◆ Top 10 American League MVP in 1994
◆ Led American League in batting average in 1991

BATTING

Year	Tm	G	AB	R	H	2B	3B	HR	RBI	SB	BB	SO	BA
1982	PHI	16	29	3	8	1	0	0	3	0	2	4	.276
1983	CLE	149	560	68	153	24	8	8	80	32	27	50	.273
1984	CLE	160	658	82	188	22	5	3	79	19	43	68	.286
1985	CLE	160	636	97	183	33	4	6	90	13	54	74	.288
1986	CLE	149	599	80	183	30	5	10	74	10	32	66	.306
1987	CLE	128	495	86	158	24	3	8	52	32	57	56	.319
1988	CLE	152	613	88	186	23	6	10	54	25	56	72	.303
1989	TEX	150	548	80	173	31	5	13	92	21	66	69	.316
1990	TEX	157	582	96	172	27	1	11	69	31	82	83	.296
1991	TEX	146	589	108	201	27	3	15	78	36	65	78	.341
1992	TEX	35	107	19	25	7	0	2	8	1	15	17	.234
1993	TEX	144	532	85	154	31	3	14	84	9	62	95	.289
1994	CHW	112	433	72	138	19	2	20	98	8	62	75	.319
1996	CLE	112	432	72	139	20	1	14	76	8	61	82	.322
1997	CLE	78	289	46	82	13	1	3	25	8	38	75	.284
	MIL	42	141	22	34	3	0	4	19	7	131	41	.241
	TOT	120	430	68	116	16	1	7	44	15	69	116	.270
1999	TBD	1	1	0	0	0	0	0	0	0	0	1	.000
2001	ATL	25	90	13	27	4	0	3	11	0	10	20	.300
17 Seasons		1916	7334	1117	2204	339	47	144	992	260	763	1026	.301
Career High		160	658	108	201	33	8	20	98	36	82	116	.341

JOSE VIDRO

Jose Angel Vidro Cetty

BATS: Both **THROWS:** Right
HEIGHT: 5' 11" **WEIGHT:** 175 lbs.
DEBUT: June 8, 1997 **POSITION:** Second Base
BORN: August 27, 1974, in Mayaguez, Puerto Rico

◆ All-Star in 2000 and 2002
◆ Second in National League in hits in 2000
◆ Second in National League with doubles in 1999

BATTING

Year	Tm	G	AB	R	H	2B	3B	HR	RBI	SB	BB	SO	BA
1997	MON	67	169	19	42	12	1	2	17	1	11	20	.249
1998	MON	83	205	24	45	12	0	0	18	2	27	33	.220
1999	MON	140	494	67	150	45	2	12	59	0	29	51	.304
2000	MON	153	606	101	200	51	2	24	97	5	49	69	.330
2001	MON	124	486	82	155	34	1	15	59	4	31	49	.319
5 Seasons		567	1960	293	592	154	6	53	250	12	147	222	.302
Career High		153	606	101	200	51	2	24	97	5	49	69	.330

SELECTED BIBLIOGRAPHY

Augenbraum, Harold and Ilan Stavans. *Growing Up Latino,*
    Houghton Mifflin Company.

Bjarkman, Peter C. "Martin Dihigo: Baseball's Least-Known
    Hall of Famer," *Elysian Fields,* Spring 2001.

Breton, Marcos, and Jose Luis Villegas. *Away Games: The Life
    and Times of a Latin Baseball Player.* New York: Simon &
    Schuster, 1999.

Carew, Rod, with Ira Berkow. *Carew.* New York: Simon &
    Schuster, 1979.

Cepeda, Orlando, and Herb Fagen. *Baby Bull: From Hardball to
    Hard Time and Back.* Dallas: Taylor Publishing Company,
    1998.

Dark, Alvin, and John Underwood. *When in Doubt, Fire the
    Manager: My Life and Times in Baseball.* New York: E.P.
    Dutton, 1980.

Dickson, Paul. *The New Dickson Baseball Dictionary.* New York:
    Harcourt Brace & Co., 1999.

Echevarria, Roberto Gonzalez. *The Pride of Havana: A His-
    tory of Cuban Baseball.* New York: Oxford University Press,
    1999.

Fainaru, Steve, and Ray Sanchez. *The Duke of Havana: Baseball, Cuba, and the Search for the American Dream.* New York: Villard Books, 2001.

Holway, John. "Cuban Baseball Greats Stifled by Politics," *USA Today Baseball Weekly,* July 22, 1992.

Jackson, Reggie, and Mike Lupica. *Reggie: The Autobiography of Reggie Jackson.* New York: Villard Books, 1994.

Jamail, Milton. *Full Count: Inside Cuban Baseball.* Carbondale: Southern Illinois University Press, 2000.

Johnston, Dick, and Glenn Stout. *Ted Williams: A Portrait in Words and Pictures.* New York: Walker and Company, 1991.

Klein, Alan. *Baseball on the Border.* Princeton, N.J.: Princeton University Press, 1997.

———. *Sugarball: The American Game, the Dominican Dream.* New Haven: Yale University Press, 1991.

Koenig, Bill. "Delgado Dynamite During Super Year," *USA Today Baseball Weekly,* September 30, 1992.

Le Batard, Dan. "Beyond Words," *ESPN Magazine,* July 8, 2002.

Lupica, Mike. *Summer of '98: When Homers Flew, Records Fell, and Baseball Reclaimed America.* New York: G. P. Putnam's Sons, 1999.

Markusen, Bruce. *The Orlando Cepeda Story.* Houston: Pinata Books, 2001.

———. *Roberto Clemente: The Great One.* Champaign, Ill.: Sports Publishing Inc., 1998.

Mulrenin, Patrick. "Vlad's visibility doesn't match talent." MLB.com, September 9, 2002.

Musick, Phil. *Who Was Roberto? A Biography of Roberto Clemente.* Garden City, N.Y.: Doubleday, 1974.

Myles, Stephanie. "Expos could have been better." *The Montreal Gazette,* October 1, 2002.

Nack, William. "From Shame to Fame." *Sports Illustrated,* July 26, 1999.

Nightengale, Bob. "Oh, to be young and a Yankee." *USA Today Baseball Weekly,* May 15–21, 2002.

———. "Abyss to Awesome." *USA Today Baseball Weekly,* September 11–17, 2002.

Ortiz, Jorge L., "Second Language in Major Leagues." *San Francisco Chronicle,* July 7, 2002.

———. "Miguel Tejada Profile." *San Francisco Chronicle,* August, 16, 2002.

Price, Scott. *Pitching Around Fidel.* New York: The Ecco Press, 2000.

Regalado, Samuel O. *Viva Baseball!.* Urbana: University of Illinois Press, 1998.

Robertson, Linda. "Miami's Alex Rodriguez draws cheers at UM." *The Miami Herald,* October 11, 2002.

Rodriguez, Alex. *Hit a Grand Slam!.* Dallas: Taylor Publishing Company, 1998.

Rodriguez, Richard. *Brown: The Last Discovery of America.* New York: Viking, 2002.

Ruck, Rob. *The Tropic of Baseball: Baseball in the Dominican Republic.* Westport, Conn.: Meckler Publishing, 1991.

Rucker, Mark and Peter C. Bjarkman. *Smoke: The Romance of Cuban Baseball.* New York: Total Sports Publishing, 1999.

Shorris, Earl. *Latinos: A Biography of the People.* New York: W.W. Norton & Company, 1992.

Sosa, Sammy, and Marcos Breton. *Sosa: An Autobiography.* New York: Warner Books, 2000.

Sullivan, Jerry. "Soriano proves high price tags are overrated." *The Buffalo News,* July 13, 2002.

Verducci, Tom. "Three Dimensional: Carlos Delgado." *Sports Illustrated,* August 28, 2000.

———. "The Power of Pedro." *Sports Illustrated,* March 27, 2000.

————— and David Sabino. "400 Reasons: Nomar Garciaparra." *Sports Illustrated,* March 5, 2001.

—————. "The Producers." *Sports Illustrated,* June 4, 2001.

Vizquel, Omar, and Bob Dyer. *Omar! My Life On and Off the Field.* Cleveland: Gray & Company, 2002.

White, Paul. "Spring cleanings finally give way to spring training." *USA Today Baseball Weekly,* March 6–12, 2002.

Will, George. *Men at Work: The Craft of Baseball.* New York: Macmillan, 1990.

INDEX